Tryweryn:
A Nation Awakes

Ar herw ers Tryweryn – 'roedd yno,
   'Roedd yno'n y dyffryn,
  Y glew a barha'n y glyn,
  A'i arf yw'r gair yn erfyn.

ALWYN PRITCHARD

Tryweryn:
A Nation Awakes

The story of a Welsh Freedom Fighter

OWAIN WILLIAMS

In memory of my parents

First impression: 2016
Reprinted: 2016

© Copyright Owain Williams and Y Lolfa Cyf., 2016

Cover illustration: Osian Gruffudd

ISBN: 978 1 78461 246 7

Published and printed in Wales
on paper from well-maintained forests by
Y Lolfa Cyf., Talybont, Ceredigion SY24 5HE
website www.ylolfa.com
e-mail ylolfa@ylolfa.com
tel 01970 832 304
fax 832 782

Foreword

IT WAS DURING my formative teenage years in the sixties that I first heard of Owain Williams (or 'Now Gwynus', as he was known). My eldest brother was frequently mentioning this ardent nationalist from Llŷn who'd emigrated to Canada to work on a ranch. Owain Williams was disillusioned with what he maintained was a lack of backbone among his fellow Welshmen, after the government in Westminster had decided to drown a valley near Bala even though an overwhelming majority in Wales were against the scheme. Recently he had returned to his native land and was running a very trendy cafe in Pwllheli whilst driving round in an American Ford Customline. Now became headline news when he was jailed for planting a bomb in Tryweryn in 1963.

During those heady days when revolution was in the air even in the dour, grey slate mining Nantlle Valley in north Wales where I was brought up, Now Gwynus sounded like an exotic specimen. And to us, young macho boys from working-class backgrounds who'd been fired up by the nationalistic awakening in Wales, he became a legendary figure – a Welsh Che Guevara. Chapelgoers and 'respectable people', of course, labelled him a 'terrorist', and warned us impressionable youngsters to keep well away from him and his influence.

I went to college in 1970 and left my home village of Penygroes, never to return there to live. But I've always kept in touch with Now. Practically, I've spent all my life as a journalist and Now was always a very good sounding board on local as well as national issues.

Throughout his life he's been in the frontline of the battle for the preservation of Wales and the Welsh language. Even

5

though this has meant a considerable personal sacrifice, I've never heard him complain. Although his contribution has been substantial, he's always been seen as an outsider by the nationalistic Welsh middle classes. This is mainly because he never embraced the long-held pacifistic views of the Welsh Non-conformists tradition when it came to fighting for Wales – principles, as he reminded me more than once, that evaporated over night when it came to standing up for Britain.

About three years ago Now told me that he'd started writing his autobiography. He'd written a short book about the Tryweryn episode years before. That was turned into a popular film on S4C, but with this fuller version he said he couldn't stop writing and it was fast becoming a *War and Peace*. Over 100,000 words had already been handwritten and there was loads more to tell, he said. Knowing a little about some of his adventures and colourful personae I strongly encouraged him to carry on, saying I was adamant that this book would make a Hollywood spectacle!

The last time I met up with Now was on the road on top of the Llyn Celyn dam in April 2013. I'd arranged for him and the other two 'Tryweryn bombers' to have a reunion. By then I was a television producer on the verge of retiring, and filming a programme about their militant protest fifty years ago. It was raining and a bitterly cold day. I was holding up an umbrella over the cameraman to shelter the lens from the rain and Now was moaning about the cold and the preferential treatment given to technicians. He had recently been to hospital for skin cancer treatment on his forehead and was wearing a leather cowboy-type hat for protection. Time had taken its toll on him. But the old warrior still had that aura of the freedom fighter and revolutionary of the sixties.

He's also got a tale to tell that will not only entertain you and keep you turning the pages, but will hopefully reinforce his dream of inspiring you to dedicate your services to Wales and the Welsh language.

Eifion Glyn

Introduction

WHEN PEOPLE ASK me why I followed the path that I did during my lifetime, the answer is quite simple: there were issues in Wales in the 1960s that required addressing.

That decade changed the course of modern politics and history more than any other: it re-shaped the global political map and, more importantly, changed how human beings in many parts of the world viewed themselves and their existence. The shackles of colonialism and servitude were about to be smashed, not only in Africa and other distant points of the compass, but nearer home, as in Cyprus, and right on our doorstep in the north of Ireland. Events that were vividly brought into our homes via television news and current affairs inevitably influenced the way people thought about their lives here in Wales. Although it's true that the levels of physical persecution and oppression here were nowhere near what occurred elsewhere, nevertheless the psychological consequences of cultural, linguistic and ethnic deprivation resulted in a national inferiority complex.

Following the death of Llywelyn II in 1282, attempts had continuously been made to turn the Welsh populace into obedient English people. Intermittently, serious levels of resistance would erupt, culminating in Owain Glyndŵr's War of Independence at the very beginning of the fifteenth century when, during a period of around twelve to fourteen years, a Welsh parliament was established at Machynlleth. Later there was co-operation on a diplomatic level with France, resulting in military support for Glyndŵr's armies, such as occurred in the siege of Caernarfon castle.

Wales had, over the last 200 or 300 years, been subjected

7

to a massive dose of pacifist Non-conformity; turning the other cheek was an accepted fact. A few miles across the sea, Ireland was a completely different story. Standing up to fight and defend that nation was expected from true Irishmen and women. History and tradition was instilled in its people from one generation to the next; to fight for their country was, and is, an honour. Martyrs and heroes are hailed and honoured.

Owain Glyndŵr is certainly a Welsh hero. His vision went far beyond the military struggle. Apart from setting up a Welsh parliament, he also foresaw the setting up of university colleges and a separate Welsh church. Despite the eventual demise of that struggle 600 years ago, the dream of nationhood has remained alive amongst sections of the people. Nevertheless, it was a massive leap from the year 1404 to the 1960s, the first period of time when evidence of mass national reawakening was noticeable. Tryweryn was the watershed. For the first time in centuries large numbers of ordinary people identified themselves with a small, threatened community in an obscure part of rural Wales.

In the early 1960s three young men, Emyr Llywelyn Jones, John Albert Jones, and me, set up a secret underground movement called *Mudiad Amddiffyn Cymru* (MAC – the movement for the defence of Wales). MAC's first act was to plant a bomb by the Tryweryn dam, and the explosion destroyed the transformer that supplied electricity to the site. This awoke the nation.

MAC's formation was slow at first. We had no recent examples of Welsh rebellion to guide us! After we'd been arrested for planting the bomb, it took a few years for the movement to regroup and intensify its campaign. Recruiting new members who could be trusted became difficult, particularly since Special Branch and other intelligence agencies began preparing massive surveillance operations in lieu of the looming 'investiture' that was to be held in Caernarfon castle in July 1969. There was growing opposition in Wales to the costly plan to crown Charles Windsor of England as 'prince' of Wales. More bombings of public buildings, water pipes to English cities, etc, were taking place, courtesy of MAC, whilst more openly, groups organised protests and rallies opposing the investiture plans. Amongst the more vociferous of these were members of Cymdeithas yr Iaith (the Welsh Language Society). It is a little-known fact that the then prime minister, Harold Wilson, seriously considered cancelling the whole ceremony because of concerns about security, not to mention the spiralling cost of surveillance, including extra policing (by this time there was a round-the-clock watch on water pipes to England!).

So it's against this background that my story unravels...

1

Stop Press:
January 1968

A BITTER ICY January wind laced with a flurry of snowflakes met me at the corner of Shaftesbury Avenue. I was greeted by a shrill cry: 'Evening Standard! Evening Standard!' The wet slippery pavements were mainly deserted, apart from motley couples scuttling for home after an evening at the West End's cinemas or thatres. I glanced at a clock in a shop window. 10.30.

'Late edition, late edition: Standard!' I then noticed a short squat figure, a woollen cap pulled over his ears, and an old khaki overcoat reaching down to his feet. He seemed to be no more than 4 feet tall. Reaching into my pocket I fished out a few pennies (it was pre-decimal times!), handed it over, grabbed the newspaper and hurried on my way.

I dived into the entrance of Picadilly underground station. A forlorn would-be busker, voice like a rusty rasp, was murdering the soul of a popular Bob Dylan ballad. I dropped a few coppers into the dirty piece of material that served as his cash register, then proceeded at a brisk pace towards the escalator, glancing over my shoulder a couple of times. As I descended into the bowels of London I was engulfed by much warmer air rising from the busy subway. There wasn't far to travel on the tube. Checking the route map on the platform I noted the Bakerloo line that I needed to take me to Russell Square, where I was staying at the Russell Hotel.

Within minutes, my train screeched to a halt, doors opened,

and I leapt aboard, made my way to a corner seat, as my ears began to thaw with the comparative heat. I unfolded the newspaper and my eyes fell on a **STOP PRESS** story headlined: 'Three men held on charges relating to explosives in North West Wales...' There wasn't much more. There wasn't need for much more. For a moment I froze – only it wasn't the weather this time. The names of these men were there in front of my very eyes.

I knew all three. Two had lived not far from my parents' farm on the Llŷn peninsula, and the third lived on Anglesey. Trying to maintain my composure, I quickly glanced round the half-empty carriage, habitually screening in my mind the occupants of each seat. As I did so, that cliché 'Trust No One' came to mind.

The 1960s were memorable in many ways; it was a turning point in modern history, bringing upheaval into the behaviour of society where youth rebelled against centuries of doctrines and codes of conduct. The age of free love had dawned; not only was religion being questioned and challenged, but also politics worldwide was being redefined and reshaped as new nations changed the global boundaries almost daily.

The Vietnam war was at its height, bringing with it protests both peaceful and violent. New world leaders emerged from the shadows. Young nations in Africa and beyond were smashing the shackles of colonialism...

2

Reflections and Back Story

I was born in Bangor Hospital in the mid 1930s, with the Second World War somewhere on the far horizon. My mother was Jane Mary Williams from Cwmystradllyn and my father Griffith Williams, from Cwm Pennant. I was the youngest in our family.

Mam was one of four sisters and one brother. Her father, Morris Edwards, farmed a very small smallholding called Cefn Bifor, which nestled on the shores of a natural lake at the foot of Moel Hebog. Life was tough on those few bleak acres. During the late 1940s or early 1950s, the old Llŷn District Council acquired it to provide water for the peninsula. When a dam was constructed at the southern end, the waters rose and my Mam's childhood home was submerged.

Mam was no more than five feet tall, small-boned, with long plaited brown hair and a round, friendly face. She had mischievous blue eyes that did not miss a thing. My earliest memories of her are engraved in my mind: baking all the bread, making butter in the cold, damp cellar under our farmhouse. I can see her now in the summer, lugging large heavy metal buckets filled to the brim with skimmed milk, to feed the calves waiting by the back field gate. Every day she would don a sack cloth over her apron in order to keep clean. One sound I will never forget is that of her wooden-soled clogs, clicketty clonk, clinketty clonk, on the concrete yard outside the kitchen door, or along the stony farm track as she hurried along. She was astute, sincere, inventive and industrious – she had to be, in order to raise a family of four growing sons on meagre funds. The whole farm, a beehive of activity, hummed around the queen bee that was Mam.

My father, Griffith, was from a long line of tenant farmers who hailed from Cwm Pennant, the youngest of a family of four sons and two daughters. He was born on the 14 July, the anniversary of the storming of the Bastille during the French Revolution. He could get volatile and could be hot-tempered. The way I see it, my father was a workhorse, labouring from morning till dusk, seven days a week. Mam, on the other hand, was the original entrepreneur. As well as working around the clock, she had vision and ambition.

My father was a born shepherd. I think that most people from Cwm Pennant and surrounding areas were. I can remember him standing on top of the stone wall by the sheep pens, where a thousand ewes and almost the same number of lambs would be crammed into the farm lane which acted as an impromptu pen. Stepping carefully along the top of the wall, his sharp eyes sweeping along the flock below him, suddenly he would call out: 'Catch that ewe over by the far wall... the one next to that spotted faced one – it's not ours, it's got a different earmark!!'

My brother and helpers would gaze at each other, bewildered: 'Which blinking sheep does he mean?'

Out of almost a total of 2,000 sheep, he had noticed a stray. Now that is a gift that does not belong to anyone, it is handed down from one generation to the next. All the hill and mountain farms have their own earmark, each one different. The one at Gwynus was called 'Cara ar y chwith a bwlch tri toriad dan y dde' (roughly translated, it means 'slice off top left ear and three-sided cut below right ear'). These cuts were made with a pair of shears – wool shears – and nobody was allowed to participate in this most holy of functions, except my father. Diwrnod nodi – earmarking day – on our farm was an event and a half; with a thousand lambs to be done every year, it was a very long day.

13

When I was born, my parents were farming Treigwm, a medium-sized stock farm outside the village of Sarn. The land was of good quality and we grew arable crops including cereals, barley and oats. The large stone farmhouse also had well-maintained outbuildings, including a big barn. My first memories on this planet are of playing in an outside loft where maize was kept. But when I was about three years old, my family were ready to move once more. This time it would be permanent.

My Mam had seen in the local paper that a large farm was going vacant about two miles north of Nefyn. She was adamant that a family with four growing sons needed more land – my older brother Morris was now fourteen. My father was quite reluctant to take the plunge into a vast undertaking as he obviously had no funds or savings at such a time of depressed markets.

Gwynus, a tenanted holding like most farms in the area, was one of the biggest farms on the Llŷn peninsula, around 440 acres, which is as near as can be to a square mile. It had been owned by the Lloyd family of Anglesey for centuries. Although it can't be proven, I'm convinced it was a part of land confiscated from our last Welsh prince Llywelyn, after he was killed by English troops near Builth in mid Wales in 1282.

Since I was too young to remember our arrival at Gwynus, I cannot recall the day or how we got there. All I know is that the farm had deteriorated from its former glory. The house itself was in a state of disrepair, windows were boarded up with cheap plywood, hinges were broken on all doors, slates had fallen from walls and roofs. As for the fields and land in general, bracken, gorse, nettles and dock had encroached from the banks and stone walls, leaving only small patches of grass in the middle. All this had to be rectified with painful hard labour.

Only horses were available for the first few years to plough and re-seed most of the fields. My elder brother Morris was in charge of around twelve carthorses, Shires and Clydesdale.

I think there were a couple of Percherons, although that bit of information came to me whilst listening in the kitchen as the men talked about their tasks. In those days boys of fifteen were men! At the time my father employed two other men: one helped with the cattle and general farm work and another was a *'cartmon'* – or in overall charge of feeding, harnessing and bedding the horses with my brother Morris.

My second eldest brother John – or John Griffith, as my mother called him, a combination of Taid and my Father – was still at Pwllheli County School, as it was known then. John had dark gingery hair and also worked on the farm, mainly with the cattle. We had around 100 pure bred Welsh Black Cattle by the end of our first full year at Gwynus. There were also over 1,000 Welsh ewes – that was my father's department.

My third brother, Ellis Vaughan, experienced a traumatic event when he was three years old. My parents were farming Porthtreuddyn, near Porthmadog, at the time. The whole family was out, getting the hay ready for gathering. My other brothers Morris and John would have been around eight and six years old, but doing what they could to help. No-one noticed Ellis was missing until they stopped to have tea. Since the hay field straddled the Porthmadog road, it was feared that Ellis might have walked through the open gateway on to the road. After hours of frantic searching, as dusk fell, Ellis appeared, trembling, shaking and sobbing uncontrollably. He pushed past my mother, scrambled upstairs, collapsed onto his bed still wearing his clothes and boots and pulled the bedclothes over his head. Mam and Dad were at his bedside as he tried to speak, bleating and crying at the same time.

Eventually he managed to blurt out the name of a disturbed teenager from the village. Apparently the youth had passed the hayfield and had seen Ellis sleeping by a pile of hay. Unobserved, he had crept up, put a hand over Ellis' mouth to stop him calling out, then he had placed him in a sack he was carrying. The youth said he was taking him to the river and was going to drown him. What really happened on that day, nobody knows. One thing is certain, a young boy's life was ruined forever in those missing hours.

From that day onwards, Ellis relived this incident every night of his life as he developed the worst kind of epilepsy. Not a night would pass that wouldn't involve either my father, mother or my two elder brothers having to get out of bed to attend to him when he had an epileptic fit. He was on medication for his whole life and suffered immensely, but, he always remained cheerful and could be full of mischief.

Farming meant that we were largely self-sufficient. Twice yearly, two pigs would be killed, one in early spring and one in autumn. A nearby farmer who had experience as a butcher would arrive at the farm quite early in the morning, usually on a Saturday. This meant that I was present to witness the scary proceedings. First thing in the morning, Mam would boil several kettles of water, enough to fill a large galvanized bath. The unfortunate animal would then be dragged, squealing, to the 'Gegin Foch' in Welsh which actually means Pigs' Kitchen, where pigswill was boiled in a huge cauldron over an open fire. After the pig had been successfully hauled into the kitchen, he was hoisted by means of a rope dangling from the rafter onto a wooden bench. He was tied and held down while the butcher would take a long pointed knife and plant it through his lower neck right into the heart! The pig would give an ear piercing shrill cry, wailing as its blood poured out of the wound. As soon as the animal was pronounced dead, boiling water would be poured over the carcass, and then a kind of large cut-throat razor was used to shave all the hair off the skin.

From the moment that the men entered the pigsty to catch the doomed animal, it was time for me to get away as far as possible from the bloody scene. I would sprint across several fields, over banks and stone walls, finally cupping both hands over my ears to try and block out the terrible sound of shrill screams. I guess I was rather a hypocrite since I scoffed every rasher of bacon my Mam put on my plate and even asked for more!

In addition to the ritual of killing a pig, we would also witness a few lambs suffering the same fate. There was one difference; my father would kill the lambs himself. He used a sharp pocket knife to slit the lamb's throat, bleeding it into a bucket. The lamb would then be hung from a rafter, skinned and cut before it was 'salted'. This same process was used on the sections of pig meat, with loads of household salt being rubbed in to preserve it. The salted ham sides would then be hung from meat hooks on the kitchen ceiling. Since there were no fridges or freezers, it was the only way of securing a supply of meat throughout the year. As I vaguely recall, it was an offence to butcher meat for one's own use in wartime, but most farmers did it.

In addition to providing meat, my father had a large vegetable patch in one of the fields beside the house. As well as potatoes and carrots, swedes and turnips, he grew cabbage, lettuce, sprouts, beetroot, onions, parsnips etc. During the spring months he would spend hours toiling in those long vegetable rows, weeding and thinning. He was very proud of his gardening accomplishments – and so he should have been. How he managed to maintain a garden and tend a couple of thousand sheep at the same time, God knows. Surely, there weren't enough hours on the clock to accommodate all this very necessary work?

To cap it all, at a time when farming itself was coming out of a recession, Mam decided she would venture into the world of tourism. Despite the deprivations of the second World War, she set out to establish the old large farmhouse as holiday accommodation, offering 'full board'.

Not everyone at Gwynus was entirely happy about Mam's intention to keep visitors. My Father tut-tutted the whole idea, playing it down as some modern fad that had no future. He was particularly annoyed at the thought of giving up his spacious bedroom for some squashed attic! He shook his head, furrowed his brows and puffed vigorously on his pipe – the only luxury he allowed himself. But all protests were in vain. Mam's mind was made up and that was it. She knew that the farm's income had to be supplemented during our first few years at Gwynus.

When the guests came, the whole family was temporarily evacuated from the main house. Mam and Dad, my brother Ellis and myself were moved to a small, cramped attic above the kitchen. My two elder brothers, Morris and John had to sleep in an outside loft above the barn. Water for washing had to be carted all the way across a dark unlit yard, then up a long wooden stairs, the only light being a small oil lamp that provided an anaemic flame.

On the other hand, the farmhouse, even the small attic, had the comparative luxury of an oil fired generator. This cumbersome piece of engineering would ingeniously start up when someone pressed a light switch in the house. Only when the last light bulb was switched off at night, would the noisy motor stop. When it was actually running, it produced a thunderously repetitive rat-a-tat that was audible from a fair distance. I well recall farmers, lost uncles and aunts we hadn't seen for ages and others suddenly appearing to view this strange contraption that generated electricity where no mains supply was available. The Lister Start-o-matic transformed our lives to a great extent, as it did hundreds of other isolated farms and dwellings in Llŷn and far beyond. This, above all else, enabled my Mother to embark on her venture into the world of tourism. One other major contributory factor was the arrival of an AGA, replacing an open fire grate that had ruled the hearth for ages.

Then, when I was eight, we had running water in the house! – thanks to Mr Moss, of Blakes of Accrington. As it turned out, Mr Moss – I never did get to know his first name – was to stay with us at Gwynus for several days, maybe weeks even, I just don't remember. He slept in a small parlour downstairs which my Mam had temporarily converted into a bedroom for him.

Blakes of Accrington built and supplied equipment that enabled water to be piped to mainly isolated farms all over the British Isles. They also provided engineers to install the system. The main component was a heavy cast iron pump called a 'hydram'. Pieces of machinery had arrived during the cold winter. These were then loaded onto a battered trailer pulled by a little green Fordson tractor and taken to a far-off corner of the farm, almost a mile away. A drain had to be cut all the way from the source of the water supply, a natural spring, before long metal pipes could be laid in the trench. The spring was quite far from the house and at a much lower altitude, so the hydram would pump the water uphill into a brick-built reservoir holding around 2,000 gallons, which could then flow downhill to the farm. Mains water was not available on such isolated farms as ours – indeed it had only just arrived in most villages.

Eventually the great day arrived. A local plumber had already installed the taps and fittings in the house. Mr Moss stood by the new galvanized kitchen sink and turned the tap on. After a few bursts and shuddering as air was forced out of the pipes, water gushed out, much to everyone's delight, particularly my smiling mother who was nodding in approval. Installing a reliable source of water was a blessing which improved not only the quality of life for everyone but also made it possible for her to develop her tourist business.

Long winter evenings could be most depressing, but in general, the atmosphere in Gwynus was quite relaxed. When darkness fell and the farm work was completed, we would have supper and retire into the front parlour. We sat around a glowing coal fire in the inglenook fireplace. My father would read one of the two Welsh-language newspapers then available – *Y Cymro* or *Herald Cymraeg*. We had an old wooden radio, or wireless as we called it, which, depending on the signal quality or even the weather, often produced an irritating crackling sound. Probably the main centre of our 'entertainment' was the draughts board. Hours and hours were spent puzzling and plotting new moves in order to lead an opponent into a trap. Morris was the family champion when I learnt to play the game. As a child I would end up frustrated when he would kindly 'give' me one of his kings, only to take three of mine in exchange! Following months of struggling, I gradually acquired some of his skills and on the odd occasion actually beat him – although I sometimes wonder if this was a ploy on his part to stop me losing interest!

During Mr Moss's stay with us, he would join us by the fireside and start to play draughts. According to his initial comments, he was a dab hand at the game... indeed the local champion, no less! We were soon to discover otherwise. My brother swept the board with him. After three games, Mr Moss stated that he had a headache and went to bed early. Doubts were cast on his sudden ailment – and his claims to being a 'champion!'

When I was five years old, despite my protests, I had to start school. I have vague memories of sitting on the crossbar of my brother John's bike as he pedalled furiously downhill into the village of Pistyll at the foot of a steep hill a short distance from the sea. Pistyll Elementary School was two or three hundred yards from the village. It stood in a concreted yard, surrounded by a high wall with iron railings on top. As my brother took me through the tall iron gateway, my heart sank. From the moment my mother had mentioned the word SCHOOL, panic had set in. I was already planning my escape from this much talked-about institution – before I had even seen it!

Miss Owen, the only teacher, seemed friendly enough, dressed in a long blue cotton dress, wavy brown hair, permed. She was quite tall (well, tall for Wales, that is), about 5 foot 6, which seemed to me to be about a yard taller than my Mam at five foot nothing! Having said 'bye' to my brother, Miss Owen took me inside the school cloakroom and hung my coat on a hook alongside some other coats and caps. As for the actual school classroom itself, there was only one, no bigger than a lounge in an ordinary house. That was a memorable day – not just for me, but the whole school population, as it climbed into double figures – there were now ten pupils!!

I was introduced to the others; Tecwyn, Ron, Loreta, William,

Maggy, Jane, Rose, Elizabeth, Eileen. A couple of them were my age, while the rest would be anything up to eight years of age. Then they had to leave for Nefyn school and get ready to sit their eleven plus exams. I was placed to sit at a wooden desk like the others. Before formal lessons had even begun, I'd already decided that school was definitely not for me! When dinner break arrived I wasn't really hungry, being too stressed out with this completely alien environment. Maybe the fact that I was already five, or that I lived on an isolated farm where I never saw another child had something to do with it. Whatever the reason, I wanted out.

One of the slightly older boys, with curly hair, red cheeks and buck teeth, had been sizing me up. We were on the school yard and the other kids had formed a sort of circle around us. This particular kid was definitely looking for trouble. This situation was new for me, so then and there, without warning, I lashed out at Buck Teeth, catching him bang on the nose. Blood spurted out. As he fell on his arse on the hard concrete, I bolted for the school gate, watched by the other kids, mouths agape. I was probably more scared than any of them. I scrambled over the rusty wrought iron gate and legged it down the steep hill. Halfway down the road, I turned my head and saw four or five of the other kids in hot pursuit. I thought they were going to kill me. My little feet accelerated to full throttle, my heart pounded and I gasped for breath. While in full flight, one of my boots caught in a pothole and I flew headlong through the air, landing face down on the tarmac, grazing both my knees on loose chippings. The pursuing mob arrived at the scene, followed by Miss Owen. To my amazement, they weren't chasing me to finish me off. On the contrary, they wanted me back in school. I noticed 'Buck Teeth' was missing, apparently bathing his battered nose at the school's only tap. My eventful first day thankfully came to a close at 3 o'clock – the sight of my brother John's bicycle coming through the school gates to fetch me home brought my first smile of the day.

After that first day at Pistyll school, I was taken there by bus. At that time I was the only one to disembark at Pistyll. One day, a stranger arrived in a large black car and took out several small cardboard boxes from the back. We all watched with innocent curiosity as the contents of these boxes were revealed – they were gas masks! Until then, all we had in the school to remind us that a war was going on were a few posters issued by the government – there was one showing an RAF pilot in the cockpit of his fighter plane. One larger poster stood out. It depicted dozens of paratroopers dropping from the sky, stood out. Presumably it was to remind us of the danger of a German invasion. We were given brief instructions on how to put the gas masks on. To us it was a novelty which we found amusing. Little did we realize that the authorities were taking precautions in case of a German air attack using poison gas! I had to carry the gas mask to school every day, tucked into the cardboard box with a string attached which fitted over my neck.

I must have been about seven or eight years old when a long, black shiny car drew into the farmyard and out climbed a short, strangely dressed man, accompanied by his chauffeur, and two women. Major Roger Lloyd was the landowner of Gwynus, a tenanted holding. He habitually wore a tweed jacket, check plus fours and a deerstalker hat. Brown brogues and canary yellow stockings completed the outfit. My Father walked across to greet them and took off his cap! Then shook his hand! My father was my hero – why had he shown such respect to this weird stranger? I was dumbfounded. This minor incident disturbed me, contributing towards formulating my radical political beliefs later on, no doubt!

Politics was not a subject often mentioned in our house; my parents were too busy trying to make a living, working hard around the clock. I was aware that a war was going on somewhere in Europe and that men and women from our community were 'over there' fighting a guy called Hitler. As far as my immediate family was concerned, no-one was involved in active service as farming was a very essential part of the war effort and they were exempt from military duties. There was one exception; my elder brother Morris was drafted into the Home Guard when he was eighteen. He was given a khaki uniform, just like the 'regular' soldiers, and had a rifle which he kept at home.

Life could be lonely on an isolated hill farm; but it changed when I moved from Nefyn primary school and passed my eleven plus to enter Pwllheli Grammar School. To say it was a cultural shock would be a vast understatement. While Nefyn was a close knit, pretty rural and entirely Welsh-speaking community – in fact most of the kids were monoglot Welsh – Pwllheli Grammar, by contrast, was a much anglicised institution. English was the language of the classroom. The teachers would address us in English inside school and on the yard and playing fields. It is difficult to comprehend such a situation because at that time, even in Pwllheli and surrounds, more than 90 per cent of children could speak only Welsh.

To understand the origin of such an unbalanced and unnatural situation, one doesn't have to delve very far back into history. As recently as the 1860s, children in Wales were punished and actually beaten for speaking Welsh either in the schools or out on the school ground. When a child was 'caught' speaking Welsh in the school yard he would be reprimanded and a wooden board with two holes drilled each side to fit a piece of rope through, would be placed around the victim's neck. Printed on this board were the words 'WELSH NOT'. The other children were encouraged to jeer at the child bearing the board. Should another child dare to utter one word of Welsh, the 'badge of shame' would be handed to him or her. Finally, the last child to be in possession of the 'WELSH NOT' slogan when break-time was up, would be taken to the front of the class and beaten with a stick.

Incidentally, during that period, my grandfather Morris Edwards was himself a victim of the 'Welsh Not' policy. Ironically, I discovered later that his father was half Spanish and that his real surname had been Eduardes! I remember him

23

speaking English with great difficulty. On one occasion, while staying with his daughter near Manchester, he was mistaken for a Russian by a shop assistant! So much for that attempt at enforced assimilation and integration.

So once I had mastered the art of reading English at the age of nine or ten years old, I soon took an interest in history and politics. When I was ten years old, I was possibly the youngest member of Plaid Cymru – or Plaid Genedlaethol Cymru, as it was known.

3

Secondary school and adolescence; love

WHEN THE SECOND World War ended in 1945, I was in Pwllheli Grammar School. As soon as we entered the building, we were addressed in English – the exception being the twice weekly Welsh-language lessons and religious instruction. At least 95 percent of the children were Welsh-speakers. There is no doubt in my mind that confining our language to the classroom at that stage in our life was detrimental, ill-judged and discriminatory. Despite the forcing of English down our throats, it didn't work out that well, since most of the kids would have only basic knowledge of that language on leaving school at sixteen.

There were, however, a few bright spots shining through the gloom. I was a fanatic sports fan – I know I'm called a fanatic for other reasons! I took advantage of the school facilities. Here I could practise the long jump in a proper sandpit. When I was around sixteen years of age, I was aiming to jump twenty feet but never quite reached that distance – being almost two feet short! In order to practise at home, I dug a long hole in the ground in a field alongside the house, which I re-filled with a combination of sand and fine soil I found lying around. This was my 'sand pit' of sorts! Dreams of future glory sped before my eyes as I measured the distance I had leapt each day with an old tape measure of my Mam's. Weekly the distances increased inch by inch. As I sprinted and leapt, I dreamt of standing on a podium proudly holding the Welsh dragon flag above my head, with the Welsh national anthem playing in the background. When I opened my eyes, instead of the cheering thousands, there stood my father's sheepdog Gelert, head on one side, studying the spectacle before him with his one remaining eye.

Rounding up sheep on a 440-acre holding required a lot of running, and an equal amount of shouting and swearing! We had sheepdogs of varying degrees of competence, and it's hard to believe that this gave me my first lesson in athletics. I was totally useless in running long and middle distances – but sprinting, that's where I came into my own. My father soon discovered I had the ability to sprint like a hare; not a hare in overdrive, perhaps, but still pretty nippy. I had to be a good runner in order to cut off the escape of young lambs, which would seize any opportunity to break away from the flock. I can hear him now calling out 'Da iawn!' when I had successfully intercepted one of the usual culprits; heart pounding, gasping for air, the shirt on my back wet from sweating – but I really enjoyed it.

I played football at almost every position, forward, back, even a spell at keeping goal. We had a sports teacher called Mr Williams – Big Boy we named him, and he WAS big, in his mid forties, with dark short curly hair, always looking tanned and fit. One day, he decided to put me in goal. A penalty was awarded against our team. I had been practising for such an event. A tall scrawny lad came up and banged the ball into the left hand corner while I dived to the right!

To my embarrassment Big Boy yelled out for everyone to hear, 'Owen Williams makes a spectacular dive to the WRONG side after the ball hits the back of the net!' All the kids from both teams laughed, except me.

Rugby was introduced in our school only during the last couple of years of my stay. On one of my trips to the cinema, I had seen a couple of clips of a match when the Welsh national team was playing. The game seemed exciting and appealed to me. One day, Big Boy threw us a rugby ball, brightly instructed us on the basic rules, and away we went. It took less than ten minutes for me to become a casualty. One of the boys from the opposite side ran towards our try line and in an effort to stop him, I took a flying dive to grab his ankles. As I hit the ground, there was a sickening crack. A teacher came over, took a quick look and pronounced it was definitely a fracture.

He took me to Richard Williams the bonesetter, a scrawny, elderly gentleman with wavy snow white hair, rimless glasses and a slight stoop. For a moment I writhed as he sat me down in a chair facing him and held my arm in his hands, calmly saying 'This may hurt a little...' Without further warning, he jerked my wrist upwards for a fleeting second, then a slight twist – I shouted... no, actually I swore, a combination of Welsh and English, though the 'f' word hadn't quite found its way through the school gates then! Unfolding some bandages, he wound them round my wrist a few times, and then put my arm in a sling which was held together by a huge safety pin. That was it; no hospital visit, no X-ray, no plaster of Paris, but miraculously, it gradually healed! The incident put an end to my sporting ambitions for some time. The pain lasted for several days.

Incidentally, this was the second fracture for me in a three-year period. Riding my pony Seren outside the farmhouse one evening, I decided to try and race a motorbike along the farm track – not the most sensible of choices. This particular motorbike was old – no, that is an understatement, it was antique! Hugh Hughes the local rabbit catcher owned it. It had a tendency to backfire. On the day that I decided to throw down the gauntlet and challenge him to race Seren, the motorbike let out a resounding Bang! like a fired shotgun. My pony leapt and sent me flying, landing on my elbow, suffering quite a serious double fracture. As a result I spent three weeks at the Bangor Infirmary.

I was nine years old and had never spent a night away from home before. Time passed very, very slowly, although Mam came to visit me a couple of times a week. Knowing that I was lost and lonely, she used to bring me books to read. One book still stands out: *Owain Glyndŵr* by Thomas Pennant. I must have read that book a dozen times. It had pictures or artists' impressions of our warrior prince, also pictures of battle sites and of his former home. This book, more than anything else, aroused my interest in my country's history and struggles. I am indebted to my Mother for buying it: it changed my life and set me on the path of patriotism.

At school in Pwllheli, I certainly wasn't a brilliant scholar. The subjects I excelled at were geography, history, art, Latin, English and Welsh. As far as physics, chemistry, music and written arithmetic were concerned, they are best forgotten! There is one exception. I had a knack for mental arithmetic and could calculate in my head quicker than most people. Originally my Father wanted me to stay in school and maybe become a lawyer. Unfortunately, my obsession with sports meant I was not paying attention to subjects that mattered academically; as a result, my marks diminished and my standing in class plummeted from as high as third to about fourteenth. Dad made his mind up: I would have to leave school to help on the farm. I was still a month short of my fifteenth birthday.

At the time I hated the thought of having to work on the farm. Since I was about ten or eleven, I'd had to milk cows by hand after coming from school, churn the milk to make butter, feed pet lambs and carry out a myriad of chores. Frankly, the very thought of having to work full time, seven days a week, doing jobs I was not happy with, scared me.

Because I had now left school, it meant losing contact with all my friends and associates. I did not have the means to travel to town. To overcome the isolation, I would walk down to the village some nights after work to play football with the other children. One good friend of mine, Bob, lived on a farm over the hill by the sea, about a mile away. Bob used to walk over to our house and we would spend the evening playing draughts or talking about this and the other. Eventually, Bob joined the Merchant Navy and would travel to all points of the compass, much to my envy! He would send letters and cards to me from as far away as South America, Europe and even Russia. I missed his company at the time.

On Saturday nights and Wednesday evenings, I would visit Pwllheli, our nearest town. One of my two older brothers would drive there. I would invariably visit the cinema, usually accompanied by my cousin Owen Pennant. We were extremely good friends and had a laugh together. Sometimes we'd visit a cafe or milk bar to pass the time before the cinema opened. At the time it would have been unthinkable to visit a pub since both our families were devout Welsh Methodists and drink was taboo! Girls were not on the agenda at that period of my life. I made up for that later on!!!!!

I was a member of the Young Farmers' Club. We had a small branch at Pistyll, and would hold social evenings as well as lectures on most things, from animal husbandry to managing grasslands. We had quiz nights and sometimes we would visit other clubs in the county. It was a way of meeting people and socializing. Eventually, when I was around twenty years old, I became leader of our club. One of my pastimes was driving my little Ford Prefect along our narrow country lanes. I taught myself a few skills and considering the size of the engine, attained a decent level of performance from it. Like most young men, I sometimes imagined myself a better and faster driver than I really was. I did survive a couple of crashes, usually taking a bend too fast, discovering that a car does not necessarily round a bend on two wheels without repercussions!

During this period of my life I had but briefly come into contact with members of the opposite sex. Shyness was my pitfall. I found it difficult to start a conversation with girls my age. Quite a few young females, some quite attractive, would come to stay at the farmhouse with their families. The first brief encounter I had with one of them didn't happen until I was in my late teens. Her boyfriend had been staying with her and her parents over the weekend, but had to leave on the Sunday evening. I noticed she would smile and say a greeting each time she would see me around the farm. Then she started following me around and I thought, is she flirting with me?

One day I picked up the courage to ask did she fancy taking a walk that evening – she gladly agreed. Great. I thought, I'm getting somewhere here! After an early supper, I slipped quietly out of the house. (My mother didn't think it was a good idea to 'fool around' with young 'hussies'.) When I got outside, she was waiting for me. Shyly, I held her hand as we walked across the fields towards the top of our hill. We sat on the grass and talked. She mentioned her boyfriend; that made me feel slightly guilty, although, when the cat's away... and all that! We ended up with a little goodnight kiss – more of a peck in reality. These walks continued for the rest of her stay, much to my Mam's annoyance. She still referred to the young girl as 'that hussy'. We never did get into any really passionate clinches, just holding hands and a few innocent cuddles. When it was time for her to leave, I thought that my world would collapse!

My cousin Owen Penant was still an important part of my life. While I was greatly influenced by politics, Owen on the other hand was infatuated with motor bikes, mechanics and engineering in general. He actually built his own bikes out of bits and bobs he managed to acquire on his limited budget – very limited, since we were allocated about 50 pence a week pocket money. Still, we did not complain, as we supplemented this by catching rabbits and taking them to Pwllheli where Miss Clark, an octogenarian, would buy them from us to sell in her fish and game shop in the town's Gaol Street. We were paid a shilling for each rabbit.

Occasionally on Sunday evenings in the summer, I used to go down to Nefyn, walk along the cliffs or on the beach, where we would sometimes visit the cafe halfway down the hairpin bend above the sea. With one of my friends, Alun from Pistyll, we would chat up visitor girls who stayed in the area for a week or two during the summer months. When autumn and winter returned, it was back to the old routine, cinema on

Saturday and a Wednesday evening, Young Farmers' Club on a Thursday.

I met my wife Irene when she and her sister were staying for a week's holiday in Nefyn. Alun had encountered the two sisters the previous evening and had arranged a date for the next day. He rang me to tell me about the two 'stunners' and we were to meet them in Nefyn. As it happened, I had plucked up the courage to ask a girl from Cricieth out that evening – and she'd agreed! But Alun was very persistent. 'When you see these two, I'm telling you...' Oh well, I thought, if they don't live up to the description, I can always go back and see that Cricieth girl. I was almost twenty-two years old and it was the day of the Cricieth Fair, 28 June, a big occasion in a rural community. I picked Alun up in my Ford Prefect car. The girls were waiting and as soon as I saw Irene, I thought, 'This one's mine!' She was medium height, slim, and her short, curly brown hair was bleached by the sun. She had beautiful, clear skin and two huge brownish green eyes. She seemed very pleasant and laughed a lot – I liked that!

We jumped in the car, went to the fair and had a whale of a time on all the rides, eating candyfloss, ice cream, talking a lot. She said she worked as a dental nurse in a clinic in Halesowen, more or less a suburb of Birmingham. She told me her surname was Howell, that she had one Jewish grandmother, and one Italian. She was just seventeen years old... and I was already falling in love with her!

But there was a serious setback to romance; they were both going home the next day – their holiday was over! As we said a passionate goodbye, I wondered if we would ever meet again. We exchanged addresses and I promised to visit her. Summer passed painfully slowly – I was smitten, no question. Once or twice my mother scolded me for acting like a 'love struck puppy' and ordered me to pull myself together and find a nice Welsh farm girl! Alun and I drove to Halesowen and rented a room above a rather noisy pub. I phoned Irene's work number and we met. Then she said that I wouldn't be able to visit her

31

house because her father would object – and what's more, she had to be home by 10.00 every night, with an extra half hour on Saturday. When I asked about this, she dropped a bombshell – she was only sixteen!

She'd known that I wouldn't have had anything to do with her if she'd told me her real age when we met. She was sorry. Of course, I believed her. No matter how many times I turned the matter over, my heart overruled my head. Besides, I just couldn't turn back the clock – and I was a romantic, in my personal and political life. Since we both wanted to be together all the time, we agreed that when she was seventeen, she would try to find a job in Caernarfon.

I met her at Bangor station. She stood on the platform, looking diminutive, carrying a suitcase containing all her worldly belongings. My heart swelled with a combination of love and sorrow; she had left her home and family to be with me. I prayed that we had done the right thing. When we're young, we follow our hearts and to hell with the consequences, I suppose. On reflection, my life has been full of decisions taken on the spur of the moment. I act first and think after!! But I have 'no regrets', as Edith Piaf famously sang.

Irene found work with a local dental practice and a room in one of the town's B&Bs and soon made friends with two local girls. We'd meet up almost every evening after I finished work. I'd drive her to various places in Snowdonia. Two weeks after she'd arrived, Margaret, one of her new friends, asked if she'd like to stay in her house. I thought it was a good idea and Margaret and her family were very good to her. This arrangement worked well and we were very happy. I was head over heels in love and I thought it was mutual.

But my mother considered I was paying too much attention to 'that girl' and felt I was drifting away, even though I still worked very hard at home. At times, I started to feel I was being smothered. My parents were doing all they could for me, but somehow I was not leading my own life. I wanted to be in control and had the feeling I was being pressurized – though this was probably not true. One evening I asked Irene if she would marry me. She looked at me wide-eyed. 'Are you serious? Where would we live?'

I really hadn't given such a basic necessity a thought – which I suppose says something about my romantic personality. We couldn't afford to buy a house or pay rent at that point as I was paid £4 a week. I lived at home, didn't have to buy food or pay for electricity, didn't smoke or drink. My car was my biggest expense. Eventually, I had what I thought was a brilliant idea. I'd buy a caravan and site it in one of the fields on the farm, since Mam had already established a small caravan park there.

Our marriage was very private and quiet. Irene's parents, who occasionally spent holidays at Nefyn, called up at the farm to meet my parents – and me! We were from completely different backgrounds in a way, worlds apart. I found out afterwards that Irene's father George used to refer to me as 'that Welsh hillbilly'.

We were married at Llanbeblig church in Caernarfon and the reception was held at the home where she'd stayed for the last couple of months. Doreen, her sister, was bridesmaid and Doreen's boyfriend was best man. With the church warden as witness and the vicar officiating, we were six in total – a very modest affair. We did have a honeymoon – a week in Prestatyn!

Life in a caravan during spring and summer was a novelty – almost a holiday, except I worked a ten-hour day. Irene coped well in her new environment, though there were some odd moments. She complained that she'd been chased across the farmyard by 'a bloody massive chicken!' I burst out laughing – that was a turkey! Spring turned to summer and Irene became pregnant.

When autumn came with its cold winds and endless rain, living in the caravan was not so attractive, especially with a baby due in January. We rented a small house in Nefyn. It was a struggle, since the rent was half my weekly wage, but we managed. December was very cold; fine powdery snow would blow into the house through the door and window frames. We managed to stop this but the house was like Siberia. It was the last day of the year. We weren't going to celebrate New Year's Eve anyway, but it became obvious that the baby was going to arrive earlier than expected. We grabbed some things and drove to the maternity hospital in Bangor. Irene had to stay in overnight, but since the birth was not imminent, I could go home.

The next morning I rang the hospital early and was astonished to be told I had a baby daughter. I rushed in to Bangor and found Irene, sitting up in bed, with a carry cot alongside. And there was my little girl, Iona, looking very beautiful with big brown eyes. Though she only weighed five lbs and was a little premature, she seemed very alert.

My parents were very excited with their very first grandchild and doted on her. One Saturday afternoon my father said he was giving me £1 a week pay rise, which meant I was now getting £7 a week. Looking quite serious, he asked, 'Well, Owain bach, are you able to save much of your wages?'

I smiled and said,' Of course, father.'

4

Canadian Adventure Part 1

I NEEDED TO break free. It wasn't that I didn't value my parents' care and concern for me and my new family, far from it. Since I could remember, I had always meant to travel one day and see a little of the world. But I was now married and had a small child, so obviously options were restricted.

I loved my country dearly and wanted to make some political contribution to its future, but it was difficult. Unfortunately at that time, the end of the fifties, Wales was very stagnant. I had been a member of Plaid Cymru since I was ten years old, but I increasingly thought it was bankrupt of ideas. There was no vision, no leadership, just nice men in nice suits making nice speeches. Of course nobody took any notice of them, except a handful of middle-class academics and a few mavericks who were regarded as 'nutters' by the public.

When I was around fifteen, I joined the Welsh Republican Movement and used to get their monthly newsletter. What was revealing for me was that almost all their members were products of the south-east Wales valleys. They would organise protests whenever the Welsh identity was under threat, burning the Union Jack and challenging the Labour party. Once they succeeded in penetrating security and placed an explosive device on a Birmingham water pipeline near the Claerwen dam in mid Wales. A couple of their members were arrested and served time in prison. Several other members of the WRM served prison sentences for refusing to be conscripted into the British army. Strangely, there were hardly any members in the Welsh-speaking regions of north and west Wales. Eventually, mainly due to police harassment and adverse publicity in the unionist press, they faded away in 1959. So, since there was apparently no united front which could galvanise and give expression to Welshness, I decided to leave it all behind for a while and concentrate on my new family life.

I noticed an advertisement in a newspaper inviting applicants to settle in Canada. I contacted the address shown. Most work opportunities were either on the eastern side, around Toronto, or else in the prairie provinces of Manitoba, Saskatchewan and Alberta. The flat prairie lands did not excite me, as I was used to living not too far from the sea with the mountains of Snowdonia in the background. However, there was one post in British Columbia, on the Pacific coast. It sounded idyllic, working on a large farm just a few miles from Vancouver – and a small cottage went with the job.

Irene and I were both excited, like two kids. In less than an hour we had made up our minds to apply for the job in British Columbia. There were several matters to deal with before any final plans were made. We had to visit Canadian immigration, sign forms, update our passports, etc. All these necessary chores were quickly accomplished and, having paid the required deposits, we awaited a date for departure.

My parents were greatly perturbed by our decision to move so far away. Mam was particularly upset, pointing out we were taking a mere baby halfway across the world, 'It's all right for you,' she kept saying 'but think of the little one'. Naturally this caused me pangs of guilt and a more than a little soul-searching. In the end I promised we would return to Wales within three years. Whether that would be on a visit or permanently, I could not tell.

On a bright spring day in early May, we set out on our great adventure. Arriving in the port of Liverpool we made our way to where the liner *Empress of Britain* was berthed. The voyage from Liverpool, picking up extra passengers at Greenock in Scotland, would take six days. Once on board we were shown into our cabin by a friendly steward who also explained to us the general routine of daily life aboard what was to us, a luxury liner. Apart from dining rooms, lounges, bars and cafeterias, there was a swimming pool on one deck, complete with sun loungers. After settling down, we emptied our cases into a large wardrobe. We did not have many items with us on board, apart from essentials, clothing, baby wear, toiletries etc. All other items had been crammed into a large old metal chest which was buried somewhere in the ship's hold, to be recovered when we docked in Quebec.

This was the first time either of us – correction, the three of us – had ever been aboard a liner, or even a ship of any kind for that matter. I don't think a pleasure boat on the Marine Lake at Rhyl on a Sunday School outing counts! I was curious to have a walk around the several decks and explore it in detail. While Irene fed Iona, off I went on a grand tour of what was in a way a floating hotel. It was impressive. There was quite a variety of passengers on board, mostly middle-aged and retired, with the exceptions of a few young couples, some with children. I wondered to myself if any of them were, like us, moving to find work or in the hope of a better life.

Since it was almost time to sail, we picked a good vantage point from where we could see the city of Liverpool disappearing behind us as we headed out to sea. Many were of the same mind, and in no time the deck was packed. A loud booming sound from the ship's hooter made us sit up. Iona opened one eye lazily, wondering what the fuss was about. We were on our way!

Apart from docking at Greenock to pick up an extra couple of hundred passengers, we now had 4,000 miles of Atlantic ahead of us. High winds, rain or drizzle dominated most of the remaining journey. Meanwhile on board, there were not many activities we as a family could participate in, since the baby could not be left on her own. It seemed that there were only the bars and daily games of 'tombola' or bingo for entertainment. Booze and 'drinking sessions' did not appeal to either of us. As for bingo, no thanks!

I won't forget our last evening aboard in a hurry. We were preparing to leave the cabin for the restaurant and evening meal. Iona, as was the usual, was screaming for more milk – the teat of the bottle didn't seem to let out enough as she sucked it vigorously. I said to Irene that the hole was too small, and found a small pair of scissors and enlarged the hole ever so slightly. It seemed to work a treat, as the milk level in the bottle plummeted. All of a sudden, the baby's face turned blue as she gasped for breath making strange gurgling noises. Panicking, I picked her up, turned her on her stomach and tried slapping her gently on the back with my open hand. Nothing seemed to work so I ran out of the cabin shouting: 'Baby's choking – help!!'

A middle-aged gentleman wearing glasses appeared. 'Let's see,' he said grabbing Iona by her legs, holding her upside down before thumping her back, hard. Next thing, she coughed all of a sudden as a gush of milk streamed from her mouth. In no time, her colour returned to normal, even though she broke out crying. I'm sure she was about to suffocate. I felt very guilty over the incident for a long time afterwards.

As dawn broke next morning, we were in the estuary of a large river, the St Lawrence, heading for the French speaking city of Quebec. Canadian Pacific Railways' gleaming silver and red train would travel night and day to cover the 4,000 miles, one of the most striking and breathtaking journeys on the planet. Once we had boarded and were shown to our seats, we had our own compartment with sleeping accommodation, surely a must considering this was our home for the next six days. Within an hour of boarding, it was time to move – the train's distinctive hooter heralding our departure with a long twin blast. If anything, I was looking forward more to this transcontinental land journey than I had been to the sea voyage.

When I awoke next day, dawn was breaking and I could just make out an expanse of water as we sped along – I gathered we were alongside one of the Great Lakes, but, which one? Could have been Erie or even Lake Ontario, I mused. What amazed me was how smooth the train journey had been throughout the night. Apart from a gentle rocking and steady hum of the engine, we could have been at home sleeping. After eating breakfast in one of the dining cars, we decided to take a walk towards the front of the train, since our cabin was further back. We were amazed at the length; it seemed to go on and on through dozens of carriages. Right at the front almost was the observation car. Climbing a short stairway, we emerged in a glass domed chamber, complete with seats.

Already, even as such an early hour, the sun's warmth penetrated the glass roof. Considering that it was only mid May, it seemed pleasantly warm. Since the observation car provided an ideal vantage point, we were able to see large tracts of the countryside around. The lake seemed tranquil enough, surrounded by evergreen forests of spruce and sitka mostly. There didn't seem to be many signs of houses or villages – or even life. Just like the week-long sea voyage, the prospect of six days on a train, after the initial euphoria, began to seem a little daunting. Maybe the fact that we were very young and had a 4-month-old baby daughter to care for twenty-four hours a day was a factor. Most of the other passengers seemed to be pensioners. On the second day we awoke, we were still alongside one of the Great Lakes. I assumed this was Lake Superior, more of a sea than a lake. I marvelled at its vastness and realised Wales would fit within its boundaries three or four times!

By the third day we had seen the last of the Great Lakes, having crossed from Quebec and through Southern Ontario. We were now heading into the prairie provinces, Manitoba being first. Canadian prairies are vast in area, completely flat. Millions of acres are cultivated each year and sown with wheat or other cereals; the dust generated by the massive farm machines as they churn up the soil is incredible. After Winnipeg, a bustling city, the scenery changed dramatically as huge cereal farms stretched further than the eye could see. We sped past isolated farms with a few trading posts, shops or filling stations, not villages in any sense of the word. Scattered here and there would be the odd windmill, generating power for a farm or small settlement

It was an extreme engineering feat to carve a railway line across the Rockies, and it is surely spectacular. On the edge of the Rockies lies the town of Banff, now a world-famous skiing and winter sports resort centre. On the fifth day of our journey we left Banff and entered the mighty Rockies. We were now beginning to feel the excitement as our eventual destination came closer. From our seat in the observation car we could see deep ravines and canyons at least a mile below the conifer clad hills. Rivers snaked along the bottom in deep gullies, swelled by melting snow from high up on the lofty peaks. One of the most spectacular sights was watching huge brown bears in their natural habitat, playing with their cubs on steep rocky cliffs, literally yards away from where we sat. We were soon brought back to earth by Iona screaming for her milk. This was our last night on the train, as we were scheduled to arrive in Vancouver the following evening.

Eventually, as night fell, we saw Vancouver's city lights in the distance. We were approaching the Pacific Ocean. After almost two weeks' travelling, with the last six days in a rather confined space, we were both completely shattered. I imagine that Iona was probably feeling the same, but could not express it in words.

As the train glided into Vancouver's busy terminal, the platform was awash with humanity. We would be met at the station by my new employer, but how in God's name was he to recognise us? All I knew was he would be driving a station wagon – I did not even know its colour. I had been given a name: Mr Stevens. We pushed our way through the throng of people.

I juggled the carrycot and a suitcase while Irene dragged the other case. There was a large car park outside, overflowing with vehicles of all kinds, including at least two dozen station wagons. Most of the cars were unoccupied and I assumed Mr Stevens might be either sitting in his car or standing alongside it. Squinting through the semi dark, I made out the tall, slightly stooped figure of an elderly gentleman on the very far side of the parking lot. Walking over, I half heartedly enquired: 'Mr Stevens?'

He straightened himself up to his full height of about 6 feet 2, looked me up and down. 'You're Williams I take it – not very tall are you?', as if disappointed.

I dropped the suitcase but hung on to the carrycot and tried to stretch to my full 5 feet 8 – I was about to say 'No, but tall enough', but decided it would not have been the best time for such a comment.

Mr Stevens was old, very old, probably late eighties. He had a long face, deeply wrinkled and very weather-beaten. I decided straight away that he must be a tough old bastard. I told him we would have to pick up our heavy chest from the luggage office. He grunted his discontent but agreed to wait while I made arrangements to collect it. As I left, he growled, 'Don't be long now!'

Once we retrieved our trunk and managed to load it on to the back of the station wagon, we set off for Mr Steven's farm, which, if I deciphered his monosyllabic grunts correctly, was some twenty miles up the Fraser river. Driving at a steady forty miles an hour, he was no Stirling Moss or Michael Schumacher; bends, narrow lanes or freeway didn't make much difference, it was always forty miles per hour. After leaving the city limits, we took a sharp turn (at 40 mph!) and we came to one traffic light on red. Did he stop? He did not, just drove through – at 40 mph! About half an hour after leaving Vancouver's main station, we arrived at what seemed to be a dead end. Squinting through the unwashed windscreen, I could vaguely make out a faded sign with a logo depicting a ferry crossing – we had stopped on the bank of a large river. I enquired 'Where are we, do we take the ferry?'

Slowly removing the pipe from between his teeth, he half turned towards me. 'Yep, unless you wanna swim,' came the facetious reply.

'So,' I continued, trying to remain calm, 'Your farm is on the other side?'

Silence again, momentarily, then 'Nope. It's right in the middle!'

Hold on now, I thought, are you taking the piss here? Before I completely lost control, since I felt like grabbing him by his skinny throat, he added: 'It's an island... we live on an island'. Well, bloody hell, I thought, this was complete news to us. Where in hell's name was he taking us?

A short, thickset man appeared out of a shabby-looking wooden shed – he was the ferry man. He removed a barrier and switched on a powerful overhead lamp. We could now see the ferry. Mr Stevens drove his vehicle onto the rickety looking deck, which emitted unhealthy creaking sounds from the weight of its cargo. We were in mid river, moving at a very leisurely pace, when I decided to ask him what the hours would be like at work, and when would I start?

'You start tomorrow,' he croaked. 'We begin at 05:30'

'Mr Stevens,' I began, 'don't know if you are aware, but we started off two weeks ago from home... just been six days on that train journey alone. Would it be possible for me to start a bit later on the first day? Or maybe start work the following day?'

Removing his glasses methodically, he half-turned to face me, and said in what sounded an angry tone, 'Nope. I need you to start tomorrow morning. The other worker's gone, so we're short of hands.' Then silence: 'Tell you what though, since you tell me you've been on the road awhile, let's make it half six tomorrow!'

Wow, I thought, his generosity is overwhelming!

We drove from the ferry along a very narrow lane. Half a mile further, the farm came into view. Driving past the farmhouse, the old farmer headed for what looked like a wooden cabin – this was to be our new home. It was small, one bedroom, a small kitchen and a tiny living room with a wood burning stove right in the middle. There was no bathroom, an outside toilet and we would have to carry all the water from a well a hundred yards away. Welcome to Canada!! Since it was almost ten o'clock and the three of us were absolutely shattered, we would have to wait till next day to find out exactly what our situation was.

The next morning, heavy banging on the cabin door made me jump out of bed. This was followed by a stern voice shouting 'Time to get up, it's six o'clock... you start work in half an hour!'

I was still feeling the effects of our long journey and we'd had little sleep. The noise woke Irene although the baby slept through it all.

'Shit, I don't think I'm in a state to do much work' I said, though realising there wasn't much option. The old miser had us over a barrel; if I didn't work, he would throw us out of the cabin – in reality it was no more than a shack. On the other hand, it was a roof over our heads.

My wife put the kettle on an old gas stove to make some tea before I went outside. We had unearthed a few items stored in boxes in the cabin. There was a small pot of coffee, tea, a bottle of milk, a loaf of bread and a dish of butter plus a small packet of cornflakes. I gulped down the tea and ate a slice of bread before going out to start my new job.

Once outside, I saw a range of farm buildings, a large barn, cow sheds etc. In a large field stood around three hundred dairy cows, Holsteins, waiting to be milked and to be fed, a mixture of maize and barley with added molasses.

A short guy in overalls ambled across to meet me. 'I'm Hermann, farm foreman – what's your name by the way?' I introduced myself. They didn't do handshakes in this place, I noticed! 'OK... your job is to feed the cattle every morning.

They get five pounds of meal, you load it into this wheelbarrow and take it to them troughs. Once you've finished, you open the gate for them to come from the field.'

The wheelbarrow was not like the ones at home – this was king-sized. I reckoned it would hold around a hundredweight. Working it out quickly in my head, it meant three quarters of a ton to be wheeled out each morning. That would be fifteen trips. The distance from the storage shed to the trough was around 200 yards. This was equivalent to over three miles for each feeding session. The bad news was the procedure had to be repeated every evening! Luckily for me on the first day, Alec and another named Hank had done the work.

Ah well, I thought, there's hope for me yet! Most of my first day consisted of being shown around the farm and buildings. Since I already knew I would be starting work at 05:30 and was also aware that I had to repeat that duty each evening, starting at 17:30, which meant at least an hour and half work, I would not be finished until after seven in the evening! Christ, I thought to myself, can this be real? That's almost fourteen hours a day, six days per week... I was to be given Saturday off one week, Sunday the week after. An eighty-four hour week! No bloody way, I decided. However, during one 'tour' of the farm, Herman Schulz, a German prisoner of war who had stayed behind after the war had ended, told me after morning milking and feeding that I was off for four hours before resuming work at around two in the afternoon. Well, at least that was some relief. It would give me a respite and a little free time with my family. I was also told a ferry crossed from the island once a day and there was a small store on the other side, selling groceries etc.

By ten o'clock I was already feeling drained and starving. When I returned to the cabin, my wife had already started to clean up the kitchen and living room and Iona was sucking away at her bottle. There was one wash basin and an old metal bath tub which had seen better days. After washing and a quick change of clothes I felt slightly better. We would need to take the ferry first chance that arose, as we were desperate to get in some food supplies. Luckily Irene came across a couple of cans of baked beans on a window sill. Those with a couple of slices of toast made our first breakfast.

We both sat down later to work out how much I was being paid. At the time a pound sterling was worth two Canadian dollars and eighty cents. My wages were fifty dollars a week. Not a fortune, but there was no rent to pay and no electricity charges since the farm was powered by a small windmill. The major drawbacks were the hours and the location – we were right in the sticks. Having eaten, we decided to walk across to the ferry, find out the times and cost etc. It was a beautiful spring day. This part of British Columbia, the delta region around Vancouver, boasts a very temperate climate, warm summers and mild winters. As we strolled down the narrow lane strewn with potholes, the fields on both sides were covered with lush pastures, cows grazing contentedly. A variety of birds sang out of the hedges and colourful butterflies flew from flower to flower.

When we arrived at the jetty, the ferryman was slumped half asleep in an old deck chair, a straw hat covering his face. On hearing our approach he lazily removed the hat, squinting against the sun's glare, 'You're the new folks?' he began. We enquired about the ferry times and were told there was a daily crossing for passengers at noon, returning an hour later. As for cars, it seemed there were no strict rules. Since we were desperate for some items, it was decided that Irene would cross over to the store, which was but a short walk on the other side. Luckily, we had changed our currency to Canadian dollars as we docked in Quebec, so we had a grand total of 295 dollars and 28 cents!

I watched the ferry depart with Irene and Iona aboard, waved goodbye and returned to our cabin. Soon it would be time to start the second shift of the day. That evening after work, we had a feast, bacon, eggs, sausages, homemade potato chips. Irene had even splashed out a dollar on a bottle of Californian wine! Later we decided on an early night, since 5:30 would soon arrive, and it would mean back to the grind. Before dozing off to sleep, my wife took me by complete surprise when she said 'Owain – I'm pregnant again!'

I think I was only half awake. At first, I thought it was a dream... 'WHAT?... Are you sure?' There was no doubt about it. Even before we left Wales she was almost sure. Now it was an absolute fact. We tried to calculate a date. Irene was barely four months gone and now it was late May. Suddenly we realised we couldn't stay on this island in a wooden cabin with a baby on the way. Working out a strategy, we decided to save some more money to tide us over while we searched for somewhere more accessible to live, where I could also find work.

Working long hours in a very physically demanding job meant I was ready to drop almost every evening. The hard work was not a problem for me. After all, I was brought up in an environment where long hours and physical demands were the norm. My father's motto was 'hard work never killed anyone'. But apart from the work itself, it was a lonely existence. Both the other farm hands were not very talkative, being middle-aged and rather sullen. Me, I like to talk, have a joke and a laugh; I find that helps me to carry out my work without feeling the weight of the world on my shoulders. Although my heart had never been 100 per cent into farming back home, I was literally 'forced' to work at home at fifteen because my father decided I was not putting enough effort into my lessons. But, if I had one pet hate, it was dairy farming. I hated bloody cows!

5

Canadian Adventure Part 2

ON ONE OF my rare days off, a boiling hot Sunday in late July, we decided to catch the ferry and get a bus on the other side which would take us to New Westminster, a fairly large town on the banks of the Fraser estuary. Just a few miles from the city of Vancouver, New Westminster had docks and, according to the *Vancouver Sun* there was a demand for unskilled workers in and around the port. Iona was now almost seven months old and we had a small collapsible pram to wheel her around.

We bought a local paper and sat in a cafe to scour the ads for accommodation and work. An elderly man sat at the next table. 'You folks from the old country?' he queried. Irene looked at me, then at the stranger.

'Well,' I replied, 'my wife is English but I'm Welsh.'

His reply would not be the last we would hear in the next three years. 'Well', he drooled, 'we're all the same aren't we?'

Irene smiled wryly at me. She knew what my answer would be on that one. But, at this particular time I was in no mood for a discussion on any subject, apart from finding a job and a room!

'Mind if I join you?' Before we could answer, he had dragged his chair across and sat down. In the space of twenty minutes, he told us his life story. Born in the north of England, brought up in an orphanage, he'd left for Canada when he was a teenager. We told him we were on an island up river, that we had no car and were looking to find accommodation and work. His

47

name was Bill Woodall –and he turned out to be a very friendly, generous person. He said he had a small business servicing heating boilers. All of a sudden he asked us to come over to his house for a meal and he said he might be able to find us work and a place to stay. Thanking him for his kindness, we decided to take up his offer. Leading us up to his vehicle, an old Buick station wagon, he said, 'Take no notice of my wife, she's a bit cranky and can be a bitch at times, but she's got a good heart really!'

We arrived at a large bungalow with a well-maintained garden full of shrubs and colourful flowers in neat borders. Mrs Woodall, when she appeared from the kitchen, turned out to be a tall, skinny woman with a long, deeply-wrinkled face, grey hair tied up at the back, and wearing rimless glasses. When Bill introduced us, she eyed us up and down and nodded briefly. We felt we were being scrutinized. She did not seem over-pleased to see total strangers appear unexpectedly and unannounced in her home. Bill broke the ice: 'How about some tea, Mildred?' he asked. 'These kids are starving!' I suppose to him, we were all children. After all, my wife was only eighteen. Mildred – the name suited her somehow – leapt into action. In no time, the table was laid with an immaculate white linen cloth. Sandwiches, cakes and scones appeared and we all tucked into a welcome feast. Mrs Woodall turned out to be a much friendlier person than we had been led to believe by Bill's earlier comments. He was such a talker, no one else could get a word in edgeways.

Before it was time for us to leave, he had gone through the newspaper columns and identified a couple of 'For Rent' ads. There was one in New Westminster, another in nearby Burnaby. He kindly used his home phone to enquire for us. Following the second call, his face broke out in a triumphant smile, 'There's this apartment in New Westminster, it's an attic conversion, should do to wait before you get something better,' he beamed. 'We could drop by now on the way to the bus depot, if you like?'

Irene and I looked at each other – this had happened so suddenly. We hadn't expected to find anything so soon. Besides, there was the problem of finding a job to pay the bills.

As if reading our minds, Bill cut in: 'I need a hand with the business. Getting up on them roofs at my age is risky – a young fellow like you it's no problem... what ya say?'

'Well, I guess there's no harm in looking,' I replied, 'but we'd have to sort out with the foreman, all our stuff is out there!'

Driving back through the busy streets, Bill knew every road on the delta, having lived in the area for close on fifty years. We came to an end house, rather in disrepair. When told we were looking for an apartment, Mr Koslowski, the owner, vanished into the house and returned clutching a bunch of keys.

'Last son of a bitch I had were fucking thieving bastards!' he growled, spitting as he mounted a wooden staircase which led to the attic. Opening the door, he ushered us inside, switching on a light bulb dangling from the low ceiling. It was sparsely furnished with an old settee, a couple of wooden chairs and a table. There was one small bedroom and a shower room which also contained the toilet. Since the asphalt clad roof overhead was low, it was very warm in the attic with the July sun bearing down and no air conditioning.

After a hurried discussion we decided to take it, but had to give the farmer a month's notice as well as pay a month's rent in advance to secure the room. It was in an accessible location and Bill had offered me a job, maybe not full-time, but at least enough to keep the wolf from the door.

Back on the island, old Mr Stevens was none too pleased when told we would be moving in a month. 'Darned young people these days, just don't wanna work... and you blasted limeys – you're the worst of the lot!' We didn't argue with him. I suppose he had a point, since he'd have to find someone else to take my place.

Mam wrote us a letter each week, enquiring how we were getting on and how 'that poor little baby' was, obviously concerned about our welfare, probably thinking we couldn't cope being so far away with no family or friends. I replied to her letters regularly, since I didn't want her and Dad fretting about us. My account of our living accommodation and surrounds was slightly amended; cabin/shack became a 'nice bungalow', no mention of lugging buckets of water from down a well, or being stuck on an isolated island etc.

A few days before we left the farm, a small parcel arrived. Mam had packed a few local Welsh newspapers together with a note. There was a front page story in *Y Cymro*, reporting on a proposal to build a huge dam near Bala to supply the city of Liverpool with water. The plans entailed evicting around a hundred people from their homes, including a small village called Capel Celyn, with a school, post office and chapel, in order to create a massive lake. According to the newspaper, there was strong opposition to the proposals, not just locally but apparently throughout Wales. I read the story several times until I had grasped the real implications of this insensitive and arrogant proposal. It seemed that an Act of Parliament had already been passed in the House of Commons, despite opposition from all Welsh MPs, with the exception of one Conservative. Of course there were well over 600 MPs in the Commons – English, Scots and Northen Irish – so a mere thirty-six Welsh MPs had no influence whatsoever! At this time Wales did not even have a Secretary of State, in contrast to Scotland.

Unquestionably, this story re-ignited the flame and passion within me for my country. I realized then that this single event could shake up the whole Welsh political establishment. It could be the catalyst for devolution of government from Westminster to Wales for the first time since Owain Glyndŵr's parliament in Machynlleth early in the fifteenth century. But how could we get people to listen and understand? It was during those last few days on the island farm that I decided the years of talking were over! Someone needed to do something dramatic to make people listen – some kind of 'direct action', perhaps.

Once we moved, life became much easier for us, with shops

close by and a bus stop across the road. Bill helped us move in and gave us a large carpet he didn't need any more. The next day I was picked up by Bill in a small wagon with a sign XL FURNACE AND CHIMNEY SERVICES printed in bold red letters on both sides. We had to go across the town to an estate in North Surrey, crossing the Patullo Bridge which spans the Fraser river. Arriving at the house, ironically on Bangor Street, we unloaded the gear, consisting of a large vacuum cleaner, rods and various spanners and grips. Cleaning and servicing the boiler was a simple task. The tricky part was getting on the roof and sticking rods down the chimney pot to make sure they were not blocked by nesting jackdaws or any objects. This is where I came in – never having done this work before! I raced up the ladder and scrambled along the shingle tiles to reach the chimney. Heights did not worry me and old Bill seemed quite impressed by my agility. 'Son of a gun, you're like a cat!' he yelled at me. I shouted back that the chimney looked clear enough, but stuck the broom down anyway. Most people clean a chimney from below, but Bill was adamant. 'With those oil burners, it's the best way... saves damaging delicate piping.' Well, he was the boss.

We managed to service six boilers and chimneys that first day. Bill Woodall was more than pleased since he was no longer able to get on the roofs. 'Darned rheumatism killing me... when I was your age I'd run on top of 'em roofs like a monkey on hot cinders,' he boasted.

Ever since I was seventeen, I had been driving. So Irene and I decided to look for a car that could take us about on weekends, since our finances seemed healthy. Bill drove us out towards Burnaby just off the Trans Canada highway, where there were three roadside car lots. He was no fool and knew the ropes, warning me against rogue traders and car sharks. Typical suit shining, teeth flashing salesmen were everywhere. 'Don't be fooled by the polish, son,' he warned, 'it's underneath them hoods you gotta look, that's when you find out what's what.' Checking several vehicles, we finally chose a Chrysler

De Soto – it was something we could afford. Driving from the car lot, following Bill, stuck to his tail like a leech in case I got lost, I felt as proud as if I was driving a brand new Cadillac!

I only worked five days a week, with Saturday and Sundays free. When my wife heard there was a part-time job going for her, Friday evenings and Saturdays at a shoe shop, we decided we could manage it if I looked after Iona at those times. Now we had an extra income, we could visit a drive-in cinema on Sunday evenings. There was no need for a babysitter as Iona slept through it all on the back seat, oblivious to the events on the giant screen in front. Some Sundays we would drive down to Bellingham, a summer resort on the American side of the border in the state of Washington. Since it was barely an hour's drive away, it allowed us to do something different.

But a month after we moved to New Westminster, Bill dropped a bombshell. He'd have to give up the business as his wife had suddenly been taken ill and was bedridden. He asked if I wanted to buy the business, which would involve the pickup truck, equipment, ladders etc. But it wasn't something I wanted to do, though I thanked him all the same. I really did have a lot to be grateful for, since we'd still be stuck on the island, but for Bill's kindness and concern.

So I had to find another job. Canada's economy relied heavily on the timber industry, farming, fishing and mining – all dependent on the weather conditions. Winter would not be a great time to find a job of any kind, and certainly not in the unskilled sector. However, winter was still a couple of months away, leaving me little time to search for work. Along the dockside of New Westminster were several warehouses, and a couple of smaller mills. I decided to try my luck here. Following a series of 'Sorry, no vacancies, call back in a month', I stumbled upon a large animal feed mill called Brackman & Kerr Milling Co. The mill's supervisor, a tall bespectacled Swede, interviewed me. He was a straight talker, which I liked. The hours were long, the work was hard, no slacking and no missing shifts! I told him he could rely on me, that I needed the work, had a young family and when could I start? The pay was a dollar an hour for a forty-four hour week. I figured that would be around eighteen pounds a week and a dollar an hour was the very bottom line in pay terms. There was a downside. It was shift work and there were three shifts, day, evening, and night, which they termed the graveyard shift.

On my first morning I was shown the production line, where various sacks of animal and poultry feeds came cascading down a metal chute, two a minute. My job was to stack these bags, five at a time onto a hand trolley, wheel them across the warehouse, stack them up and run back to the chute where two or three sacks would be waiting,. This would last for four hours. After a half hour's dinner break, I would return to where I'd left off.

Sometimes, I was sent to empty box cars off a railway siding. Usually this would mean shifting 20 or 25 tons of wheat or barley or rye. This procedure meant one man each side of the wagon holding a large square board at the back of the pile, pressing it down, while a winch would then drag the board, pushing the cereals out and into a chute where a conveyor belt carried the contents up to the hoppers under the building roof. This was laborious and dirty work, as the grain dust would stick to the sweat of the workmen's bodies. When I first did this particular duty, my partner was a Dutchman named Bernie – apparently he was under the illusion that people coming from the British Isles were either too lazy or too weak to do manual jobs. I think I destroyed this belief when he doubled up, gasping for breath from trying to race me to the top of the pile. I pointed out to him that it wasn't a competition.

One day I was told to accompany one of the wagon drivers to deliver cattle meal up river on the delta. The driver's name was Hank, one of the few Canadians at the plant. Hank was a very good natured guy, cracking jokes, asking about my family and about Wales. Compared to most jobs at the mill, this was easy going. Driving from one farm to the next along a small rural road, I noticed a sign in the field saying 'Cow Manure For Sale'. I commented, 'Why, they even sell manure here.'

Quick as lighting came the reply, 'Yeah, believe me man, you get a lot of bullshit with it an' all!' I laughed my head off.

It had been rumoured that they needed someone to volunteer to clean inside the corn silos. This process involved a worker being strapped into a wooden seat, then lowered by a winch into the silo. A layer of crushed meal would stick against the sides from time to time and it had to be prodded free with a long paddle. When told there was twenty cents an hour extra for this, I volunteered; five hours down there was an extra dollar. Once lowered down into the bowel of the silo, the heat was tremendous. Sweat poured from my body. As I rammed the paddle against the side, great chunks of caked meal would crash down to the bottom. After one hour, I was hauled up for a break. Five minutes later, after drinking a litre of cold water, I was winched down again. At the end of five hours, I was feeling drained. Almost on the verge of fainting, I decided that the extra dollar wasn't worth the effort – no wonder they kept looking for new volunteers!

Brackman & Kerr turned out to be a real human melting pot. On my shift there was a Ukranian who swore like a trooper in broken English, a Frenchman, two Germans, an Austrian, one Hungarian, a Czech, a Pole, one Scot, one Englishman, and a Swiss named Herman. There were also a few native Canadians as well as a Japanese-Canadian. There was also one Italian called Andreas Scalabrini – I was involved in a fist fight with him later on.

When you're in Canada or the States, if you say you are from Wales... you get a vague look; 'Oh, England, you mean!' 'No, no, no, not fucking England, WALES!' Hermann Schmidt was Swiss. Although not tall, he was a heavy guy, probably eighteen or nineteen stones. Herman worked one floor down from where I was. Sometimes my work entailed sending heavy sacks of grain down a chute to where he'd handle them. Since I first met him, he never missed a chance to goad me – in a friendly way. He knew how to get under my skin. Every now and then he'd cup his hands over his mouth and holler, 'C'mon, Englishman, what's with you, have you gone to sleep up there?' This was followed by uncontrollable laughter. At first I tried to take it with good humour, but he kept on and on until I was pissed off.

On this particular day I was not in the best of moods and I was standing by the chute with half a dozen hundredweight sacks of cattle cake, waiting for Hermann to give me the OK to chuck them down, when all of a sudden I heard: 'OK Englishman, let's have you!' I suddenly saw red. He was in stitches, thinking he'd upset me, half bending over, hands on his knees. No way could I miss this chance. I grabbed a sack with both hands and hurled it down, deliberately missing the chute. It landed on the back of his head and he went down like a skittle – and stayed down!

'Oh my God,' I thought, 'I've killed the fat bastard!'

Running down the steps, three at a time, I arrived at Hermann's side. His face, usually red, was now ashen. I knelt beside him to feel for a heartbeat before shouting, 'Help, there's been an accident!' Rolf Miller, one of the foremen, ran to the scene, told me to get some water whilst he searched for a pulse. Returning with a glass of water, I was glad to notice Hermann's bulky body sitting on the wooden floor. Soon he was sitting up as Rolf put cold water on his lips. 'What the fuck happened?' he enquired still dazed – looking round he saw me, then the corn sack lying alongside him. 'Mad fucking Welshman!' he blurted as he staggered up. I was so relieved and thankful when he came round, I wouldn't have minded what he called me. Strangely enough, he always called me 'mad Welshman' after that incident. I think there is a moral there somewhere!

When I reflect on my time in Canada, I believe my job at the mill was the most rewarding – people had come from all corners of the globe to try for a better life. They were, for the most part, the salt of the earth. Despite having a hard life, Hector Barcello was one of the kindest persons one could meet. I shall always remember when my wife went to hospital to have the baby, Hector and his second wife took Iona into their home for three days to allow me to keep working.

Christmas was fast approaching. Irene had long since given up her part-time job at the shoe shop because of her pregnancy. I was earning a regular wage. At weekends and for one evening a week, I also laboured for a small builder, doing a variety of jobs, including building a fish pond with stones for his garden. I was paid a dollar an hour which made up for the money lost when Irene left her job.

One evening as we were having supper, suddenly my wife complained of stomach pains. Iona was almost a year old. Luckily the Royal Columbian Hospital was only a short drive away and on reaching the hospital's maternity unit, we were shown into a small consulting room. A doctor arrived on the scene shortly to examine my wife and we were told the baby would arrive within the next twenty four hours. Having stayed three hours, Iona became restless and started yelling for her bottle, so Irene suggested I'd better take her home to feed, put her to bed then call in the morning.

When Iona was in her cot, I decided to ring Hector and tell him the news. It was then he suggested leaving Iona with them for two or three days, until Irene was back home. Hector and his wife had two young sons of their own. I thanked him and said I would discuss it with Irene the following morning.

I rang the hospital early next morning to be told my wife had had a restful night. I was allowed to have a word with her. She sounded in good spirits and I told her about Hector's offer. At first she hesitated, reluctant to let Iona out of our care, but she knew Hector and his wife were loving parents so she agreed. The day passed slowly. I waited by the phone for a call which never came. Twice during the day we visited the hospital but the baby seemed no nearer. On leaving the hospital that evening I decided to take Iona over to Hector's house. Packing a few baby clothes and nappies, powdered milk and canned food into a carrier bag, I drove over the bridge to his home. We had a great welcome on arrival, with everyone making a fuss of Iona. Hector insisted I stayed for supper – we sat talking for hours.

Next morning I was awoken by the shrill ringing of the phone and a woman's voice, excited, told me to come to the hospital right away. When I got there, the baby – an eight pound boy – had arrived before me! Irene, as expected, looked shattered but managed a weak smile. We decided to call him Griffith, Gruff for short, after my father. Both he and Mam would be overjoyed when they heard the news. Looking at the calendar on the hospital wall, I realised it was the shortest day of the year, 21 December; four days before Christmas.

Since we needed the money for presents and a Christmas dinner etc, I decided to return to work the following day and each evening I would visit Iona in Hector's house. Iona saw her new baby brother, but she was too young to take much notice. Irene said she wouldn't be released from hospital until Boxing Day, so I said we'd visit the next day.

We had a friendly young couple next door, Shirl and Karl, who helped me prepare Christmas dinner despite having to cope with their own. Since they had no children, they would fuss over Iona and were looking forward to seeing Gruff. Shirl asked me 'What are you going to call the baby – Owen?'

I said 'I think his first name will be Gruff...'

'If I was you, I guess I'd call him Quits!' she quipped... That of course was a dig at me because Iona had been born only eleven and a half months earlier!

Our small attic was really getting too small now we were four. I thought, Christ, at this rate we'll be ten in six years! Scanning the housing columns in the *Vancouver Sun*, I saw a two bedroom bungalow for rent, just across the river in North Surrey, close to the Trans-Canada highway. OK, it wasn't Beverly Hills, but it did have two bedrooms, kitchen, bathroom of a sort, no flush toilet. Ah, what the hell, there was a large back garden with a mammoth hole in the ground at the top end; so one emptied the chemical toilet in there, after dark naturally!

It was a nice tidy area, little shop on the corner, quiet, a good place for the kids to play, we thought. What was also good was the fact that my work was barely three miles over the Patullo Bridge. We moved within the week, and it was the best accommodation we'd had so far.

Home was never far from the back of my mind throughout this period. The newspaper article from my mother about the threat to drown the valley at Capel Celyn gnawed at my conscience. Problem was, there was no one I could really discuss it with. To be fair, my wife was English and she was not political – most people are not. Of course she would give her tacit support because she was my wife and the mother of my kids. I longed for a rational discussion with people who felt like I did. Passion and commitment was what we needed. I wondered to myself, was there anybody else out there who was ready?

There was one other blessing in our new house. We had a telephone and on rare occasions my mother would ring us, while on rarer occasions I would ring her. The cost of transatlantic phone calls in those days was almost indecent. Whenever we spoke on the phone, I knew how the conversation would end. 'When do you think you'll be coming home?' It was hard listening to the pain in her voice. Parcels arrived regularly, clothes for the children. Mam never missed a birthday or Christmas. In a way it was Christmas all year round for the kids, because the amount of clothing we received was almost enough to start a shop.

Five months after starting work at Brackmann & Kerr I was made foreman. I would not call it promotion as it meant I worked even harder for six cents per hour extra! That is roughly the equivalent of £1/hour in our money today; no wonder Hermann the Swiss called me 'mad Welshman'. My work now consisted of doing shifts in various departments, production line, storage, distribution, plus the feed mixing and silo maintenance. Apparently a senior floor manager mentioned my name to the Swedish supervisor saying I was 'not afraid of hard work'.

We worked shirtless because of the heat. Maybe it was overwork or just being exposed to so much grain dust on my bare skin, – but the end result was severe dermatitis. So bad was the itching that I scratched large patches of skin off my arms, chest and neck until I bled. When examined by a doctor, I was told that I was suffering from a severe allergy to grain dust, which meant giving up work. I was absolutely gutted, not just because was I losing my job, meaning no wages or any compensation whatsoever, but also, I'd be losing friendships which I valued dearly. I had made friends with people from around the world, but my best buddy was Hector.

On my very last day at work, Hector said he had a surprise in store for me. Half way through the evening shift he came by, whispering 'C'mon, let's go!' I looked up and protested, saying 'There's four hours to go.'

'Don't worry about that, I've fixed it OK... Joe and Andy are going to clock us in... and out!'

I looked rather bewildered, knowing we 'clocked in' halfway through every shift, also when we left work.

'Well, are you coming, or do I have to carry you?'

I followed him rather meekly – one did not argue with Hector!

'Where are we going?'

'Let's go shower and change,' he replied. We always brought clean clothes with us to change into before going home.

Once outside, he said 'We're going to downtown Vancouver... I wanna show you China Town!' We both clambered into my old Chrysler, Hector guiding me away from the heaviest traffic areas. Driving down Granville Street, we parked not far from the city centre. 'Right!' he said 'We're going to visit some bars.'

I hesitated, 'But I don't drink – I've never had a drink in my life!'

'Jesus Christ... are you jokin', every sonofabitch drinks!... don't they?'

'Well, I don't,' I insisted.

'Well you can come in with me... have a coke or somewhat...'

In we went to the flashing neon and loud music. Hector ordered a beer and a coke, taking a large sip saying 'Christ, I needed that,' before taking another swig, as I toyed with the bottle of coke between sips.

Next he ordered two lagers, passing one along the bar to me. 'Go on, try it,' he insisted 'won't kill you!' Just to please him, I took the glass and tried a little. I must have pulled a face because he retorted 'CMMMON... can't be that fucking bad surely!'

Minutes later Hector had downed two pints of lager, I was struggling with my first, having abandoned the coke. 'Let's go to another bar.' I managed to finish my drink, before scurrying after him in the crowded streets. It was Friday evening and all the young people were out to enjoy themselves – also many who were not so young!

Hector waited for me by the open doorway of what seemed like a club. The bar was fairly small, but packed. Hector shoved his way through the mass towards the bar with me in close pursuit. He ordered two more lagers and two 'chasers' – I did not even know what a 'chaser' meant!

'Cheers,' he called, holding the 'chaser' up above his head, I followed suit, clinked our glasses, he gulped his down. I copied him... wow, the whiskey burnt my throat till I was gasping. Hector laughed aloud.

Two girls in very short black leather skirts were edging closer. 'Dya wanna meet a friend?' said the one with fair hair and a deep plunging neckline'. I looked up and realised she was addressing me and replied, 'No, no, I'm already with a friend.'

Hector looked at me with astonishment, 'Jesus... don't you know what she's after?... She's a hooker... Christ, you must be right from the fucking sticks!'

As I'd told him previously I'd never drunk any alcohol, he couldn't believe that I'd never met a prostitute in my life. 'Well, Hector, I've lived a very guarded life, Sunday School, Welsh Methodists!'

'Well I'll be damned... sheltered you call it? Where I grew up, half the girls on our street were on the game... the other half were just generous!!' he quipped before adding 'OK, let's move on, we've time to visit a couple more.'

After drinking all that lager my head was feeling a bit light, but it didn't seem to matter, I was having fun. By the end of the evening I reckoned I had drunk twelve pints of lager and downed at least four chasers. I had never before drunk any alcohol in my life, nor visited a bar! Oh my God, I thought, Irene will be wondering where I am. Normally after this shift I would be home by half past nine. In those days there were no breathalyser tests in Canada, although, of course there was harsh punishment when caught driving under the influence.

We made our way back to my car, and, I am ashamed now to admit, I drove all the way home, dropping Hector off at his house. When I arrived at our house, switching off the engine and car lights, I staggered out. The cold air seemed to worsen the effects of the alcohol. Suddenly, I heard sobbing coming from the half open bedroom window. It was my wife. After I'd knocked on the door for several minutes, she eventually appeared to let me in, her face covered in tears. I really could have sunk into the ground. Never have I felt so guilty and ashamed. Saying sorry did not help much since I knew that her father had a severe drinking problem when she was a child – he used to come home drunk and cause havoc. I had promised her I would never drink! Now that I had broken that promise, words did not help.

After that episode I can truthfully say I didn't drink again whilst in Canada, and even to this day it is very seldom that I visit a bar. Of course I will have a drink with a meal or sometimes at home, but for someone who has been termed an 'extremist', I am most 'moderate'!

It was a combination of several factors which made us decide to return to Wales at the end of the year. One of these was the fact I had to give up work because of my allergy to the grain dust. Another factor was that the house was a little bit too small for a growing family. Undoubtedly though, the main reason was that I was getting homesick. I missed my friends, family and my country.

And I wanted to see if there was anyone who would fight with me for Capel Celyn.

However, there were a few months to go before that, so in the meantime, I trod the streets of the dockland area around Vancouver until there were holes in the soles of my boots. It was autumn, and the weather would cause an economic downturn in winter. Hector told me one day that there were a few vacancies in logging camps up-river. My ears picked up! I had always fancied a stint at such work, maybe because of all the romantic stories and pictures engraved on my mind as a child. One weekend, Hector and I decided to drive up to the camps. After passing thousands of acres of cleared forests, we eventually turned off onto a rough track until we came upon a clearing where there was large machinery, tractors, trucks, huge stacks of timber and two long wooden sheds. We saw a sign marked OFFICE and hurried towards it – inside was a thickset 40-year-old man, wearing a red and green tartan windjammer and a white safety helmet. Getting up from his chair, he greeted us in a gruff voice: 'What can I do for you?' We said we were looking for a job, was there anything going? Shifting his eyes from me to Hector, noting he was the strongest-looking, he replied there were a couple of jobs, but only temporary, for maybe a month or six weeks. It would consist of constructing an extension of the track into the forest to gain access for large machinery etc. Hector asked about the pay. It was a dollar and a quarter per hour, which wasn't too bad, although we realised it would be hard graft and out in all weathers.

On the way out we passed a square reinforced shed with a

sign EXPLOSIVES, DANGER in large red letters on the door. I was most interested and knew explosives were widely used when building new tracks through rocky terrain or uprooting massive tree trunks left in the ground after felling. My interest in working in the timber forest was slightly more complex than just earning a wage! What I was hoping for was a chance to work with some dynamite and detonators which would, hopefully, stand me in good stead when I returned to Wales.

During the first week, I was called on to drive one of the heavy tractors and a fork-lift since I had previous experience. We were travelling over fifty miles each way, every day; most of the roads were very basic. Still, we enjoyed the work and the company was good, typical Canucks: rough, tough, most with foul mouths, calling each other sonsofbitches, arseholes, mother fuckers and worse, but all good-natured.

One day, quite unexpectedly, my chance came... Joe Kelly, a foreman in charge of building a new track, called over and asked which one of us could handle a big dumper truck. I knew there was blasting going on in that part of the forest, so I jumped at the chance. 'I can handle that, no problem,' I said.

'OK, follow me... both of you might as well come' Kelly commanded.

The dumper was massive, several times longer than any I'd ever seen before, but I knew the basics, fired it up and awaited instructions. Kelly pointed out where a digger waited by a large pile of soil. I was to carry the pile and dump it down a crevice on the open side. An hour later the whole pile was shifted. 'Hey, you handled that OK,' said Joe, 'You can lend a hand to Hank and Art over by them rocks. They're getting ready to do some blasting soon.'

There was an exceptionally large rock jutting out of the ground, so bore holes were needed to pack explosives in and around it. They handed us a couple of steel chisels and lump hammers. Luckily I had used a hammer and chisel at home on my father's farm, so it was nothing new. Hector, on the other hand, had not. He started with plenty of enthusiasm but suddenly there was a yell! 'Sonofabitch' – he had missed his chisel and caught his thumb! It took a good hour and a half before the holes were up to standard.

'OK, that should do,' Hank said, moving across to his left, where he lifted a small green tarpaulin to reveal three boxes, two containing plastic explosives and one containing electric detonators. I had never been this close to explosives before and I must say my heartbeat quickened as I walked up closer. Hank quickly opened the carton revealing roughly two dozen round sticks of commercial gelignite. Opening one of the other boxes, he pulled out a handful of white, plastic-coated wires attached to copper heads, about an inch long – these were the detonators. Watching with increasing interest, I tried to absorb everything he did, clipping the wires to shorten them before stripping a couple of inches of plastic covering to reveal copper wiring. Handling the gelignite with great care he proceeded to insert a stick in each of the bore holes in the rock, finally placing the copper head of a detonator into the sticks. It all looked so easy, but I realised he was a professional who'd spent years at his job, since he never took his eyes off his work until he was finished.

'OK you guys, make yourselves scarce,' he ordered. 'We're about to blast this goddamn rock off the planet!'

We scurried past some boulders and uprooted tree trunks into the safety of a small cliff, bending down, hands on our ears until... BOOM!!' Crashing chips of rock rained down yards from where we stood. The ground was littered with chunks of smashed rock, and smoke was still drifting but there was nothing left of the protruding mass. It had been levelled.

On the way home that evening, Hector quizzed me as to why I had been so very interested in the blasting. I replied that it was something I'd read about in a magazine years ago and always wanted to see. There was no point trying to explain my plans for the future. He would not have understood and I didn't want anyone in on my secret.

Six weeks later, work ended in the forest and I found another job in a dockside warehouse for the remainder of my stay in Canada. Before that, I tried a stint knocking doors trying to sell encyclopedias. After receiving a few hours' training, we were driven in teams of four and let loose on the streets of Vancouver. The tactics they practised and encouraged were not my style – pressure selling, bribery, sticking a foot in the doorway to prevent the door being shut in your face etc. I lasted a week, sold one volume, earning myself a grand total of forty-five dollars! I quit.

On the eve of flying home, we had very mixed emotions. We had made a number of such good friends, ordinary people, hard-working, kind and loyal. After saying our goodbyes back in the house, I shed a few tears. Before leaving I sold my old car to a local lad and we left what little furniture and kitchen utensils we had to friends and neighbours. Early next morning, a taxi called by at six and drove us to the airport. The flight would be over a distance of 8,000 miles and would last twelve hours, with one stop at Toronto International Airport.

6

Tryweryn

WITH A MIXED sense of eagerness and trepidation, we boarded the flight, an Air Canada Boeing 747 with the distinctive red maple leaf emblazoned on the fuselage. This was the first time for us to fly and my wife was slightly nervous. Soon the giant engines were roaring skywards as Vancouver and its surrounds shrank below us. We took one last nostalgic look through the window as the plane half-circled before setting its course eastwards towards Toronto. The two children had been fast asleep throughout, oblivious of the long journey ahead. Watching them, I smiled, thinking we were three when we left, now we were four! We stopped at Toronto after about seven hours flying. Within less than two hours we were on the final leg of the journey, crossing the Atlantic, arriving in Manchester within eight hours. Throughout the whole flight, I never slept a wink. As for the children, they were awake for just long enough to take their milk and a small amount of food.

Since it was close to being the shortest day, night had fallen before we reached Manchester's Ringway airport. My father had arranged for a car to pick us up. I knew the driver, Dic Pant, so this time there wasn't a problem of identifying us on arrival. Everything went to plan as we walked out of the arrivals building. I spotted his tall form amongst the crowd. We shook hands and for the first time in two years, I spoke Welsh!

It was already pitch black when the car turned in to Gwynus' drive and three minutes later Dic Pant had pulled up outside the house. I clambered out, feeling exhausted after the journey, followed by Irene, carrying Iona who was still fast asleep, while

I had Gruff in his carry-cot. No sooner had the car stopped outside the house than my parents ran out to meet us, wanting to see the children. My Dad was anxious to see Gruff. He lit a match and peered inside the carry cot to see the baby, who was now almost a year old. *'Duw annwyl, edrychwch, Jane!'* – 'Good God, look here, Jane!' to my mother who was already fussing over Iona. I shall never forget the joy on their faces that evening when we got in the house, Mam had cooked a big supper for us as if we hadn't eaten during the last two years! Ellis, my brother was also all smiles and doting on the two kids.

Since we had no other accommodation, we stayed with my parents for a couple of weeks over Christmas. My mother spoilt the children with toys and clothes, while at weekends, my wife and I would visit the cinema in Pwllheli. Mam loved babysitting for us.

It was during one such visit to the town that we came across a coffee bar and grill called Espresso. We dropped in for a couple of milk shakes before going to the cinema. Inside was quite modern but a bit noisy because of a juke box blaring away. I thought at first it was very North American and trendy. Business seemed to be booming. True, it was a Saturday evening, but young people were virtually queuing to get in. When we found a vacant table, the owner, a rather short middle-aged man with an English Midlands accent, came over for a chat. He told us his name was Harold and that his coffee bar was similar to ones in Canada.

Unexpectedly, he remarked, 'Do you want to buy it? I'm going to sell as it's getting too much for me and the wife to handle.'

It took us a bit by surprise. I looked at my wife as if to say, 'Buy it... what with?'

It was then, as if reading my mind, he added, 'You wouldn't have to pay it all in one lot. I'd take a deposit, and you could pay the rest through the bank in stages.'

I said that I didn't know. I hadn't really collected my thoughts together since coming back.

'Well, think about it. By the way, there's a nice two-bedroomed flat above!'

Now that made the proposition more interesting. Our priority had to be somewhere to live, as we didn't want to impose on my parents for longer than was necessary. During the next few days we discussed the matter over and over. We had to let my parents in on the project. Following our journeys across to Canada and back, which I had financed out of my meagre savings, there wasn't that much left to start anything more than a market stall. Fortunately my parents offered to help with a deposit, and through that I could secure a loan. Things moved very quickly after Christmas and by the end of the year, contracts were exchanged.

On 1 January 1960, Iona's second birthday, we moved in! During the first week, Harold offered to lend a hand, showing how all the machines worked, how the kitchen operated, where to order goods, contact numbers and addresses etc. We decided to keep the staff employed by him: a cook, kitchen helpers and two waitresses, who were full-time. Since the coffee bar was open seven days a week, it meant long hours for all of us and I had to be present when the staff had finished. Not only was the establishment run as a coffee bar, catering mainly for young people, but also there were around twenty regular customers, professional people, such as solicitors and accountants who came for their lunches.

We soon settled down to life in the flat above the business. The only negative side was the sound of the juke box below which, particularly at weekends, could be heard permanently. We partially cured that problem by controlling the volume and when our television set was switched on, it muffled the sound. Strangely, the children didn't seem concerned about the juke box and they loved running about laughing and screaming all day.

Winter was not the best time to judge how a business such as ours was performing, but when we compared figures with the previous couple of years, we were pleased to note an increase of 40 per cent since we took over. We were both very young, and compared to the previous owner we were easy going. Mixing with people is all-important in such a business. Being able to understand young people, talk with them and listen to them – that was the key. Another factor which helped us increase our turnover was people's curiosity. The fact that we had just returned from Canada seemed to spur many to come in and have a look. Although I didn't realise it at the time, many of the old established cafes and milk bars were envious of our 'roaring' trade, since at weekends there was a queue back towards the Palladium cinema as young people waited for room to enter. The cinema was only two doors away, which also helped, as it was just about the only entertainment in the town.

When Easter came around we received our first taste of the holiday season and the extra trade that generates. Not only were we busy in the evenings, but dozens would come in during the mornings for coffees or cold drinks. By the time the season was in full swing, during July, August and early September, we were flat out. On Wednesdays, Pwllheli market days, we sold up to a thousand cups of coffee. Since the coffee bar had seating for only fifty, plus around ten on the outside tables, it gives a picture of how hectic trade was.

During the first few months running the business, there was hardly time for any other issues or distractions and my political activity was on hold. With the onset of autumn and winter looming on the horizon, all summer visitors vanished for another year.

But in November of that year, I was re-initiated into the world of Welsh politics.

It happened quite unexpectedly one evening: a student at Aberystwyth University who lived locally, used to call at the cafe when he was home. His friends called him 'Twm' and he was studying law. At the time there was a certain amount of turmoil amongst Welsh students who were demanding rights for the Welsh language, forming Cymdeithas yr Iaith Gymraeg (the Welsh Language Society). They staged protests and sit downs, blocking streets and roads, all non-violent, modelling their activities on the tactics used by Gandhi in India. Twm was a brooding, studious 20-year old when I met him, and although mainly involved in the language battle, he was also very much opposed to Liverpool Corporation's plans to drown Tryweryn valley. During our conversation I discreetly enquired were there any students with deep convictions about the Tryweryn valley, and were they genuine or just 'pint pot patriots'?

During our long discussions, 'Twm' went through a handful of names. He seemed reliable. There were a couple of 'head cases' roaming around Aberystwyth in those days, probably still are. However, one name kept coming up – Emyr Llywelyn Jones. This guy seemed to have not only a political and cultural 'pedigree', being the son of a chaired National Eisteddfod bard... but he also had the bottle to act!

A few days before Christmas, a short chubby student with a mop of unruly curly hair knocked on the door of our flat. From the description given me by 'Twm', I knew straight away that this was Emyr Llywelyn. This was our first meeting, but not the last! 'Emyr Llew', as he is known, outlined his plans, which, strikingly, were almost a mirror image of what I had been contemplating. I explained to him I had already made contact with a local lad named John Albert Jones who was keen to take part in an attack on the dam site.

John Albert Jones was a tall dark-haired young man in his late teens when I first met him. We got to know each other well when John, a regular customer at the coffee bar, used to discuss his political leanings (in between cups of coffee and sizing up all the pretty girls, who showed a lot of leg during the miniskirt era). When we met, he was on leave from the RAF and used to stay at his sister's house. His mother had died tragically when he was just two years of age and he had also lost his father before he reached fifteen. Life had not been easy for him and he learnt to cope for himself from an early age. John's philosophy was quite straight and to the point. He had no time for 'spongers' but believed in an honest day's work. I got the impression John was a little more to the right than me, but we shared many common beliefs and on the Tryweryn Valley issue we agreed: a radical approach was needed.

Since I had met John over a year before I met Emyr Llywelyn Jones, we already had ideas on what to do, when and how. Talking and 'politicking' were getting nowhere, and the valley was still under threat. Time for some 'direct action'.

During the harsh winter months of 1962–1963, we surveyed the Tryweryn site at night and during the day. In order to get acquainted with the workings on the site and where various items and equipment were stored, we took a rather risky step. On a cold windy weekday shortly before Christmas, we dressed up as 'navvies': donkey jackets, steel-capped boots and yellow safety helmets. We even found some TARMAC badges, stuck them on our jackets and calmly walked into the site. TARMAC was one of the big contractors on the dam site. Although John is half Irish on his mother's side, it was left to me with my version of a County Cork accent to do the talking.

Seeing a corrugated shed which acted as the company office, we made a beeline for it. It must have been lunchtime as it was completely empty, with no lock on the door. Apart from a few dumper trucks around, the odd lorry loaded with soil and rocks, and maybe a half dozen labourers hurrying along, we could have, more or less, done as we pleased. We turned the handle and calmly walked in. There was a long wooden table covered in maps of the site. Some were very detailed, showing the fuel storage, lorry and van parking lots. They even showed where the main electric transformer was situated. Before leaving, we decided to take a quick peep and find out where the security guards were holed up.

Just as we rounded a corner, we almost collided with an important-looking official wearing a suit and clutching a thick folder, on his helmet in bold letters: TARMAC Site Manager!

Wow! We thought, this is it – but he seemed as surprised as we were. He stopped and peered over his thick glasses, saying, 'Haven't seen you two around here before, have I?'

I replied in my best attempt at a County Cork brogue, 'Ah, sure we're with Mick's gang, our first day.'

Believing our luck was about to run out, we vanished behind some sheds and made our exit through a patchy hawthorn hedge, stunted by prevailing easterly winds and poor clay soil. It had been not only an 'interesting' excursion but quite a beneficial one, since we had unexpectedly stumbled upon a complete layout of the site, with important details which would come in useful in days to come. For several evenings we kept the site under surveillance, using different cars or vans in order to confuse both local police and site security. There were a few narrow escapes, like the time we drove up Cwm Prysor, near Trawsfynydd on the Bala road, parking in an unfrequented lay-by, leaving the car and walking over the foothills of the Arenig. As we were returning to our car, headlights appeared out of nowhere, through the low-lying mist. We dived into the car just in time to see a police patrol car pulling into the lay-by. In an instant I threw my arms around John, pretending we were two lovers, our faces obscured from the two officers inside. Ever so slowly they drove past us into the night: 'You know your breath smells fucking awful! Besides, you're not my idea of a good snog!' said John as we both burst out laughing.

Despite the seriousness and possible dangers of our planned mission, we both managed to retain our sense of humour and this helped us cope with the stresses. Since our initial meetings with Emyr Llywelyn, we had all decided on a date to strike. It would be 8 February 1963, a Saturday evening when all of the workers would be away, leaving only the watchmen behind. Before finalising our plans, I had been in contact with the two men from Gwent who had been arrested for causing the oil leakage from the transformer. From contacts I had in Merthyr Tydfil, I learnt that one of the men, Dai Pritchard, had expert knowledge on electrical timing devices. Following a secret meeting in Tredegar, Dai volunteered to travel up north and meet us in Pwllheli.

One Sunday evening in mid winter we took a trip along the coast towards Penychain, which was the location of Butlin's Holiday Camp – now Hafan y Môr. When we reached an isolated small headland with a rocky cliff, we emptied a small rucksack containing sticks of Par Ammo gelignite and a couple of electronic detonators, plus a battery and a clock. Dai expertly demonstrated how to assemble the clock and connect it to the detonator, using an old alarm clock as a timer. Placing the small pack of explosives against part of the rock face, he covered it with a clod of turf, then connected it to the detonator and set the clock for five minutes. Retreating to the other side of the rocks, we waited anxiously for the result. A loud explosion echoed around us as chunks of rock were hurled into the sky and smaller chips rained down like confetti. 'Wow'...! said the two of us in chorus, whilst Dai Pritchard calmly wiped the steam off his glasses with a satisfied half-smile on his sombre face.

One detonator we used came courtesy of an earlier raid on a granite factory near Nant Gwrtheyrn, where the Language and Heritage Centre is now established. During the raid, we took a large chest which we at first believed to be full of explosives – but later found it held hundreds of electrical detonators. The actual gelignite was 'borrowed' from another quarry in Pembrokeshire.

During our preparations for the pending attack, I found out Irene was pregnant with our third child. Because of this, the situation became much more complicated and caused me a great deal of soul-searching. I understand that many people still believe that our actions at Tryweryn were done on the spur of the moment. That certainly was not the case. In all, the planning, finding the materials, surveillance, finding contacts and transport etc, took the best part of a year. Others have commented we were amateurish and left too many trails behind us. All too true, of course; we were not a professional team of saboteurs with a bank roll behind us. All our efforts, including the costs of financing it all came from our own meagre pockets. I am aware that years later an ex-detective sergeant who was involved in the case accused a South American Welsh-born multi-millionaire of financing us. That is a blatant lie – and I should know.

When I returned from Canada, I had set about trying to find out who were the true patriots – not the pint-pot patriots, or even the piss-pot patriots, mostly daubing English-language road signs with green paint. I soon came to realise that true patriotism in Wales was a rarity. However, through various contacts I had half a dozen names to go by. Hywel Hughes' name was at the top of this list, so I decided to try and contact him at his ranch (or hacienda) in Colombia. Since I was not too sure what his reaction would be to a complete stranger approaching him, I decided to use a pseudonym. Jones is undoubtedly the most common Welsh surname and William as a first name is still widely used, so I decided Bill Jones would do. There must be hundreds, possibly thousands bearing that name in Wales. When I mailed my letter to Colombia, it was signed Bill Jones, care of Espresso Cafe, Lower Cardiff Road, Pwllheli, Wales. Months passed and I had forgotten about it more or less until one day in August 1962, the twin doors of my coffee bar swung open. In the doorway stood a well-built middle-aged man, dressed in a dark cloak, wearing a large brimmed hat, – not so much a ten gallon hat, more like a twenty gallon! As he stepped inside, he whipped off his sunglasses and in a booming voice said, 'Hywel Hughes from Bogota. I'm looking for a Bill Jones!'

'*Blydi el!*' said Hefina, one of the waitresses. 'Who the fuck is this?'

Rushing out from behind the counter where the espresso coffee machine was sited, I ushered him into the kitchen out of sight of the two dozen customers, mostly local teenagers who were gaping at the charismatic 'cowboy'.

Once we were out of sight and hearing in the kitchen, I

shook hands and confirmed I was Owain Williams... alias Bill Jones! However, that smart idea backfired badly, although I later told the staff and a couple of curious customers that 'Bill Jones' had used the coffee bar as a cover address – naturally without my knowledge!

It turned out Hywel Hughes was very well acquainted with the Tryweryn Valley issue and was very angry about the proposed drowning of this traditionally Welsh community. I told him that a handful of patriots opposed to the flooding were contemplating 'direct action' to try and stop the project and he was very much in favour. I gathered that he was most disappointed by Plaid Cymru's lack of backbone on the issue, believing that had Saunders Lewis still been leader, he would have advocated a much tougher line. Hywel had been a generous contributor to the party for decades, but was now wavering. What we were looking for was someone with patriotic values and a little extra cash, who would be willing to contribute towards supporting the families of patriots who could be imprisoned, or worse, in the future. Hywel Hughes did not hesitate in committing himself to such a possibility. Indeed a few months later he wrote me a letter from South America in which he expressed these sentiments in quite dramatic prose... 'You deliver the action and I will supply the silver bullets.' Rather naively I kept this letter as a memento, but when the police raided my flat when arresting me for my actions at Tryweryn, they took the letter and tried to interpret it as an offer of payment for committing political acts. Nothing could be further from the truth.

Over the last few decades I have remained silent over the incident, basically in order to protect Hywel Hughes from police harrassment, particularly as he was a Colombian citizen and the authorities could cause problems when he travelled back and forth to Wales. Unquestionably this larger-than-life patriot was an enigma, who rose from being penniless to a position of wealth and power, counting senior political figures in Colombia as his friends. Despite living so far away he never forgot his homeland, travelling to Wales for the National Eisteddfod every year. Hywel Hughes passed away several years ago now, and no one has quite taken his place. Undoubtedly he was a benefactor to many Welsh causes and was a staunch nationalist.

Early February 1963 was particularly cold. Several inches of snow lay thick on the ground, while drifts several feet deep blocked roads across Meirionnydd. As if the weather conditions were not enough to contend with, a serious complication happened nearer home. My wife was rushed to hospital following loss of blood just weeks before the baby was due, and she had to stay in for a couple of nights. Whether to abandon the whole plan and ruin months of careful preparation caused me much soul searching. To this day I have asked myself – did I do the right thing that night?

I talked it over with my wife, who was obviously aware 'something' was about to happen. She realised that other people were involved and it wasn't something we could easily postpone to the next night or next week. At the same time she needed me at her side. Because of police surveillance and phone-tapping etc, we did not contact Emyr Llew and he was expecting to meet up with us on 8 February. He had already hired a red Vauxhall car at an Aberystwyth garage. Torn between loyalties, on the very eve of our proposed rendezvous, I decided to proceed. Irene was taken to hospital again the day before and it seemed like an omen to scrap the whole plan. When I visited her in hospital, she told me to do what had to be done, to be careful and to visit her the next day. I said goodbye and left the hospital, praying everything would turn out alright.

Emyr Llew had parked the red Vauxhall on some waste ground, which was also the back entrance to Pwllheli Post Office. John Albert Jones and I joined him, climbing over a low fence that led to the back door of the coffee bar. Once in the car, we moved at a leisurely speed so as not to attract attention from the occupants of the police station directly parallel to the back entrance.

Even in Pwllheli town, there was a covering of snow, but as we left Porthmadog and entered the vicinity of Meirionnydd, matters quickly deteriorated. Snow ploughs had been busy piling snow on both sides of the road, leaving just one narrow lane in many places. As we approached Dolgellau, several feet of snow had been bulldozed to each side, giving an eerie look to the landscape. When we took the road leading to Bala, we were moving further from the coast and climbing, which meant even more snow and drifts. It was getting so bad in places we wondered if we would make it through the narrow lanes leading from Bala. Suddenly, there was an almighty bang and the car skidded across the road!

Somehow we managed to push the car off the main road onto a clearing near a field entrance and saw that the rear off side tyre was well and truly flat. Rummaging in the back of the car, to our horror we discovered there was no jack! Two of us would have to lift the car on one side while the other slid on the spare wheel. Thank God, there was at least a spare. It was bitterly cold. The packed snow was frozen solid underfoot and crackled as we struggled to lift the car. Finally, after twenty minutes of heaving and pulling, we had the new wheel in place. During this time, one explosive device was stored on the back seat and the timing device ticking away. It wasn't connected yet, but...

Traffic was very sparse on that Saturday evening. The thick snow had discouraged all but a few from venturing out. Driving through the small sleepy town of Bala, we saw a small police car parked near the memorial in the main street. Emyr Llew kept well below the thirty miles an hour speed limit; to be stopped at this stage would have been a disaster. Taking a left turn near the end of the main street, we were now on a much narrower side road leading towards Tryweryn and the dam site. As we climbed higher, the going became ever harder. The small Vauxhall struggled to stay on the road, skidding at times as the snow on the ground became deeper.

When we reached the small hamlet of Frongoch, we took

a right-hand turn onto an even narrower road. Here we planned to park our car, safely out of sight, in the school yard at Cwmtirmynach. We then walked to the site, carrying the explosive device, timer, detonators, and the gelignite, which was strapped with adhesive tape onto the lid of a Jacobs biscuit tin. Leaving the road, we climbed over a farm gate into a field with at least a foot of snow covering it. Soon we saw the actual dam site, brightly lit by strong overhead lamps, creating an eerie picture against the white surroundings. We paused behind a high stone wall, scanning the site for any guards patrolling the perimeter fence. Once over the wall, we were in a position where the bright lights of the site were shining on to us. To avoid being spotted in the glare, we continued for the rest of the way crawling on our stomachs, inching forward through the thick snow. Our target, a large transformer, loomed before us, surrounded by tall iron railings, spiked at the top, with two powerful lights shining brightly on either side. Staying glued to the ground, almost afraid to breathe, we waited and listened. There was only the deafening throb of a generator in the distance and a shallow humming sound from the transformer itself. Eventually, after several minutes of waiting which seemed forever, three figures appeared out of a large shed. One had a large Alsatian guard dog on a lead, which seemed to be straining to get free. John and I looked at each other; we'd got it right during the past few weeks when we had monitored and timed the watchmen. It seemed there was a half-hourly walk around the installation to check all was well.

Once two watchmen had passed the transformer compound and vanished into the night, we set about the last leg of our mission. We had estimated it would take approximately twenty minutes to get into the compound, place the device and get back to where we were. That left ten minutes before the watchmen returned. Slithering along on the snow, we climbed over a barbed wire fence, directly opposite the transformer compound, another twenty metres and we were standing by the iron railing. Emyr climbed over the high fence first, followed by myself. John remained outside keeping watch and listening for any sounds or movement. Emyr and I then decided the best place for the explosive device was under the large square tank, which we assumed held the oil. The detonator wire was quickly connected to the gelignite and the wire at the other end attached to the timing device. This was set to explode at three o'clock next morning; by now it was half past eight in the evening. By setting the timing six and a half hours in advance, it allowed us to travel back before it got too late. Once the device was planted, we hurriedly got out of the compound, climbing over the railings once more and jumping to the ground on the outside where John was nervously waiting.

Losing no time we trekked back towards our car, a distance of over one mile. Once out of range of the powerful lamps we straightened up and proceeded to walk or stumble through the thick snow. As we climbed over the last barbed wire fence, Emyr let out a small cry – he had caught his leg on a strand of barbed wire which left a nasty gash on the back of his leg. Blood kept spouting out of his wound, which was at least three inches long and deep. Emyr fished out a white handkerchief from his pocket, then pressed it hard against the wound. This unfortunate accident lost us valuable time, almost a quarter of an hour. John and I managed to half-drag Emyr along, even though he was in some agony. He gritted his teeth and hopped on one leg. When we eventually reached the road which led to Bala, the bleeding had almost stopped, although there were a few patches of red on the snow. During our struggle to get Emyr back, his handkerchief had slipped off, lost in the snow. This would have some significance later on... the letter E was embroidered on one corner!

Once on solid ground we made easier progress, although the side road had hardly been touched by snow ploughs or gritters. A few minutes later we were back in the grounds of Cwmtirmynach School and the car. This time it was left for me to drive as Emyr's leg was too painful for him to manoeuvre the foot pedals. Deciding not to return via Bala, but rather aim up the side road towards Cerrigydrudion and hit the A5, I drove carefully in that direction. We had travelled less than half a mile when we realised this road was much more treacherous and had even more snow on the surface. As we seriously contemplated turning around and heading back towards Bala, suddenly rounding a sharp bend, our path was blocked by a small white van stuck in a snow drift!

'What the hell do we do now...?' said John, as a youth of around nineteen or twenty appeared in our headlights. Squinting and raising a hand to shield his eyes from our car's headlamps, he walked slowly towards us. I turned to the other ones and said 'Leave this to me. Don't either of you say a word. I'll pretend we are English and lost in the snow!'

I was fairly good a mimicking accents. I must have picked it up from my elder brother Morris, because he was always doing impressions of all kinds of people including Churchill, and even local preachers like Tom Nefyn Williams, for example.

'I see you're in a spot of bother,' I began.

'Yes, car stuck in snow... not go anywhere,' he stumbled in broken English. After all, there were still a few monoglot Welsh-speakers in the area.

'Don't worry – we'll soon have you out of there. Charles, Steve, give us a hand here, just a little push...'

Emyr and John at first looked confused then, realising they'd just been re-christened, padded through the snow towards us, telling the youth to get into the driver's seat and start the engine. The three of us pushed and shoved until eventually the small van inched forward, slithering from side to side. Once out of the drift and onto a clear part of the road, the driver stopped and walked back towards us. I had told him earlier that we had taken a wrong turning and we needed to head back towards Bala. This meant we had to turn the car around, no easy task with all the snow. This time I got into the car, started the engine while the other three pushed. After several attempts we finally had our car facing the other way. 'Charles' and 'Steve' climbed back inside as the hapless youth waved us goodbye.

Valuable time had been lost and it meant crossing through Bala just after the pubs had shut. Most of the streets would be empty, making us vulnerable and more noticeable to the local police. But once in Bala, we found the main street was pretty much deserted apart from the odd drunk and a handful of noisy youths. Slowly making our way through the town, we passed a parked police patrol car on the outskirts. My heart beat a little faster, as I watched in my rear view mirror for any signs of being followed. At first all seemed well, but suddenly the patrol car we had passed switched on its headlamps and started to follow...

For a gruelling ten minutes the patrol car followed us and finally less than five miles from Dolgellau, it parked in a lay-by and we breathed a sigh of relief. It had certainly been an 'eventful' evening: first a flat tyre, then getting stuck in that snowdrift on the way back. In hindsight, it was a major error of judgement to try and head for the A5 to Cerrigydrudion considering the road conditions. The blame for that rested squarely on my shoulders. Not only had we wasted valuable time, but we had been seen by the youth who was stuck in the snow with his butcher's van. What would he do the next day, when news of the explosion broke? For the rest of our homeward journey, hardly a word was spoken. We were all thinking the same thoughts. When we finally arrived at the back of the coffee bar in Pwllheli, it was gone half past eleven. Having parked and locked the car, we entered the flat, exhausted and ready for some sleep. Before getting into bed, I rang the hospital to enquire how Irene was. I was told she was asleep and would be ready to come home during the next couple of days. Soon I too was asleep – barely three hours to go before our device would shatter the peace of the doomed valley.

Next day, a Sunday, we got up at around nine o'clock before switching on the radio to hear the news. I rang the hospital once more and told the staff nurse I would be visiting Irene later that afternoon. Having listened to all the local news bulletins on Radio Wales, we were beginning to think something had gone wrong as there was no mention of an explosion. Maybe the timing had ceased? Or maybe the device had been disarmed and the authorities were keeping quiet? Finally after hours of agony and worry we switched on the television national news; pictures were shown of a badly damaged transformer with oil leaking onto the snow-covered ground while a team of detectives sifted through the fragments.

A sigh of relief from all three of us broke the silence and we then congratulated each other and there were smiles all around. Then we went our separate ways. Emyr had to take the hired car back to Aberystwyth, John had to return to his sister's house and I had to visit my wife at Bangor Hospital.

When I reached the ward, Irene was sitting up in bed looking very cheerful and feeling much better. I knew from her face that she had also heard the news, but she whispered in my ear not to talk about it. Apparently staff and patients had talked about little else for most of the day. Having been told she would be allowed to come home the following morning, I stayed until visiting time was up and then returned to Pwllheli, as the coffee bar opened on Sunday evenings even in winter time.

Next day, I fetched Irene from the hospital before dinner time and Iona and Gruff from their grandparents where they'd stayed the weekend. Most newspapers carried stories of the 'sabotage' with many pictures of Detective Chief Inspector Humphry Jones who was leading the investigation. Several of the papers referred to footprints found in the snow – there were three sets – one was wearing climbing boots – that was Emyr Llew – two were wearing 'winkle-pickers' – a fad of the day, shoes with pointed tips – that was John and myself. Not ideal footwear for extreme winter weather conditions, true, but John and I had discussed this and thought this might confuse the police. I don't know about confusion, but the flimsy shoes certainly caused both of us much pain, as our feet were frozen stiff with the cold since the snow seeped though the thin leather. The week rolled by without much out of the ordinary happening, then about seven or eight days after the explosion a news flash appeared on the local TV station... a student had been arrested in Aberystwyth in connection with the bomb blast at the Tryweryn dam site!

We had already agreed not to use the telephone to contact each other because of possible 'bugging'. That evening John called at the coffee bar. We had a quick chat – he was thinking what I was thinking; how much longer before we had a visit from the police? As it happened, there was no visit. We knew Emyr Llew would remain tight-lipped under questioning. Besides, we had sworn an oath that if one of us was caught, the other two would bide their time and hit back at the first appropriate opportunity.

7

Tryweryn Aftermath

EMYR'S REMAND HEARINGS at Bala were attended by hundreds of supporters, many of whom were fellow university students from Aberystwyth. Finally, several weeks after his arrest, he was taken before the Dolgellau Assizes Court and sentenced to one year's imprisonment. Meanwhile, John and myself had been busy reconnoitering the electricity line that fed into the dam site. There were a couple of large steel pylons near the small village of Gellilydan, between Trawsfynydd and Blaenau Ffestiniog. These were far enough away from the busy main road, but not far from a small stone bridge which could offer cover. The road itself was hardly used except by a couple of farms.

On the night Emyr Llew was sentenced to one year in prison, John and myself drove to Gellilydan, parked the car in a disused yard and proceeded to wire up the four 'legs' of one of the pylons. Since we had no timing device and it was too dangerous to try and find one, we decided to detonate the explosives at the base of each 'leg'. Once we had placed a device on each of the four 'legs', I took cover behind the bridge wall and John raced downhill towards a disused building, shouting as he went: 'Look out... when the pylon hits the ground the whole place will be live...'

Waiting till he was safe, I touched the wire against the terminals of a small battery. All of a sudden there was a deafening explosion as bits of the pylon mixed with shattered pieces of rock whipped through the air, some landing with a crash on the corrugated roof of an old shed. However, despite the blast, the pylon was still standing. Only one 'leg' had been destroyed because the circuit had been broken with that first explosion; three of the 'legs' were still intact.

There was no time to gather up all the loose bits of wire lying around. Soon someone would come to see what had caused the explosion, so it was time to get out, quickly. We turned back for the A487 which would take us through Porthmadog. Since it would have been foolhardy to use my own car, I had borrowed my father's Vauxhall Cresta, because its metallic silver colour made it inconspicuous. Obviously he was not aware of this.

We had worn Korean combat boots over our ordinary boots and shoes. We took off these outsize boots, placed them in a plastic sack that John was supposed to dispose of after I dropped him off at his sister's house in Penrhyndeudraeth. We had visions of the local police looking for two giants wearing size 13 boots – quite a change from size 8 or 9 winklepickers! But things had not gone according to plan. Because three of the pylon 'legs' had not been damaged, that meant three packages were still in place, until they were found by someone. A third party had been instructed to notify the press and media that there had been an explosion at one of the electricity pylons feeding the Tryweryn dam site. The spokesman had also been instructed to say the attack was a response to Emyr Llew's gaol sentence the previous day.

During the following days, I found it hard to keep my mind on running the coffee bar and my family. I had a gut feeling that too many clues had been left behind and our arrest was inevitable. Exactly one week following the pylon attack, I noticed strangers wearing long macs and wide-brimmed hats circling past the coffee bar. Less than half an hour later, one of my regular customers rushed into the coffee bar and tried to tell me that a friend, Tex, had been taken behind the cinema car park by detectives. His name was all I wanted; Tex had been involved in an earlier raid at a nearby quarry when detonators had been taken. Someone or something had led the police to him, so it was only a matter of time before he and another local lad would crack under questioning.

Although it was a Sunday evening, the cafe had been busier than usual because there was a *Gymanfa Ganu* (hymn singing festival) at one of the town's chapels. Shortly after ten o'clock I was shutting up shop for the day. Without warning, half a dozen plain clothes officers, together with a couple in uniform, entered the premises. Trying to appear unruffled, I calmly said 'Sorry, afraid we're closed for the day... coffee machine's off.'

'We don't want coffee,' said a plain clothed officer in Welsh.

'Oh. OK, do you want fags, then?'

'Cut the chat, Williams, we're not here for fags... we're here for you!'

Amongst the eight cops was Inspector Shaw, head of the police in Pwllheli town and Llŷn. 'You'll need to come to the station with us. We want to ask you some questions,' he said.

I was allowed to go upstairs to tell my wife what was happening, accompanied by two detectives. Although aware there was a strong possibility I could be arrested at some point, it was still a big shock for her, coming at such short notice. Tip-toeing into the two older children's room, where they were fast asleep, I took a last look and then opened the door to our bedroom where Teleri, the baby, was also sound asleep. There wasn't much time to say goodbye to my wife since the police were insisting we get going; a quick hug and a peck on the cheek and down the stairs. Although Pwllheli police station was barely 100 yards around the corner, I was whisked into the back seat of a police car and driven the short distance.

Having entered the police station, I was taken upstairs into an 'interview' room. Here around ten officers, again mostly plain clothes, were huddled around a small table and I was placed to sit in a chair facing them. I noticed a large wooden crate, lid shut, lying on the floor of the room. I immediately recognised it as the one containing the electric detonators we had taken from a nearby quarry almost six months ago.

'Recognise the box, Williams?' said a thin-lipped man. Later I learnt his name was Detective Sergeant Hughes.

Pretending I was focusing on a box of England's Glory matches lying on the table, I replied, 'Yeah... yeah, we see loads of those in the coffee bar!'

DS Hughes, alias 'thin lips', was not amused. 'Think you're clever, eh? We'll bloody see how clever you are when you get locked up for ten years! We know all about you, we've got two in the cells over there. Been singing like canaries, they've told us everything.'

Now it was Inspector Shaw's turn. *'Well Owain bach, da ni ddim yn ffyliad. Helpa di ni yn fan hyn, a mi helpa ni chdi wedyn, iawn?'* ('Owain, we're not fools. You help us and we'll help you later, right?')

This game of cat and mouse went on for several hours. After threats that they would return to my flat, wake up my wife and children and 'turn the place over', I finally agreed to sign a statement admitting my part in the campaign. Although in two minds about the wisdom of such action, I had at least ensured my family was left alone. At least for the time being.

Tired and drained, I was taken downstairs and half pushed into a cold, dirty cell. The door slamming behind me was the very first realisation that my days of freedom were coming to an end. A dim light shone from a naked bulb dangling from a bare cable. As my eyes got accustomed to the surroundings, I noted several examples of graffiti scribbled on the brick walls including the letters S L. For a moment I assumed they were a reminder that Saunders Lewis had spent a night in custody at this very station following the burning of the bombing school at Penyberth, near Pwllheli, in 1936. If this was the case, it made me feel better; despite being alone in my cell, I was still in good company!

Ever so slowly daybreak arrived; it had been a long and sleepless night. For the first time in my life I had experienced what 'being deprived of one's freedom' meant. My life had always been one of roaming wherever I pleased, over wide open spaces, private and uncrowded. When that cell door slammed shut, I was like a caged animal, I wanted to be free. I kicked the door and banged my fists against the bare brickwork. Of course, no one would listen.

A remand hearing was hurriedly arranged. Before I was led from my cell, I heard someone calling my name. It was John Albert. He was locked up a couple of doors down from where I was. Although I was disappointed that he had also been arrested, it was still a good feeling to hear his voice. He was already cracking jokes about the local cops. 'When they found those giant footprints in the snow, they must have thought they were looking for a couple of yetis.'

It was a very short hearing. Three magistrates sat on the bench, two men and one woman, just to go through the legal technicalities of detaining us for another week, while police enquiries continued. My father, wife and my elder brother Morris were in court, all pretty distressed as would be expected. I was allowed a few minutes to say goodbye before John and myself were whisked away in a waiting Black Maria and taken to Shrewsbury prison. If a Pwllheli police cell had been an eye-opener, Shrewsbury gaol was a total culture shock. John and I were split up, although on the same floor. I later found out I was in a cell where my 'neighbour' was a psychotic murderer, while on the other side was a pervert and child abuser who had murdered a little girl. 'Ordinary' convicts do not take kindly to child abusers, rapists and child killers. I witnessed some of these perverts being physically attacked and even hospitalised by other inmates.

Life in prison is not a 'holiday camp' experience. The food left much to be desired – porridge consisted of third grade oats complete with mouse droppings! I recall once doing a stint in the kitchen when one of the prisoners triumphantly hoisted a frozen shoulder of New Zealand lamb above his head shouting 'It's got 1946 stamped on it... that makes this bloody lamb a teenager...!'

The remand hearings were held at Blaenau Ffestiniog,

Aunty May, Mam,
Aunty Anne, Uncle Jac

My mother on the right,
with her sister Anne

A rebel at five years old

Old family photo

Children at Pistyll School
around 1940 (11 pupils)

My father and 'Ossie'
Crowden from Tasmania
at Gwynus, 1953

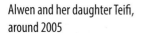

Alwen and her daughter Teifi,
around 2005

'Remember Tryweryn' became a popular slogan

Monika Hibler from Darmstadt, my partner from 1976 to 1984

Special Branch parking spot, opposite Gwynus

From left: Phil ap Siarl, myself, Cayo Evans, Gethin ap Gruffydd and Twm Twm (from Caernarfon), 1969

Geraint Jones,
RS Thomas, myself
and Neil ap Siencyn
in 1988

A 1985 portrait

Dennis Coslett, Keneth Griffith and myself outside the
Independent Wales stall at the Llanelli Eisteddfod, 2000
(photo: Rhobert ap Steffan)

Doran with Rhys and Enlli, 1992

With Enlli (1½ years old) and
Rhys (4) at Erw Wen, May 1992

Rhys Fychan and Enlli
Fychan, Corfu 1997

With John Humphreys, ex-editor of the *Western Mail*, and on the right, my cousin, John Roberts Williams, journalist and broacaster, 2000

At the Llanelli Eisteddfod working for a Welsh identity box for the 2001 Census *(photo: Robin Griffith)*

John Roberts Williams and myself at the Llanelli Eisteddfod *(photo: Robin Griffith)*

Rhys and Enlli outside Erw
Wen on Enlli's first day at Ysgol
Uwchradd Dyffryn Nantlle, 2002

The family on holiday
in Florida, 2003

With my 4 year old grand-daughter
Efa Teleri Fychan, daughter of Enlli

With Geraint Roberts, Awen Bryn,
Councillors Evie Hall Griffiths, Dafydd Guto
Ifan and others, 2005

Llais Gwyned
Christmas par
2014

At Gwynus,
Sumer 2010

With Gethin
ap Gruffudd,
Pwllheli, 2015

With my brother
Morris at
Gwynus, 2010

because of its proximity to Gellilydan, scene of the pylon attack. Both John Albert and I were committed to stand trial at Dolgellau Assizes Court in June. Despite police objections, we were given bail to await that hearing. It was a relief to be allowed home for a few weeks to be with my family.

All was not well at home. My youngest child Teleri had been suffering slight convulsions that weren't thought to be serious, but we decided to take her to see the specialist in a hospital in the Wirral. Following some tests, it was confirmed that she had hydrocephalus, a condition whereby surplus fluid converges around the brain, causing swelling and other complications. We were later told that she would need immediate surgery and this would take place at Alder Hey children's hospital. On the day in question, we travelled to Liverpool with our baby daughter, then barely four months old. We were assured by one of the surgeons that the medical procedure was fairly straightforward and the chances of success were better than 50 per cent.

Hours of anxious waiting followed while our baby was being operated on, but we were fairly confident that the outcome would be positive. When the operation seemed to be taking much longer than we were told, we did start to exchange worried glances. Finally, after what seemed to be ages, a young Irish doctor called us to a consulting room and we were asked to sit down. Apparently an unexpected snag had occurred. Somehow during the operation it had been discovered that they could not treat the problem and consequently Teleri was almost in a vegetative state. This was a devastating shock to us both. There was no doubt her brain had been damaged during the operation. The surgeons told us that she probably could not distinguish between day and night; she would need constant care and would have to be spoon-fed for the rest of her life. The hardest thing for us to digest was being told by the young surgeon, 'As far as you're concerned she is basically brain-dead and you should try to forget about her. I know it's cruel but it's a fact.' We were completely stunned.

Sadly, the doctor was proven right. Teleri lived to be seven years old and stayed most of that time at Heswall Children's Hospital on the Wirral. She spent her entire life in a cot, cared for by loving nursing staff, to whom I am eternally grateful.

Despite our desperate personal situation, the clock kept ticking away as the time given me on bail drew to a close. My trial was set to take place at Dolgellau Assizes Court in mid-June 1963. When the day arrived, I was amazed to see several hundred supporters gathered in the town's square and on the main street – a psychological boost for John and myself. Knowing there was such overwhelming support went a long way towards lifting my flagging spirits, which had been severely tested by the family events of the last few weeks.

Basically the 'British' legal system has no provision for recognising political 'crimes'. Several European nations do differentiate between the criminal and political. Preliminary posturing and tit-for-tat exchanges between prosecution and defence soon gave way to senior barristers solemnly attempting to intimidate the jury. When it was time for the crimson-garbed judge to sum up, he surprised even the most optimistic of supporters in the public gallery when he unexpectedly made a most conciliatory speech, saying, for example, that 'being patriotic is a very fine thing' and referring to 'legitimate grievances'. He ended his speech in an extraordinary manner, when he decided to grant me a further period of time to 'consult with those of the same beliefs' in order to try and end the violence, although he did not use those words. I could not believe my ears and I could not comprehend why he took such a stance. It was only later that I realised he was making a political statement, probably by direction of the Home Office, since the establishment had been surprised by not only the militant action taken by the few, but also the mass support shown by the Welsh public, who had felt betrayed and ignored by Westminster.

It was with a mixture of joy and bewilderment that I walked out of the court. My family and friends were overjoyed and were even beginning to believe I would eventually be conditionally released without serving a prison sentence in due course. On the other hand, despite the judge's words, I was prepared for the inevitable, since no court in Britain would stomach such a climbdown. The final act in the drama would take place at the next Assizes Court in Rhuthun on 1 July, barely a week later.

On the surface, the scenes in Rhuthun town were not much different from those in Dolgellau. Again, hundreds of supporters turned up, waving the Welsh flag and singing our National Anthem. But this time around, the judge adopted a much tougher line. In fact he was at pains to explain that what he had said last time in Dolgellau 'should not be misinterpreted' and the offences were serious and that we – John and myself – had shown 'defiance' in attacking the electricity pylon on the very night that Emyr Llew had been sentenced. Dealing with John first, he took into account that he was younger and that his role was a 'minor' one. John was given a conditional discharge. When dealing with me, he referred to Emyr Llywelyn's sentence and stated I could not be treated differently, so I was sentenced to one year's imprisonment on each of the three charges (the sentences to run concurrently).

Following a hasty farewell to my family and friends, I was unceremoniously marched to the large Black Maria, handcuffed between two screws. So this was for real, no more weekly excursions from a prison to a courtroom and back again, always in hope that, just maybe, the authorities would climb down in face of such continued public support for our cause. From now on I was on my own, no packed courtrooms of solid rank and file nationalists and no more strains of *Hen Wlad Fy Nhadau* ringing in my ears from the large contingent filling the streets outside. Again a total of eight tight-lipped screws accompanied me, including the two attached to me by two pairs of 'cuffs'. Oh well, they were at least taking me seriously, almost as if I was a piece of rare and valuable Clogau gold. By the time we reached Shrewsbury gaol it was late afternoon.

The July sun was high in the sky as I was transferred from the vehicle into the shadows of the prison's high entrance.

After the heavy metal gates clanked shut behind me, I was led along long red tiled corridors, passing through several locked gates along the way. Eventually I reached what was termed 'reception'. Here I was required to strip in front of three, supposedly 'medical' officers. One of them seemed to take an unhealthy interest in my genitals while another made a snide comment about wellingtons and sheep! However, this was to be expected and I had been used to such comments before, during my previous times in prison. Having handed over my clothing and shoes and any other personal items, I was given the standard prison uniform, a pair of boots, bed-clothing, a couple of blankets, a sheet and a pillow. It was tea-time. Most of the prisoners were queuing up outside the 'canteen', each holding a metal tray. After trundling up a couple of flights of stairs, I was stopped in front of another cell door and pushed inside. The door slammed shut as I viewed my new 'home' and its contents – a metal framed bed, a small table, a chair, a basin for washing and a metal 'pisspot'. I lay on the hard mattress, hands tucked under my head, gazing out through the tiny iron-barred window and thought of how slowly the next months would pass.

Several weeks into my sentence, I was summoned into the governor's office and told I was being moved into an open prison. Drake Hall Prison is located not far from Stoke in Staffordshire and, as an 'open' prison, is run on quite different lines. There were several Welsh prisoners among the inmates, although being the sole political prisoner, I was at first regarded with some degree of cynicism by a few. However, once we had got talking and I had explained the situation to them, it was amazing how many of them were won over to our cause. In fact I can truthfully say that several of the Welsh prisoners became 'politicised' and I taught Welsh to half a dozen lads from the valleys of south-east Wales, along with one from Swansea and another from Cardiff. There was one colourful character named

Bishop who, once made aware of the flooding of a Welsh valley for the benefit of an English city, became quite agitated and used to admonish some of the English inmates in four-lettered rhetoric.

One day I will never forget occurred just before Christmas. I was suddenly called to the Governor's Office and politely asked to sit down. Gwilym Griffiths, a modest and unassuming man, was a native of Pembrokeshire. He had been a submarine commander, had travelled the world and was broad-minded. A message had been sent from Heswall Children's Hospital, stating my daughter Teleri's health had deteriorated sharply because she'd contracted pneumonia and her life was in grave danger. Gwilym Griffiths told me he was authorising my release for one day to travel unescorted to the hospital to visit my child.

Early next morning a car awaited me outside the prison gates. I expected one of the warders would be driving me to the train station. It was with amazement that I realised the Governor himself was to chauffeur me. Once inside the car he started to speak, stressing more than once that we were for the time being two equal human beings, not prisoner and governor and furthermore, he would like me to tell him what exactly my 'protest' was about? Naturally he knew the background of Tryweryn but was keen to understand how I had become personally involved. In the few brief minutes it took to arrive at the station, I did my best to explain to him what my patriotism truly meant and that I had had these deep feelings for my country from a very young age. He listened quietly as he drove, nodding his head occasionally. After I had finished he said something which has stuck with me all these years. 'I do realize, and want you to know that I understand, that you are different from the others (meaning prisoners). We can talk freely about these things while we're in the car, but of course once you're back inside this evening, I have to treat you the same as anyone else'.

I told him that was ok and I understood his position and

thanked him for allowing me to travel unescorted from the prison. Before leaving the car, he shook my hand and said, 'I believe I can trust you to come back and I shall be here to meet you off the train.'

It was a strange feeling, standing on the platform, wearing civilian clothes – to all purposes a 'free man' – well, at least for a whole day. Eventually the train arrived at its destination and I completed my journey to the hospital by bus. Once off the bus, almost directly outside the hospital entrance, my stomach began to churn. I was scared and confused and took several minutes to pluck up enough courage to venture inside. This was my first visit to Heswall Children's Hospital, since previously Teleri had been staying at Alder Hey Hospital, where she'd had her operation. Walking down several corridors, I eventually arrived at a medium-sized ward where several young children with severe physical disabilities were staying. Some were 'thalidomide' babies. As I walked through the ward, several of these children would come up to me, some actually crawling on their stomachs as they were born without legs. There were others without arms, or had deformed hands. One of the nurses explained to me that many had been abandoned by their parents on the pretext that they couldn't cope with their disabilities. Some of the kids asked me for sweets and chocolate. Unfortunately I had none with me and that made me feel pretty useless.

I was guided to Teleri's bedside, in reality a small cot, where she lay in a sort of coma. She was being treated for pneumonia, although it was too early to say whether she would survive. Looking at her helpless tiny figure in the cot made me realise how vulnerable we all are. Young or old, we are at the mercy of events beyond our control. Because of my daughter's condition, I couldn't hold her or cuddle her. The nurses were very caring and committed. They explained that even prior to the pneumonia, Teleri had to be spoon-fed and would never walk or talk even if she recovered from her present illness. It was getting close to Christmas and the hospital staff had been busy trying to bring a little joy to the unfortunate children's ward by decorating with paper trimmings and fairy lights and a small Christmas tree. They say Christmas-time is for rejoicing and merriment. I have to admit that day only made me feel all the more sad and lonely. Seeing the suffering of children must be the most depressing emotion of all; that my own child was amongst them only deepened these feelings.

It was with an intense sense of sadness and frustration that I made my way from the hospital back to the train station. I decided to forget the bus and walk the few hundred yards which gave me time to reflect on what I had just witnessed. Since the days were short, it was already almost dark as I walked. Several houses were lit up with bright lights, trees and Christmas decorations in place. Jingles and carols came with repetitive regularity from almost every shop. Suddenly, the realisation I would not be with my little family became too much. My whole body swelled with emotion and for a few minutes I seriously considered not returning to the prison but absconding and trying to get home. In the end my head overruled my heart as I realized that even if I were successful in returning to my family for a few hours, I'd have to serve several extra months as punishment.

What's more, I had given my word to Gwilym Griffiths, the Governor, that I would return. Boarding the train was hard. Although less than three months of my sentence remained to be served, it seemed like an age. True to his word, the Governor was waiting for me at the other end. Scarcely a word was spoken, although Gwilym Griffiths tried to have a conversation. I was in no mood for talking after the day's experience, but thanked him once more for his trust and kindness.

Before leaving his car and re-entering the prison, he asked me if I would teach him the words of a Welsh hymn! This special hymn is often sung at Wales Rugby International matches – 'Cwm Rhondda' (or in English 'Bread of Heaven'). The Governor had a very fine tenor voice. I had often heard him singing from a distance as he walked around the prison

95

blocks and sometimes he would whistle a Welsh hymn. A week following my day out, he called around to see me and asked me to write down the words of the hymn. Soon Gwilym Griffiths' voice rang out across the prison as he practised his newly-acquired Welsh-language hymn.

Christmas Day was tough and I couldn't get it over quickly enough. Thoughts of my family ground me down, as I pined for their company and freedom still seemed a million miles away. Letters and cards from supporters arrived by the dozen, which made me feel I wasn't completely forgotten. During my sentence I was allowed only one visit a month, usually by my wife and close friends. It was good while it lasted, but once they had gone I felt worse than before they came. My wife had stopped bringing the children to visit me for some time, as she thought that seeing me in prison surroundings unsettled them and made them unhappy. Not being able to see them was difficult for me to handle and that in turn contributed to my visits not working out as they should. Once Christmas was over and New Year's Day came and went, I believed that the remaining two months of my sentence would pass quickly. That assumption proved to be most misguided. If time had dragged during the preceding months, now it was at a stop. Minor squabbling between my wife and myself over petty issues aggravated the situation.

1 March, St David's Day, was the day of my release. This was in itself ironic, but in reality became more of an anti-climax. My father arranged for a friend to drive down to the prison in the early hours. I walked out of the prison gates at half past seven. It was a chilly morning with a touch of ground frost covering the grass verges as I strode towards where the waiting car was parked. My father stepped forward to greet me with a broad smile on his face. Handshakes followed. In my family, hugging each other was not considered a manly way of demonstrating our affection. That doesn't mean there was any less feeling or emotion in our greeting, it was just more 'subdued'.

Throughout the two-hour journey home, not many words

were spoken, apart from my enquiry about how Iona and Gruff were coping with their lives while I was away. Of course I knew that most weekends and school holidays they spent their time with my parents at Gwynus. Apart from that, I found it difficult to put into words what my feelings were at that moment. I was filled with a combination of expectancy and also a certain trepidation at the thought of dealing with this new 'freedom'. There were personal issues I had to try and sort out with my wife, who had been under a lot of pressure ever since I was imprisoned and even before. Our sick baby girl lying in hospital with no hope of recovering had troubled me greatly. For a long time while in my cell I kept thinking that maybe her situation would have been different if... It was the 'ifs' and 'buts' which gnawed at my conscience and disturbed my soul.

Finally we arrived outside the coffee bar; it had been shut for the day. My wife had rightly thought it would have been inappropriate to have crowds of people hovering around when we needed some privacy and time for ourselves.

I have already explained that our relationship did not work out following my release. Too many arguments, too much psychological pressure and personal problems all added up to cause our split. All I can say is it was a most painful period and left many scars on my mind. Since it happened at the very time I was most vulnerable and I needed my family and comfort, it left me devastated. I descended into such a low state of mind as to question the point of carrying on. Only the thought of my children carried me through, together with the support of my parents and particularly my elder brother Morris.

8

Marriage Split; MAC Activities

IN THE SUMMER of 1964, my wife and two children departed to live with her parents, who had moved to Wales and lived in a cottage outside Nefyn. Following that, I battled from day to day trying to cope. Times were very difficult, as I struggled with my conscience over the issue of having been involved in political activity which had cost me my family. I became bitter and fought continuously to retain a balanced mind.

Less than a week after our split, I decided to close down the coffee bar, at least temporarily, since I could not handle meeting people, never mind run a business. This period was one of the darkest in my life. It took a long time and much resolve to see me through. It was at this time that I began to scribble on bits of paper – personal thoughts, basically a self-analysis of the last few years of my life. Eventually, I decided to compile these notes into a book, although at that time there was no intention of seeing it published. I thought it was too personal. Strangely, putting my thoughts onto paper proved a great release and helped me emotionally. It took several weeks for me to complete this little book and throughout that time the coffee bar remained shut. As my confidence slowly recovered, I re-opened the business and the hand-written manuscripts remained in the bottom of a drawer for several years – until I talked to Eirug Wyn about them.

Eirug Wyn was a softly spoken young man who kept a Welsh book shop in Caernarfon. Siop Y Pentan was a bustling hive of activity catering for academics, scholars, Welsh speakers from every background. Bookshelves were crammed with a wide variety of Welsh-language as well as English-language books dealing with Welsh themes, from children's books to biographies, fact and fiction. Whenever I visited his shop, the conversation would soon switch to Welsh politics and the state of the nation, the language struggle, local press, etc. On one of my many visits to his shop, the drowning of the Tryweryn valley came up in our conversation. During our discussion, I happened to mention I had tried to write my thoughts relating to that turbulent period, though this was now several years past. Eirug was intrigued to hear this and asked if he could have a look at it. On my next visit I took him the battered sheets, written in my own handwriting, not typed. My handwriting is not the best in the world; at times when I write fast, even I have a problem reading it, so God help anyone else!

Despite the difficulties, Eirug persevered and when he had read the entire manuscript, he rang me and said he would like to publish it. Not only did Eirug type it all and edit it, he also had to translate it into Welsh since I had written it in English. There is a reason for that. I left school before my fifteenth birthday and Welsh was hardly taught as a subject at Pwllheli Grammar School in those days. Despite being brought up in an almost monoglot Welsh family, my grammar in my own native language was faulty. There was a gap between everyday spoken Welsh and what was acceptable as 'properly' written Welsh.

Some months later *Cysgod Tryweryn* appeared in the bookshops and within weeks the first couple of thousand copies were sold out! It was reprinted on another two occasions. In all around 3,500 to 4,000 copies were sold. Years later another local publisher, Gwasg Carreg Gwalch, printed another thousand. Incidentally two decades later, a film was made from my story. It's called *Y Weithred* (The Act) and it was shown on S4C several times.

There was one big disadvantage of having become 'well

known' publicly through my actions at Tryweryn. The media attention afterwards made me open to all kinds of approaches, some genuine and some far from sympathetic. There were Welsh men and women who blatantly displayed their hatred for me and the actions I had taken.

Sometimes, if I were to enter a bar in Nefyn or Pwllheli, I would be confronted by such comments as: 'Think you're tough, do you?'

'I fought for the likes of you in the war... bloody Welsh Nash'.

Or on more than one occasion: 'Do you want to step out the back?' always looking for an excuse to start a fight.

I still remember vividly one incident. While walking down the street in Pwllheli near my coffee bar, two rather scruffy middle-aged women came to meet me. One, came up to me and spat in my face, shouting, 'You bloody Welsh Nashies need shooting!'.

'You and your type are only fucking trouble,' barked the other.

At that particular time, I really was on a downer. As I've written above, I'd been out of prison barely three months. My marriage was breaking up, I had an 18-month-old daughter in hospital who was not expected to live, and this was only the second time I had ventured out onto the street since my release. That little spitting incident didn't do one hell of a lot of good for my confidence. It wasn't the actual physical act of spitting in my face, unpleasant enough as it was, but the fact that there were still people out there who had no idea what some of us were fighting for. We were, after all, not in some cosmopolitan or anglicised corner of Wales – we were in the heart of Welsh-speaking Wales!

Others were supportive – or appeared to be. I remember answering the phone in my parents' house and this voice said, 'You don't know me but I am an admirer of yours. I want to do something for Wales.' When I asked his name, he said 'John', which covers a lot of ground without leaving many clues.

Before hanging up he said, 'I'll be in touch again. Maybe we can meet, but I'll call you first.' Then the line went dead.

Well, he did get in touch again... and again... and again. Despite being told that I had no interest in participating in any further actions of a military nature in future, John Gwilym Jones persisted. One evening he drove up to my parents' house in a light green mini van that seemed too small for his tall frame. Dark haired and rather pallid, he wore a flat cap and a long black overcoat. He seemed to be in his mid twenties and was very nervous. He outlined his background, claiming to live on a farm in the middle of Anglesey, since leaving a private school – Rydal in Colwyn Bay. He repeated what he told me on the phone earlier, saying he had 'great respect', for me and that he had 'plans' and similar views which were shared with five or six young men on Anglesey. Among his claims was that 'they' had hold of several firearms and ammunition, 'taken' from a territorial army building on the island, and that these could 'come in handy' for an attack to take over Caernarfon castle prior to the investiture ceremony (of Charles Windsor as 'prince of Wales')! He was most keen to find out the names of people who might be ready to take part in a mini uprising! Later he related how he was dating a girl who lived not too far from my home; this would make it easier for him to come and see me more often! Alarm bells began to ring – I had not the vaguest idea who this stranger was.

On this subject it is worth mentioning that a few months following my release from prison, probably during the winter of 1965–66, a complete stranger appeared on my doorstep, unannounced. During this time I still ran the Espresso. I lived in the flat above. It was late one evening when I ran downstairs as someone was knocking on the door. A very tall, dark-haired guy in his early thirties stood there.

'Hallo... are you Owain Williams?' he enquired with hand outstretched, speaking with a very broad scouse accent. He had a small black case in the other hand.

Shaking his hand, I replied 'Yes, that's me. Who's asking?'

'Ah, sorry mack, yeah, I'm Dave Parry from Liverpool' he replied. 'Eh, could I have a quick word?' he added.

I was curious – and suspicious; suspicion had become second nature to me following the previous couple of years' experiences.

'Come on up,' I said. He followed me up the flight of stairs with long purposeful strides. Being polite and still curious, I offered him a cup of coffee. 'Dave Parry', if that was his real name, talked a lot. For over an hour I listened to him rattling on and on about Wales, about what were 'we going to do about the investiture in Caernarfon' which was still over three years away! He was adamant – the ceremony had to be stopped. Where did he come into it? He said he had the expertise and the knowhow, having served with the military. What's more, he'd done three years with the French Foreign Legion, serving in Algeria and other French-controlled areas in North Africa. Opening his suitcase, he dug out an official-looking document – his draft papers in the Foreign Legion, he said.

'Did you know that you cannot join the Foreign Legion using your own name? You have to have a nom de plume. Guess what I chose?' he asked.

But before I could answer, 'Ken Dodd? Bessie Braddock'? he answered the question for me!

'Owen Glendower!' he boasted, showing me the papers. Strange, I thought to myself, if this clown was working for British Intelligence, obviously trying to impress me, why does he spell Owain Glyndŵr's name in the bastardised English form?

However, I decided to let him ramble on for hours, trying not to yawn too much, pretending I was believing his every word. I listened until he'd finished talking about himself and his 'plans'. Turning to me suddenly, he asked, 'What are you going to do about it? Are there any plans for stopping the investiture?'

I certainly wasn't planning anything. I'd done what I thought needed doing at Tryweryn, and that was my lot, no more for me! Somehow I don't think he believed me before trying another option.

'You must have lots of friends who feel like you. Could you give me some addresses or phone numbers?' he enquired. Incidentally, he had informed me that the reason he 'cared for Wales' was because he was of Welsh blood, hence the surname Parry.

There was no question; he was working for one of the intelligence services, probably MI5 – or else he was a total nutcase! Finally, wanting to get rid of him but pretending to believe his story, I decided on a ploy, thinking about who in Wales was the least likely to take part in any illegal or militant action – I invented a couple of 'likely names' for him. One in Cardiff and one in Swansea, one in mid Wales, another in Anglesey, but said I did not have these addresses as they'd contacted me by phone earlier. Finally, in order for him to swallow my story, I fed him the names of three or four persons who actually existed; a respectable preacher with nationalist trends but a devout pacifist; an eccentric shopkeeper who kept writing letters to the press, but was harmless enough. Another 'pillar of society' whose name I threw in was a certain lady of questionable virtues, despite her National Eisteddfod bardic role, but hardly a potential female version of Che Guevera! Dave Parry, or whatever his real name was, seemed extremely grateful for my 'cooperation' and promised 'great things' before the investiture!!

Before leaving, he asked to use the bathroom. While he nipped out, I noticed that he had not shut his small suitcase – it was lying on the floor. Opening the lid, to my surprise, inside was a radio transmitter! If I had doubts in my mind before, I didn't now.

After he left, he never called to see me again and never telephoned, but it wasn't the end of 'Dave Parry'. He flitted back and forth through Wales regularly. At one time, less than a year before the investiture, he turned up at a Free Wales Army 'training camp' in mid Wales. When the FWA trial ended at Swansea, he vanished for good and hasn't been seen since. I was told afterwards that he had visited the persons I'd named. Since I knew them personally we had a good laugh about it later. By sending him to waste his time following quite innocent targets, it gave a bit of space to real activists who risked all for their country – they were the members of MAC (*Mudiad Amddiffyn Cymru*, Movement for the Defence of Wales).

One other occasion on which 'Dave Parry' showed up was in a television programme hosted by none other than David Frost. It featured members of the FWA, parading, dressed in their adopted uniforms. David Frost used the occasion to mock the participants and by implication derided the cause of the Welsh patriots. Before the David Frost TV programme was filmed, I had warned the FWA members not to take part but to no avail. Some were intent on securing maximum publicity, others felt it would help their cause.

Most of the men taking part were genuinely patriotic; some may have been misguided, but there were a few who certainly did not back the nationalist cause – one in particular was 'Dave Parry'. I know for fact that at least two other members of the intelligence services took part in Free Wales Army mock manoeuvres in mid Wales, posing as supporters. Two of them gave evidence against the FWA leaders in a subsequent trial at Swansea just a few days prior to the investiture.

(A few words of clarification would be good here: the MAC operated underground, and were not open to anyone to join. The FWA was open to all. They wore uniforms, and were involved in parades on occasions. Their leader, Cayo Evans, was charismatic and very much a showman.)

One thing that the members of MAC did not need or seek was publicity. There was one occasion only when they deviated from that course. Their Director of Operations and Chief Activist John Bernard Jenkins arranged a clandestine 'press conference' at an old mansion outside Chester. MAC leaders and supporters had been unhappy for some time that while they carried out daring and very successful operations against many targets, ranging from water pipes for Liverpool and Birmingham to Government buildings etc, it was the FWA who seemed to reap the benefit, sometimes hinting it was their work. In itself, that may not have seemed a bad thing – but because certain spokesmen of the FWA didn't have the the detailed information concerning almost all of the explosions, MAC decided to hold its one and only conference.

John Jenkins and a couple of other members of MAC, through sympathetic go-betweens, were able to get hold of one reporter, who was blindfolded and led into a darkened room where he was confronted by a masked spokesman. The reporter was given a brief account of MAC's past actions plus a summary of what could happen in the future, unless certain demands were met. When the story broke in the press, it caused some panic in high places, despite attempts by the authorities to quash it. If there had been some doubts before about the existence of an active militant movement that was organised and focused on disruption, those doubts vanished.

It is also interesting that the leader of Plaid Cymru at that time tried to point the finger at British Intelligence service, saying this was an attempt to 'discredit Plaid!' Of all the pathetic wimping by that party, this has to be the pits. They were implying that the Secret Services were working to halt Plaid's 'election progress'. What progress? The only progress Plaid had managed was to win a by-election at Carmarthen in July 1966, which took place, incidentally, around four months after MAC detonated a bomb at the massive new Clywedog dam, built to supply more water for Birmingham. I venture to say that had that blast not taken place, Plaid Cymru would never have won that seat. Anyone who challenges that statement either does not understand the politics of Wales – or else they are proverbial ostriches with their heads in the sand.

The 1960s was a memorable decade. It was probably a turning point in modern history, a time of social and political rebellion all over the world – Vietnam, Kenya, Cyprus, Ireland.

Meanwhile, in Wales, things were at last beginning to stir –

the main concern amongst patriots was the intended investiture of Charles Windsor of England as 'prince' of Wales. 1 July 1969 had been pencilled in as the fateful day for that event. There had been several 'rumblings' in the background. Water pipelines to Liverpool and Birmingham had been bombed, cutting supplies for several days. Other targets, mainly government buildings, had been attacked, for example, the Royal Mint in Llantrisant – leading to some wit re-christening it as 'the hole with a mint in it!' These were carried out by the MAC.

The National Patriotic Front (NPF) campaigned openly for an Independent Wales. It opposed the investiture by holding rallies, distributing leaflets and raising awareness amongst a populace that was in the main ignorant of its own history due to centuries of brainwashing by its English conquerors. At this particular time I was president of the NPF – which was under heavy surveillance by the British Intelligence Service, both MI5 and MI6. Special Branch had also set up a specialist unit, based at Shrewsbury, commanded by Jock Wilson from Scotland Yard. I was informed that the security services regarded the NPF as the political wing of MAC!

Due to my earlier history as an 'activist', I had been a target for these 'gentlemen' for some time. My phone was tapped, my car was bugged, complete with homing device. I was constantly watched and followed by shadowy figures who usually wore hats, or duffle coats with the hoods pulled up over their heads.

Towards the end of January 1968, I took a trip to London to find myself a certain car. This was no ordinary model I was after, but a Volvo P1800 S, which I had fancied for some time. The fact that I had resorted to a rather clandestine method of leaving Wales for London had more to do with spending years being followed by secret agents of the British government, than with any intention of participating in any cloak and dagger activities!

I was driving my father's brown and cream Vauxhall Cresta when I stopped at The Mount, a pub outside Caernarfon, where

I'd arranged to meet someone. I was sitting on a chair near the bar drinking a coffee and chatting with my friend when John Gwilym Jones walked in. I was rather surprised to see him. Ignoring me, he approached the bar. As the other person who was talking with me left, Jones moved over rather furtively to my table. I got up to leave and he followed me outside. Since I did not trust this character, I had no intention of informing him of my London trip – or of anything else, for that matter. I also didn't want him to see what vehicle I was driving. The Cresta was parked behind the pub in a large car park. Noticing Jones' green mini van parked right next to the front door alongside the main road, I casually asked where he was going.

'Listen, I have something special for you,' he said.

Opening the mini van's back doors, he beckoned me over to have a look inside. He then pulled back some sackcloth material – to reveal a selection of hand guns, at least eight, with half a dozen daggers. I noticed among the revolvers and pistols an American Colt, plus a Smith and Wesson and a Luger pistol. I was shocked. There I was, in the middle of the day, near a busy main road, standing a couple of feet away from a deadly arsenal, talking to a young idiot who was either a dangerous infiltrator or unbelievably naive. Before I could utter a word, he picked up the Luger and tried to thrust it into my hand.

'Here, I want you to have this one,' he said.

I said thanks but no thanks. I told him I didn't need it and besides, did he not realise that carrying any kind of unauthorised firearms was not a very smart idea:

'But I've given one to Robin and Eddie already,' he protested. Suddenly I realised that what I had feared was coming true. This comparative stranger in a short period of time had worked his way into a position whereby he could drive around handing out guns at random. Whether it was true or not that he had really given others some of the weapons, there was no way I could tell.

Seeing that he couldn't persuade me to take any of the firearms, he tried another angle: 'Have you seen Eddie recently?'

he enquired. I shook my head. 'Well, he wants you to go down to that house in Llanllyfni. He's got some 'chicken food' for you but I don't know what this means,' he added.

'Nor me, besides I don't keep chickens any more, they don't pay,' I replied. Chicken feed was the slang for 'explosives' in Nationalist Wales at the time.

'Well, he's waiting for you in that house, said you would know where to go,' he persisted. I started getting agitated at this stage.

What the hell was he playing at? First, he tried to furnish me with a gun, now he wanted me to pick up some explosives! If I were stupid enough, I would be arrested in possession of a gun and explosives! Wanting to get rid of him in a hurry, I decided on the direct approach.

'Look, you'd better fuck off NOW!' in as forceful a voice as I could muster. Taking the hint, he leapt in his mini van and tore off towards Pwllheli. Thank God I was going in the opposite direction! There was something very wrong going on here, I thought, deciding to give Caernarfon town a wide berth as I zig-zagged around back roads, since I felt uneasy and extremely uncomfortable after my meeting with Jones. So it was with trepidation that I had finally arrived at Rhyl station and parked the car, before taking the train to London...

9

Repercussions

AFTER READING IN the newspaper about the three arrests in Wales, I returned to my room on the third floor of the Russell Hotel where I had already spent one night. I reread the short news story two or three times. The alarm bells which had been ringing overtime began to subside. Trouble was, events were being played out almost 250 miles away and I had no safe way of checking out the details behind the scene back home. After an hour or so mulling over the options, I decided that the only way of finding out the truth would be to ring my mother at home next morning. This would not be easy, as the last thing I wanted to do was upset my parents who were not getting any younger.

'Hello, Mam.' There was a nervous pause on the other side. 'Where are you?' she asked, almost whispering. My mother was a very astute person and could read my mind 250 miles away. She had experienced the Intelligence Services' undercover activities in the past – like the tap on Gwynus' phone since 1963, when I had been arrested and sent to prison.

'I'm in London. Is there anything going on?' I asked.

Hesitating a moment, she began, 'Listen, you'd better get home – they're all over the place. There's two been parked at the end of the lane for over two days. And some Superintendent John Hughes wants to speak to you...'

For a moment I stood frozen in my hotel room. 'Yes, OK, don't worry about it, Mam – there must be some mistake. I'll sort it out when I get back.'

She was obviously most distressed. 'Well, you'd better get back right away.'

'OK, Mam, I'll call you before I get home, bye.' I hung up and sat on the bed, thinking and thinking.

Looking on the bright side, it suddenly struck me that at least I was in the middle of London. Nobody knew who the hell I was amongst the millions, so I was safe for now. I went downstairs, ordered breakfast and ate it heartily; well, dammit I'd paid for it, hadn't I? Sipping my coffee, I contemplated my next move. I'd travelled to London to buy a second-hand car. Right now I seriously needed a set of wheels to move around, hopefully unnoticed. What better way than with an unknown car? Nobody would recognize it or know its registration plate... hell, even I didn't know it yet!

Then, suddenly, I realized that by calling my Mam from the hotel phone in my room, the authorities would track it back right away. I decided to check out at once, grabbed my few belongings and threw them into a hold-all. Glancing quickly around the hotel foyer, I saw no-one who looked remotely dubious, so I left and hailed a taxi to Oxford Circus tube station.

Making my way to a sidewalk news stand, I bought a motoring magazine. There was one model of the Volvo I was looking for, south of the Thames; red and in immaculate condition. That was the very vehicle which I had come to buy. As a person, I don't like to waste my time, or other people's for that matter; when I know what I want I go and get it... within reason! The whole process didn't take too long. The salesman took me for a short run and that was it. Transaction completed, I proudly drove my gleaming almost new vehicle in the direction of the M1 towards home... but what then?

A bright red Volvo P1800 was probably not the most inconspicuous car on the M1 that fateful day. In normal circumstances I would have been engrossed by the engineering marvel I controlled. I would have tested its acceleration to the full and seen how fast it could go. I was thirty-four, adventurous and loved challenges. But now I had other things on my mind. After driving for two hours, I decided to pull into one of the service stations.

There was a girl not far from Rhyl in north-east Wales, whom I'd known for some months. We had met through 'political' circles. Her family were staunch nationalists and supported certain methods of 'direct action' as opposed to the pacifism that was preached and practised without any visible signs of success at that particular time. Esyllt was a short, slight girl with cropped dark hair, olive skin and a bubbly personality. Using a pay phone, I dialled her number. Finally she answered and after a casual hello and how are you, I asked if she could meet me in Rhyl later that evening.

'Yeah, OK... what's it about?' she asked

'Tell you when I get there, and thanks.' Then I hung up.

As it was January, nightfall was early and by five o'clock it would be dark. On my way down to London, I had borrowed my father's car, a Vauxhall Cresta, two toned brown and cream. I had driven as far as Rhyl, parked it and walked to the railway station where I'd bought a single ticket to London Euston, since I was buying a car to drive back.

As I came off the motorway and headed towards Rhyl, I had the nagging thought that the police or Special Branch might have traced my father's car and were at this very moment ready to pounce on me whenever I appeared. On the phone earlier, I had instructed Esyllt to wait for me in the car park of a public house not far from the station, where the Vauxhall was parked. I drove slowly past the public house, lights dimmed, making sure I was well within the speed limit. I saw Esyllt's small dark saloon car parked with side lights on. She had no idea who was in the gleaming Volvo when I parked directly behind her. I tapped my fingers gently on her car window. She let out a shout, 'Oh my God!' then, 'It's you... you bloody scared me. What the hell's up?' she blurted.

I climbed into the car and told her what had happened. She had already heard of the arrests earlier, as it was big news nearer home. Somehow, I had to see if my father's Vauxhall was still parked where I had left it three days ago, and check whether it was being 'shadowed' by someone. I usually carried a small pair of binoculars with me and this pair had night vision. Through the open window of our car, I could make out my father's car. It was parked where I had left it. No-one seemed to be near it. Then I saw that both tyres on the side facing me were flat! Someone, most probably Special Branch, had got tired of waiting for me, so had let the air out of the tyres.

What now? After debating the options, we decided to return to Esyllt's parents' house for the night. I followed her at a distance in my new Volvo and arrived at her home about twenty minutes later. Since her parents knew me quite well, I explained the events to them. It was decided that I would stay until the morning and then drive to my parents' farm in Pistyll, near Nefyn. During the night I slept a little but was mostly restless. In the morning I went downstairs and Esyllt's Mam had cooked me breakfast. I had no great appetite that morning but made an effort as I did not wish to offend the kindly lady. Reluctantly, I prepared to leave.

The three came outside to see me off. Esyllt and her family were patriotic folk. Although not a member of MAC, she was an enthusiastic supporter and would carry out simple tasks on behalf of the movement. She was not my 'regular' girl friend. I didn't have one at this time – but I knew several politically active women up and down Wales who would provide 'safe houses' when I or other members travelled here and there. There were other friends, male and female, who would not have any political beliefs or leanings, but would act as distractions to confuse Special Branch members who were 'tracking' me. Being hounded by shady-looking characters 24/7 can be daunting. In many people's eyes it may sound exciting, but in reality it is nerve-wracking.

As I left Esyllt standing outside the house I whispered in her ear, 'Be careful, watch out for any suspicious strangers and unfamiliar cars or vans, particularly Fords. Note their numbers if you can.' Then I added, 'I may not see you again for a while, it all depends.' We kissed, she held me tight, – then I was gone.

I decided to give the town of Caernarfon a miss because it was at the time a local headquarters for the 'political' police and local plainclothes officers attached to Special Branch within the Gwynedd constabulary. Taking the back road over the Denbigh moors, hitting the A5 at Pentrefoelas, I drove to Betws y Coed and followed the road to Beddgelert. I could have been anybody that evening, since no one knew who I was in the red Volvo coupe. I raced down the narrow twisting roads to Nant Gwynant from Pen y Pass, hardly a vehicle in sight. There were traces of snow on the sides of the road, where snow ploughs had been at work a day or two earlier.

My heart began to throb as I eventually drove through the village of Llithfaen. Gwynus and home were barely a mile away. Pulling into a rough lay-by a few hundred yards from the farm entrance, I briefly switched off the engine. I needed a moment to think what I would say to my parents when I arrived. The closer I got to home, the harder it seemed to be.

Starting the motor once more, I decided to drive casually down past the entrance. If anybody was there lying in wait, I would continue past as nobody would recognize the car. Coming down the hill, I switched the main beam on. The farm gate and lane lit up, with not a soul in sight. Taking no chances, I decided to drive past the gate as there was another lay-by ahead. This was also clear. Since the main road on both sides of the entrance to Gwynus was clear, I turned around and drove back. Stopping the car, I got out to open the farm gate.

I dimmed the lights as I approached the large old farmhouse. I could see a light burning in the back kitchen. Gelert, an old black and white sheepdog, hauled himself up to a sitting position, barking loudly once or twice until I called his name. Recognizing me, he limped across, sniffed my trouser leg then casually sauntered towards my new car, lifted a leg and pissed over one wheel before repeating the process on the back wheel. He was christening it!

My Mam had taken to locking the doors of the house in recent times, ever since police and Special Branch officers had shown more than a passing interest in Gwynus. As I walked across the concrete yard towards the kitchen door, I heard her unlocking and turning the key. She stood in the doorway looking very serious and very worried. At that moment, I truly wished I could have vanished from the face of this planet because I knew the grief and pain my parents were going through, and I was the cause of it.

We were never much for displaying emotion as a family. We hardly ever hugged another family member on meeting or parting. This did not mean there were no feelings, it was just the way we were. My father sat in his chair by the AGA. He eyed me over his glasses. 'Owain,' he said, 'So you're home.'

'Hello, Dad – yes,' I nervously replied, knowing full well that some serious questions were about to be asked and answers would have to be given.

'Some John Hughes has rung, several times, says he wants to speak to you.' It was my Mam this time. John Hughes, I knew, was head of the Gwynedd CID, Chief Superintendent. 'You'd better ring him,' she remarked, nodding towards the phone in the corner beside the TV set. 'Supper's ready, do you want to eat first?'

Wherever I went, whatever time I came home, Mam always had a meal ready for me. Since I moved back to Gwynus following the breakup of my first marriage, she had fussed over me as if I was some lost child. While I appreciated all she did for me, I often wished for the day when I could have a place of my own once more. Mam cared immensely about the family and more than anybody else, she held us together through tempestuous times. I loved her dearly.

'Think I'll ring this John Hughes,' I eventually replied, trying to maintain a semblance of normality but knowing full well things were about to come to a head!

Mam had scribbled a telephone number on a small notepad beside the old fashioned black handset – I noticed that it was a Caernarfon number. I dialled it and in no time at all a voice boomed 'Hello... Caernarfon Police station, John Hughes speaking.' My heart beat a little faster, though I tried to sound calm:

'Hello... Mr Hughes... it's Owain Williams. Mam says you wanted to speak with me,' I responded in Welsh.

'Duw Duw Owain bach, how are you? Just want to ask you a few questions,' came the reply, also in Welsh.

Hesitating a moment, thinking of my next move, I tried to choose my words carefully. 'Oh well. OK. Tell you what, my Mam's getting supper ready... but what I'll do, I'll leave it... and I'll come over now... and I'll come back for my supper!'

There was the slightest pause before he responded offhandedly, 'No, no... tell you what, you eat your meal first, then come over to the station, I'll be here for some time yet.'

Trying to decipher what this meant in reality, I quickly made up my mind and decided that the advice for me to eat my meal first meant, 'You're not going back home for some time!'

My Mother had piled a big plate with fried potatoes, beans and fish, but I had suddenly lost my appetite. 'What did he say? What did he want?'

Oh-oh, I thought, here comes the inquisition – she wanted answers. My Father remained silent. Since my Mother was no fool, it was no use trying to lie my way out of it. At the same time, I wanted to try and put both of their minds at rest. 'Like you said Mam. he just wants to ask me a few questions, that's all,' I said.

'We're not stupid, Owain bach. Are those three men who were arrested the other day anything to do with you?'

This was difficult, very difficult, as she knew only too well my patriotism, my passion, and my resolve. 'Don't worry... it's really not a big thing,' I lied.

I battled to behave as normally as possible, struggling to clear my plate, while her eyes watched my every move. Glancing up to look at an old chapel clock on the kitchen wall, I said, 'Better be off and get it over with, OK?'

I attempted a weak smile as I walked out of the door. 'See you both later on!' When, I thought, would I next see them?

Driving out of the farm entrance, I headed towards Caernarfon. What was in store for me there? I would soon find out. Parking my Volvo on the quayside car park, I walked towards the police station, which was in darkness, apart from one weak light in an upstairs room. Taking a deep breath and letting out a nervous cough, I stepped inside. There wasn't a soul in sight. Had there been some mistake? Had they all gone home and left it till the morning?

I boldly called out in Welsh, 'Anybody home?' Suddenly lights were switched on in all parts of the building. Momentarily dazzled by the glare, I heard several footsteps hurrying down the stairs to reception. At least eight plain clothes members of the police force trooped in, grim-faced and led by John Hughes.

'Take him upstairs,' he commanded in English, although seemingly ignoring me, not even a hello. Two big constables half lifted me off the ground and dragged me up two flights of stairs. I was thrown into a chair beside a table. John Hughes removed his grey suit jacket and slung it over the back of another chair before plonking himself down directly facing me.

'Right, Now bach,' he began. I should explain that many people call me Now, rather than Owain, and Now Bach would be an endearment! Endearment? I didn't think so, not in my present situation.

He then continued in Welsh, 'Let's clear all this up... all you have to do is sign this piece of paper here.' He tossed a couple of sheets of printed A4 onto the table in front of me. 'You help us and we'll help you. Quite simple, really.'

The other seven detectives stood behind in a half circle. Trying to sound composed and positive in a difficult situation, I casually enquired about the content of the papers.

'It's just really to acknowledge we've interviewed you and things like that,' he said.

Oh yeah... and things like that, I mused. Following a few more requests to sign what was to all points and purposes a 'confession', I refused to sign anything.

After a couple of hours, the whole mood changed. A more aggressive approach emerged: 'We've got three men arrested... you know them very well. They've all been singing like canaries. We know ALL about your little games. We know for a fact that you were involved in the explosion at that country club in Penisa'r-waun.'

This referred to a bomb blast which had partly demolished one wall at a club, just a few miles from Caernarfon. Apparently, the owner had moved in from the Manchester area. Apart from running the club, he had started up a 'scam' where he offered one square yard of Snowdonia for sale to 'buyers', mostly from England, complete with faked deeds of ownership, although he had never owned this land in the first place. This whole idea of a complete outsider moving in and flogging parts of land off Wales' sacred mountain, had been met by a great deal of anger locally.

'We know that these men handed you explosives... we know that you, alone or with others used these explosives to blow up this club... we need names, and we need them quick...'

Shit... what was I to do now? 'Names? What names?'

'You know bloody well what I'm talking about!!' responded the angry CID chief, red face turning purple. 'I'm warning you now. I am not wasting any more time on you. Enough is enough. If you don't co-operate now, I'll make sure when you go down, they'll throw the bloody key away! With your record, you won't have a hope in hell!'

By about two o'clock in the morning, John Hughes was sweating badly and getting more frustrated by the minute. Seeing I wouldn't budge from my silence, he suddenly declared he was leaving for home and some sleep.

I was bounced off my chair and frog-marched down a corridor towards a row of cells and pushed inside. The cell contained a rusty bedstead with a battered, stained mattress and a grey, thin, crumpled blanket lying on it. By now I was exhausted, but didn't feel I could sleep in such a mental state. Barely ten minutes had passed when the cell door flew open and two of the plain clothes officers stepped in.

The bigger one spoke threateningly, rolling up his sleeves.

'Right, Mr Hughes has left. He's told us to take whatever action that's needed to make you see sense!!'

I was lying on my back on the bed. They stood over me menacingly and the other CID guy said, 'John Hughes is a gentleman... but we're not.' At that point he pulled me up by the collar and kneed me in my private parts. This was unexpected. I felt threatened, but soon recovered.

'That's OK,' I bluffed, 'You know I'm up in court tomorrow for the remand hearing. Go on, mark me, that will suit me fine,' I boasted.

'Don't you worry, Owain bach, the way we work there won't be any marks! Tough guy are you?' he queried

'No, not tough, but not impressed by bullies,' I replied, staring into his eyes.

They must have come to the conclusion they were not getting very far with their methods because they suddenly left. Eventually, my cell door flew open as a uniformed constable brought in a tray with my breakfast. 'Bore da.' He had a friendly voice and seemed amicable enough.

In the meantime I had been informed that the remand hearing would be held at 10 o'clock – it was not anticipated to take very long. Since I had not been given a legal representative, when I had the opportunity to nominate someone I asked for a solicitor from William George & Son of Porthmadog, and within the hour Robert Price turned up. With no time for a detailed analysis of the facts, he outlined that I would be charged with possession and handling of explosives on three counts: the first in connection with the recent attack on the Country Club at Penisa'r-waun; the second, with being involved in a bomb attack on the main water pipeline from Lake Vyrnwy to Liverpool at a place called Llanrhaeadr ym

Mochnant; while the third concerned an explosion at the Temple of Peace in Cardiff the previous year. Robert Price impressed upon me that these were very serious charges, that the prosecution would ask for me to be remanded in prison and he believed it would be futile to ask the magistrates for bail.

Caernarfon magistrates court on that morning consisted of a bench of two men and one woman – all middle aged, greying, and 'respectable pillars of society'. During a brief hearing which was a mere formality, the prosecuting solicitor outlined the three charges in a very grave voice. He was a short guy with rimless spectacles, balding, dressed in baggy beige trousers, grey jacket two sizes too long, and brown sandals – no stockings. He seemed like a bohemian in this most conformist and conservative location.

The whole procedure lasted twenty minutes. The chairman announced I was to be kept in custody for seven days. From that moment on I was transferred from the 'care' of the local police to that of the prison authorities. A large Black Maria was already parked nearby ready to transport me to a remand centre in Warrington, Cheshire.

My family had been informed of these developments and my father and one of my brothers were in court to hear my fate. I was allowed less than five minutes to say goodbye – they were very emotional minutes. My father seemed quite disturbed, which was to be expected, as he was almost seventy-eight. Although he had witnessed my previous terms in prison four or five years earlier during the Tryweryn saga, he found it hard to understand this latest episode. My mother, though not in court, understood my political leanings and how my mind worked – after all, she was my mother.

Soon it was time to start the drive to the prison over the border. The prison guards who were now in charge were totally different from the local uniformed constables. For a start, they were English and obviously spoke only English. On the other hand, the local constabulary were Welsh and Welsh-speaking.

119

After all, in the late 1960s, more than ninety percent of the population of Caernarfon were Welsh-speakers.

My new keepers' first action was to handcuff me. I counted six prison officers assigned to my 'safe keeping' – one sat alongside the driver, the other four accompanied me at the back of the vehicle. There was no conversation throughout the journey. On leaving the town of Caernarfon with its massive Edwardian castle and Roman walls, we moved at a comparatively leisurely pace.

Crossing the border into England shortly after Queensferry, the four prison officers were for the most part quiet, apart from one exception when a good humoured 'debate' took place about the merits of Manchester United – supported by two, while one, a scouser by his accent, supported Liverpool. The fourth screw was not much into football, coming from Runcorn. I guessed he was geographically squeezed out! I remained handcuffed for the whole journey.

The only time I was addressed by one of them was when we were somewhere the other side of Chester. A few sheep were grazing in a field: 'That should make you feel at home,' he said with a smirk, referring to a tired English joke about Welshmen having an unhealthy relationship with woolly creatures. The other three were greatly amused, but I ignored their sick humour.

We arrived at Risley Remand Centre where I stayed for one week before reappearing at Caernarfon magistrate's court. Arriving at a prison is a most degrading experience. You are stripped of your clothes, probed and prodded bodily, before being issued with a uniform of striped blue and white shirt, dark blue trousers, tunic, a rough tatty vest and pants unravelling at the seams, together with a couple of coarse grey blankets and a pillow. Then I was marched down corridors, up metal stairways, keys jangling in the screw's hands as he opened and shut a succession of doors. Finally, having passed several cell doors, all locked, we arrived at the very end of a corridor. The screw unlocked the door, beckoned with his head for me to enter before promptly slamming the door shut. I was now alone.

I looked around the four bare walls. There was one small window at the top and a metal single bed with a stained mattress across it. In the corner was a metal piss pot, one tiny metal locker and a single wooden chair. Tossing the pillow and blankets onto the bed, I fell in a heap into the chair – it was a very bleak sight. My whole future at that moment seemed even bleaker.

10

Prison – Again!

I WONDERED HOW the other three were reacting after being arrested. One of them I knew fairly well. Robin was a truck driver in his late 30s. He had four kids and was a very colourful character. Honest and hard working, he would call a spade a spade and was reliable. One of the others, Eddie, was a friend of his. I only knew him slightly and couldn't gauge what his reaction would be. As for the third, I wasn't at all sure. John Gwilym Jones had somehow come into contact with the other two, so they were now all implicated in the explosives possession charges we were facing. And John Gwilym Jones, from what I had seen of him immediately before I travelled to London, was not to be trusted.

The first day dragged by slowly and painfully. I was 'lucky' in the fact I had already experienced prison life during my period in gaol in 1963 and 1964. I knew the prison routine. Soon they would serve lunch, then what was called tea at around five o'clock, then finally, between seven and eight, they would come around each cell with a large metal bucket containing what was loosely called Cocoa!

When all the cell doors were finally slammed for the night following the cocoa run, I lay in my bed in the dark. All lights had to be off by around nine. I could hear the prisoners talking and shouting nearby, because they would clamber onto their chairs and were able to speak to the person in the next cell through the partly opened windows. Since I had only arrived on this particular day, there was no one I could talk to. I had not a clue who my 'next door neighbour' was, and to be honest,

I couldn't care less. That first night was a very long one. Sleep just wouldn't come, although I was tired out after the previous night.

One week can be a very long time in a prison cell. At the time of my arrest following our actions at Tryweryn, the three of us had each other for moral support. The public at large supported our actions. When any of us appeared before preliminary hearings or even on remand, the court would be more than full, while at times hundreds of people packed the streets outside. Emyr Llew Jones, John Albert Jones and myself took heart from this visible and vociferous support. However, in this particular case the issues were rather more 'clouded', not as straightforward for the man in the street. After all, saving a village and community from being wiped out of existence by creating a monster dam was simple to understand. In a case of opposing an investiture, it was a different ball game. While many individuals could understand the significance of the opposition to what could be termed as a symbolic investiture, large swathes of the Welsh public were either completely apathetic or else had succumbed to the daily royalist propaganda pumped out by the media!

Before the week was out, I received a visit from my solicitor. Apparently two of the other three accused had been charged and had been granted bail. The third, John Gwilym Jones, had turned 'Queen's Evidence' and would give evidence for the prosecution, meaning he would not be sentenced. Just as I had feared, he was probably working for the security services. He would be charged with the less serious offence of receiving explosives and of handing them to me later. I was aware that both Robin and Eddie could be pressurised into giving evidence against me. One of the familiar ploys used by the authorities was: 'You help us and we will help you'. That implied a minimal non-custodial sentence in exchange for convicting the 'big fish', as I was referred to by police chiefs.

My second appearance before Caernarfon magistrates, necessary because a person can't be held for more than seven days without another remand hearing, was just another formality. The process could go on for several weeks until a committal hearing date had been agreed. It would be difficult to learn what the prosecution's platform would consist of until that date was announced. Once that happened, the defence would have access to what their barrister would be concentrating on, who their witnesses would be, and a general idea of what evidence they would provide. One week became two, then three, then four... finally towards the fifth week a committal hearing would be held. Things were not looking very promising for me. My solicitor warned that should I lose the case, a sentence of ten or twelve years awaited me!

Deciding that desperate situations demanded drastic action, on my last remand hearing before the committal date was agreed, I decided to go on hunger strike. From the afternoon of the day I returned to prison to exactly one week later, when I was taken back to Caernarfon for the committal hearing, I refused all food. Because I was not taking any meals and only drank water, I was confined to my cell and meals were brought to me three times a day. Every time I would leave the tray untouched. At first the hunger pangs were quite bad, keeping me awake at night. For the first two or three days, I also suffered from severe headaches. However, as my body became used to the situation, the pains eased and I taught myself to concentrate my mind on everything except food! Confined to a small space that did not leave much scope for exercise, I did press-ups and would walk up and down the small cell hundreds of times each day. I was allowed to leave my cell once a day for half an hour, to walk around the concreted prison yard. That supposedly constituted my 'exercise'. By the end of the sixth day, when dusk fell, I climbed into my rickety bed feeling quite weak. The next morning I was woken at around 05:30 to get ready for my long trip to Caernarfon.

Though I felt tired and weak as the effects of my hunger strike took hold, sleep just wouldn't come. For the last couple of days my body was visibly shrinking. I had lost half a stone.

Once dressed – I was allowed to wear my own clothes for the court hearing – I drank my usual litre of water, brushed my teeth and was ready for the screws to take me to the awaiting Black Maria. Driving at a steady fifty miles per hour, the journey was boringly uneventful as I sat handcuffed at the back of the vehicle. We arrived at Caernarfon police station opposite the castle and I was ushered into a cell, shortly before nine. My solicitor, Mr Price, came to tell me what to expect. An application would be made to allow me bail, but he wasn't too hopeful of achieving this since the police would be bound to object. Noticing my pallid appearance and aware of my hunger strike, he seemed to think that my shaky physical state might well swing the magistrate into a sympathetic frame of mind and bail might be granted.

I was flanked by two screws. This time there were barristers present as well as solicitors. Suddenly a court official called 'court', the magistrates filed in and I was ordered to stand, as was everyone else. We were then ordered to sit. After the preliminary opening statements by the court clerk, the prosecution began stating their case against me. One faint speck of light was that the prosecution had now dropped two of the original charges of possessing and supplying explosives, leaving only the one relating to the explosion at the country club at Penisa'r-waun, near Caernarfon. Before closing his address to the magistrate, their barrister emphasised several times the need to keep me in prison and not to grant bail as this could affect the outcome of the case; there was a danger I could interfere with witnesses, and so on.

Answering the prosecution's claims, my defence concentrated on the fact there was no concrete evidence and only unsubstantiated statements against me. This, despite the fact that the prosecution had alleged traces of explosives had been found on swabs taken from various parts of my father's Vauxhall Cresta. These so-called positive swab tests were to prove vital in the ensuing trial which would take place almost a year later. Since the hearing was taking longer than I had at first anticipated, I felt myself getting weaker and started feeling faint. I was given water to drink, and the lady chair of the bench asked was I all right to proceed, in what sounded like a very caring tone of voice. I nodded. The bench and the whole court were, of course aware of my hunger strike.

Following hours of allegations and counter-allegations, my defence impressed upon the court that it was imperative I was granted bail to (a) prepare for a proper defence, and (b) for health reasons. They argued that any continuation of my hunger strike could be life-threatening in the longer term.

When the magistrates left the main court to consider their decisions in a small room at the side, I was suffering from fatigue. The mental strain of waiting almost six weeks, together with the hunger strike, had taken its toll. Until that day it had been uncertain how the prosecution would present their case, how many charges they would bring, how many witnesses and who they would be, although we had a pretty good idea of three of them. Following what seemed hours, I heard a rustle at the back of the court, a court usher called 'order', before the three magistrates filed back in. Since I was already standing, I remained in that position when the bench chair announced the result of their deliberation. They had concluded that there was a case against me to be answered: that of receiving a package of explosives, possibly used later at the country club explosion.

Furthermore, I was ordered to appear in front of a judge at the next Caernarfon assizes court, which would be in roughly six weeks' time. When the lady chair announced that I was to be granted bail, a roar of approval rang out from my supporters who had packed the courtroom. This decision definitely did not please the police and the prosecution officials. As I left the court building, I was somewhat amazed to see a crowd of around 200 more supporters waiting for me. Amid loud cheering and shouting followed by the singing of 'Hen Wlad fy Nhadau', Welsh dragon flags were waving all around on this cold February day. Taking a deep breath as the seagulls circled above Caernarfon castle's lofty battlements, I thanked the crowd. Some were waving placards. 'NO FOREIGN PRINCE FOR WALES' said one. 'STAY HOME CHARLIE' read another, 'NO TO ROYALTY!' One was more explicit. I won't quote that one but leave it to the reader's vivid imagination!

Representatives from the press were present, both local and 'national'; also a couple of television cameras and radio reporters, Radio Cymru and Radio Wales. I agreed to say a few words in both Welsh and English. Since members of my family were present and I had been more or less surrounded by the crowd and press, I didn't have a chance until now to spot my father and brother. We eventually managed to withdraw from the crowd, who were, to be fair, most understanding, as I was anxious to see my children, Iona and Gruff. My youngest daughter Teleri was still in Heswall Children's Hospital. Once in the warmth of my father's car, I was able to digest the day's events and realised how happy the family were to have me back. Half an hour later we were driving up the farm lane to Gwynus.

I had hardly got out of the car before my daughter Iona and son Gruff ran out of the house to greet me, smiling broadly. As I hugged them tight, something I hadn't done for several weeks, I welled up with emotion. Tears of joy filled my eyes, which I did my utmost to hide. Then we walked into the old farmhouse. My mother had cooked a big meal for everyone. Mother's face spoke volumes, there was no need for words. I was home, and did it feel good!

Because of my recent arrest, not to mention my previous term of imprisonment for my part in the Tryweryn dam site bombings, my children were having a hard time at school. Kids can be cruel and words can and do hurt. Of course, children frequently repeat what they have been told or overheard at home. Often the remarks they make mirror their parents' leanings. So my two children were subjected to such taunts as 'Bomber', 'your Dad is a JAILBIRD' and so on.

Things moved very quickly following my release on bail. I knew the security services were now in cahoots with the local

CID and Special Branch and had initiated a process whereby 'evidence' against me was being fabricated, such as the nitro-glycerine 'discovered' on swabs taken by forensics from my father's car. So I had reached the conclusion that there was no earthly hope of my getting a fair trial. Somehow, I had to find a way of prolonging the date set for my trial beyond the five or six weeks pencilled in. This meant getting away from the authorities for several months, possibly a year, in order to give my defence enough time to counter and challenge the prosecution's allegations. Jumping bail and leaving for another country seemed the only option. There was no way I was prepared to spend ten or maybe twelve years in an English jail on concocted evidence.

Through various political contacts, wheels were sent in motion to initiate my 'disappearing'. The Irish Republic was a natural choice, because of its proximity and Celtic bond. Discreet telephone calls from public phone boxes to contacts and sympathisers in London, Cardiff, as well as Ireland, followed. Although the pain of leaving was colossal, around ten days after my bail, I was ready to travel.

11

Jumping Bail

As the Bangor to Euston train sped through central England's flat, neat countryside, I nervously checked my baggage: a medium-sized suitcase, shoulder bag and larger trunk. So far I had not noticed anyone I knew aboard the train, having remained in my seat for almost three hours. However, I eventually had to make my way though three other carriages to find a toilet. On my way back, I recognized a young Pwllheli student who was staring at me. What to do now? I couldn't ignore him and I couldn't very well step halfway down the corridor to chat with him. For all I knew, the man sitting next to him could be from Special Branch. With a half nod of my head I beckoned him to follow me out of the carriage, he obliged.

Once the door was shut I told him 'Don't ask questions, just – you haven't seen me, you'll understand what I'm saying in a few days, ok ?!'

Nodding his head he replied 'All right, I won't say a word – promise!'

As far as I'm aware he kept his word. I was to be met at Euston by a sympathiser to the cause. Since this person is still living, I cannot name him. All I can say he was a successful businessman and lived in a large comfortable town house. Soon after I had unloaded my luggage, a tall gangly man appeared, wearing a long trench coat and a white woollen scarf draped around his neck. From the descriptions I had, he stood out a mile. He seemed nervous and glanced over his shoulder as he approached, giving me the briefest of greetings, not even a handshake. His car was parked outside the station. With my baggage in the boot, we began the journey back to his house which was in the direction of Hampstead. 'Ianto', as I was instructed to call him, seemed to assume a sort of cloak and dagger manner and kept glancing into his car's mirror with monotonous regularity, so much so that I was fast becoming a nervous wreck. Even bearing in my mind my own limited knowledge of north London, I couldn't miss noting that Ianto took several detours and circled around Hampstead Heath more times than a jumbo jet coming in to land!! 'One cannot be too careful!' was his constant comment, which didn't make for the most stimulating of conversations.

We eventually arrived at a spacious, three-storey Georgian detached house. Since the double wrought-iron gates were already open, Ianto drove straight onto the pebbled driveway, sending stones flying, and screeched to a halt, level with the panelled side door. If his intentions were meant to deter any neighbour's curiosity, then I'm afraid the manner of his noisy arrival had the opposite effect. Curtains twitched ever so slightly next door. Ianto leapt from his seat, tugged at the collar of his trench coat and twirled his long scarf around his neck and lower part of his face in a melodramatic fashion. We entered a large hallway which led into a spacious lounge. Ianto's wife was a tall slim lady with fair hair and blue eyes, quite attractive. She greeted me with a hug and a kiss on the cheek, which was nice and helped to ease the tension that had built up inside me, thanks to Ianto's overtly dramatic behaviour. Brigitte was a German girl. Her accent did not reveal her nationality, since she sounded most upper class English. Once I was seated, she brought me a large plateful of salad sandwiches and a king-sized mug of coffee. I noticed that Ianto would often sidle up to a large curtain draped window and peer outside. On the third occasion – all in the space of ten minutes – Brigitte became irritated by his behaviour and said, 'For Christ sakes, Ianto... stop it, you're not a character from 'The Third Man', you know!'

Before it developed into a major argument between them,

I feigned a long yawn, got up, thanked them both and wished them good night and made my way to the spare room I had been allocated. Lying in bed, I wondered what lay ahead in the next few days. I couldn't think further than that at this stage. It had been planned that I would lie low in his house for a couple of days, then I was to be driven either to one of the channel ports or else to Heathrow airport. Whichever way it worked out, my final destination was Ireland.

Next morning I got up fairly early. Ianto was already up and ready to leave for his office in central London. Once he had pointed out where the coffee was, he left, but not before another sideways glance through a corner of the curtain. As he went, he half turned back and said, 'Don't leave the house in case you're seen... but if you have to, take the back door, hide behind the rhododendron bushes first, then climb over the garden wall. Keep to the left and you'll come to Hampstead cemetery, cross through there and you'll come to some shops, should you want something... and be careful!'

Sitting on a stool in the kitchen munching a slice of burnt toast, I heard a slight shuffling behind my back. Startled, I swung round to be greeted by Brigitte, dressed in a very short dressing gown which revealed a lot of thigh; the neckline was not too high either. 'Did I startle you? Did you sleep all right.?'

'Yes... thank you. I mean, I slept very well, and no you didn't startle me', I lied.

'So you're going to be staying a couple of days then... should give us time to get to know a bit about each other,' she added, in what I thought was an over-friendly tone. She was a very attractive woman but to get involved here would not have been clever – after all her husband was helping me out. Gulping the last of my coffee, I blurted, 'I have to make a phone call and it's not safe to use your house phone. I'm going out to find a public phone kiosk.'

'I'll drive you, it's not safe for you to walk!' she insisted.

'No, no really, thank you very much for offering, I won't be long!' I replied edging towards the back door.

I disappeared out through the back door, glad to inhale the sharp morning air. Taking a deep breath, I passed the rhododendrons as instructed and made my way towards the high stone wall. It was fairly quiet on the road outside since most of the morning traffic had eased off. I jumped over the wall onto the pavement and worked my way left as Ianto had told me.

Hampstead cemetery appeared through the morning mist just a short distance away. Once inside the cemetery walls, I slowed down to a leisurely pace, gazing in awe at the sheer size of the sacred grounds. It seemed as if there were thousands of head-stones and I was the only living being. However, walking amongst the dead soon brought me back to reality and made me aware of my own mortality.

I felt it better to steer clear of the house until Ianto returned from work, as I wasn't too sure I could resist Brigitte's advances next time! A small cinema at the end of the street was closed until the afternoon so I found a newsagent, bought myself the *Daily Telegraph* and walked into a coffee shop. Over a strong coffee I glanced through the paper's pages. Nothing much of interest caught my eye, so I settled for the crossword, although my brain was sluggish and I couldn't focus or concentrate much.

Time dragged by. I left the cafe after about an hour and walked aimlessly until I reached a small park, found a bench and wrenched the crumpled newspaper out of my coat pocket. I read almost every column inch in that paper, even the small personal ads. At times I would swear my watch had stopped as the minute finger seemed at a standstill. It seemed I was in a time vacuum. Time itself had frozen around me. It was more like a dream than reality.

My future at this stage was most insecure. I had no insight as to what lay ahead, or where was I heading. Yes, I knew the geographic destination. I was heading for southern Ireland, but with no distinct plan as to how I would survive or sustain myself there. How long would I have to stay in hiding? Would

I be made welcome by the Irish authorities? My head was reeling as I went over and over the same questions. Should I have stayed and stood trial? Perhaps, but then again, I knew the Special Branch had planted evidence, including traces of nitro-glycerine on my father's car. I would have no chance of defending myself in that kind of situation. My idea was to get away to give myself time and also for my defence lawyer to gather counter-evidence, probably through getting the services of a private detective. This would all take time, hard work and a lot of patience.

After what seemed an eternity, two o'clock arrived and I trundled up the steps into the cinema. The audience was sparse at that time of day. Once the lights were dimmed and sub titles appeared I settled down and shut my mind to my worldly woes. The theme song 'From Russia with Love' blasted out full force. The whole programme lasted a good three hours. After wasting another couple of hours in the coffee shop, I slowly made my way back to Ianto's house. To my relief, his black Jaguar was parked on the gravel driveway. I walked to the back door and rang the bell. Ianto appeared, firing questions: 'Where? What? When? Who had I seen?' I explained I'd been to town, seen a film etc, etc. He was convinced the house was being watched by Special Branch or MI5, as he once again raised a corner of the lounge curtain to peer outside.

'Oh, for Christ sakes, don't be so damned paranoid? Who do you think you are, James Bond?' said Brigitte, sounding angry. This began to make me feel uncomfortable but she quickly calmed the situation by announcing dinner was ready. I could sense that Ianto was finding it difficult to cope with the pressure of having a fugitive under his roof. When the meal was over, he fetched a bottle of scotch from a well stocked drinks cabinet and poured out two sizeable glasses. There was something he was trying to tell me, I could feel it in my gut, he was just trying to pluck up courage to tell me. After about three or four large scotches he falteringly began, 'Er... look, you'd better not to stay too long. There's a chap, actually works for me, he's got a much safer place, a flat in central London, easier to come and go – also better for getting to the airport – when you leave that is!'

I never expected to move to another hiding place. I believed I would leave this house and be taken straight to the airport. I didn't know what to say, so just mumbled it was fine, OK, whatever. It seemed Ianto had already decided and made the necessary arrangements to move me out.

Early next morning after breakfast, Brigitte told me her husband was paranoid and was genuinely scared of being raided by Special Branch. I told her not to worry. I understood it wouldn't have been a good thing for me to be caught hiding in their house. Suddenly there was a sharp knock on the front door. I dived into the kitchen to hide while Brigitte answered the door. There stood a tall dark-haired, 30-year-old with a wide smile. 'Shw' mae?' he greeted in a loud voice from the open doorway.

'Oh it's you... gave us a scare then, thought it was the law,' Brigitte laughed as she whisked him inside. Stanislav Rogowski was a rather unusual Pole, a fluent Welsh-speaker brought up in Cardiganshire where many of his fellow countrymen had settled following the end of World War Two. He was very jovial and friendly and immediately made me feel at ease. We left in Stanislav's battered old VW van, quite a change from the luxurious Jaguar! We finally arrived outside his flat, a modest two-bedroomed unit in a back alley not far from Oxford Circus. Stanislav had to return to his job but said he'd be home by around five.

Since I was now virtually in central London, I decided to go foraging amongst the teeming streets. Piccadilly Circus, Oxford Street and Soho were familiar enough place names as I ambled along from street to street, lost in a mass of humanity from every ethnic background under the sun. I smiled to myself. This was probably the safest place in the world to hide. I visited a book shop specialising in books on Ireland, where I bought a biography of Michael Collins, soldier and statesman.

On Shaftesbury Avenue, I found a small Italian bistro where I had some lunch. Later I walked towards Hyde Park where I spent another hour watching both the pigeons and public. Time for one final stroll around Trafalgar Square; Nelson was still perched on his tall column, I noticed, unlike his duplicate in Dublin's O'Connell Street which had been blasted off the skyline by Republicans a couple of years earlier. Before I knew it, it was dark and I started my journey back to the flat.

Rickety wooden stairs led up the door of the flat. I knocked three times, sharp raps as I'd been instructed. I could hear at least three bolts being slipped open before Stanislav stood in the doorway to welcome me, wide grin as always. 'Come in, come in!' in Welsh. 'Oh, this is Cindy, my girlfriend.'

A slim pretty girl with her hair tied in a bun appeared from behind him. 'Hi... are you hungry? We were about to eat', she spoke English with a Welsh lilt. I figured it was a south Cardigan accent. A small table was already set for three; I was ushered to a chair. Although the attic room was small with low ceilings, it was warm and comfortable and decorated with good taste. They were a very friendly couple and talked about their life in London, their work and their families back in west Wales. Cindy worked as a designer in one of the West End's stores, which explained her good taste in colour and style.

Stanislav's parents were refugees from Poland who'd arrived just before the end of World War Two. Following much persecution they had found themselves in south Ceredigion and managed to purchase a run-down eight-acre smallholding. There were a couple of dozen other Polish families settled in the area, most owning small plots of land where they grew vegetables, raised cattle and sheep. Stanislav, although born in Wales, was brought up to speak Polish as were all the other children from the same background. Later, when it was time to start school, they had attended the village school, becoming fluent in Welsh, before learning English later at the local comprehensive school. Stanislav explained that he had known his girlfriend Cindy since school. They had been in London for

over six years. Although they would have preferred to live in
Wales, it was a case of finding work, south Ceredigion was no
more a hub of commerce and industry in those days than it is
today!

I was quite fascinated by this and also the fact that there were
about a quarter of a million Welsh-speakers in London itself.
It was heartening to know that even in this huge metropolis, a
small network existed that could assist a person like myself to
get out of the country.

Over our meal Stanislav explained that he had been briefed
by Ianto earlier in the day. I was to be driven to Heathrow the
following afternoon, where a flight was booked for me using
the name Phil McBryde. A false passport and other documents
had been produced as 'proof of identity' should the need arise.

I'd chosen the name some time earlier. McBryde after all
is quite a common Irish surname, and I could master an Irish
accent to a certain degree. A weak March sun tried to break
through the haze hanging above central London as I woke up
and gazed through the open skylight. Suddenly I remembered
where I was and that today I was to embark on a journey into
the unknown. No more stalling or hanging around. This was
it.

I was, to say the least, feeling rather nervous. Cindy had
already left for work leaving Stanislav behind to deal with the
little matter of getting me onto a plane. Ianto was contributing
towards the costs of my flights as well as providing for my keep.
Ianto had incidentally lent his beloved Jaguar for the journey
to Heathrow, believing it was less likely to attract attention
than Stanislav's battered VW van. Pulling up outside Terminal
One, Stanislav leapt out and hauled my few bags from the
boot, hoisting them onto a waiting trolley. Since this was a no
waiting zone, we bid a quick goodbye as he wished me luck
and hoped we could meet again soon. Then he was gone.

I stood alone outside the entrance gazing at the tall building.
I swallowed hard and began to push the trolley in the direction
of Departures.

'Phillip Joseph McBryde... will Phillip Joseph McBryde please attend the Aer Lingus departure desk for the 5 o'clock flight to Dublin.' For a moment the words did not register; I was too busy contemplating what the immediate future had in store. Suddenly I awoke to the fact that I was no longer Owain Williams! From now on I was Phil McBryde and had all the paperwork with me to prove it. There wasn't a trace of who I really was, all documents, invoices, letters, driving licence etc had been removed and either destroyed or stored in a safe haven back in Wales. My heart began to pound... why was 'McBride' wanted at the departure desk, had someone sussed me out? Was Special Branch waiting for me by the desk? Had someone tipped them off? Taking a quick look around the departure lounge, I slowly got up from my seat, trying to act in as normal a manner as possible. As I crossed the tiled floor towards the Aer Lingus desk, I could feel a cold sweat running down my spine.

A pretty brunette with big blue eyes greeted me with a wide smile, her accent despite years of training and speech therapy failing to disguise her County Cork origins! 'Good day, sir. I'm sorry to trouble you but just wanted to check your booking as there seems to be some confusion over the seating arrangements.'

I breathed a silent sigh of relief, although wary of a tall shifty-looking character lurking just behind the receptionist, who was now seriously and methodically thumbing through my passport, raising his eyes occasionally to stare at me. Eventually I was given back my documents by the still smiling girl who wished me a good flight. Despite the somewhat trivial nature of the incident, my suspicions were aroused and I felt uneasy. Time dragged ever so slowly as I waited for the boarding call. Once aboard, I started to relax as the plane slowly filled with the other passengers.

Occupying the middle seat can have its problems. Because the well-built woman on my left was not only filling her own seat but seriously encroaching on my space, I was being squeezed even closer to the right, so much so that I apologised to the young lady for getting dangerously close. I had the feeling that she well understood my dilemma because she smiled sweetly and muttered that it was quite OK. We soon got talking. Her name was Siobhan; she was going to Limerick to visit her ailing grandmother. Time passed swiftly and soon, we were circling Dublin Airport and preparing to land. Realising the next tricky part was getting through the Irish immigration check, I decided to cling to Siobhan for as long as I could. I insisted on carrying her well-stocked hand luggage, which meant we would get off the plane together. This made me feel less conspicuous.

Everything seemed to go without a hitch as we made our way through the corridors and past the customs checks through the exit. Having bade goodbye to Siobhan, I went to the airport car park where I was to be met by two members of the Republican movement, all pre-arranged. Carrying a small suitcase and a shoulder bag, I gingerly made my way in the direction that was clearly signposted. In my free hand I carried a copy of *Time* magazine which was to be the only visible means of displaying my identity, as at this stage I was not aware of who was to be meeting me. I stopped to survey my surroundings, momentarily putting down my suitcase and switching the magazine to my other hand. An old black Ford Zodiac approached and pulled up alongside me. A tall, well-built man in his mid fifties leapt out.

'I take it you're Phil... Phil McBryde?' he enquired in a strong Dublin accent.

'Yes, that's me, how are you?' I said. Without replying, he grabbed my suitcase and shoulder bag and threw them in the boot. 'Get in,' he added, holding the rear door open for me as I clambered inside. The driver was a balding middle-aged man who didn't speak a lot. The first man who had got out to meet me introduced himself as Sean Garland, a member of Sinn Fein. I never got to know the driver's name.

1 2

Irish Interlude

I WAS TOLD I was being taken to a safe house some twenty-five minutes west of Dublin, and would stay at the home of a well-known Republican activist, Seán Mac Stiofáin. At this time, I was not familiar with the name, but later in time it would become well known, not only in Ireland but world wide. I'd read a lot about how Michael Collins co-ordinated resistance in the 1920s, and his methods had fascinated me and left me inspired. But I was less familiar with the workings of the current Republican movement.

Less than an hour after leaving the airport, the car swung into the driveway of a small detached bungalow in Navan. A tall figure appeared in the doorway, over six foot and well built. He eyed me up and down before greeting me with a strong handshake. After being ushered into the living room, I was introduced to his wife Mary, a cheerful dark-haired woman, and his teenage daughters Catriona and Moira. The two men who had brought me soon left and I was invited to sit down to dinner. Still feeling slightly nervous, I was questioned by Seán Mac Stiofáin as to what my plans were. What was the political situation in Wales? Strangely enough, at that particular time towards the end of the 1960s Wales seemed more turbulent than Ireland. However, things were about to change with the formation of the Provisional IRA, or Provos as they became known. As it proved later, one man more than anyone became instrumental in forging this new movement into the potent force it became; that man was Seán Mac Stiofáin.

During the month or longer that I stayed in his house, it

became clear that he was a dedicated and committed Irish patriot. Unquestionably he was a strict disciplinarian who expected the same high standards from others; a leader who led by example, fearless and with a brain which could read events almost before they occurred. He had the rare capacity to foresee the actions needed to create the climate for revolution.

Historically the IRA command structure had been based on traditional squadrons or platoons. Seán Mac Stiofáin had realised that any future republican military movement would have to operate in much smaller units than previously. He proposed to develop the fledgling Provisional IRA on the cell system. Ideally the cell system is a very small command network, consisting of three or four members. The cell's leader is the only contact point. The other members do not know any members of other cells. When a secret or undercover movement is formed, the enemy will want to infiltrate it. With the cell system, even to try and gain access into the ranks of such a movement is almost impossible. Each member is screened and his pedigree checked. Were his parents or possibly grandparents active in earlier campaigns? With such an elaborate system, the chances of the enemy gaining access are pretty slim.

During my stay in the Mac Stiofáin home, Seán was diligently plotting the next stage of Irish politics. He was at this time employed by the GAA – the Gaelic Athletics Association. This work took him across the country, not only within the Republic, but also across into Northern Ireland. Regularly visiting branches and clubs, he met with many members who had become disillusioned with politics, young and committed republicans. Traditionally, the GAA has produced hundreds of volunteers in the armed struggle. Indeed the movement was founded over 100 years ago to counteract British imperialist rules and regulations which barred public meetings and gatherings of any sort. But hurling and Irish rules football were revived and residents were able to get around the law by supporting 'sporting gatherings'. So strong and successful was this Gaelic sporting revival that members were banned from participating in 'alien' sports such as soccer, rugby, hockey etc. The clubs became recruiting centres for potential republican activists. Prior to the uprising which occurred in the North during the summer of 1969, Seán, together with a handful of trusted colleagues, had skilfully laid the foundations for a future armed struggle.

Seán Mac Stiofáin's background and upbringing were hardly discussed during the many conversations I had with him. Later I got to know much of those details. His mother was a Catholic who hailed from Northern Ireland, whilst his father was an Englishman named John Stevenson and he had been brought up in England. During Seán's childhood, his alcoholic father used physical violence against his mother, leaving the young Seán cowering in fright as he hid out of sight. As a result of this abuse, he became very vindictive and also became very politicised, developing anti-English sentiments, since the traumatic events at home drove him closer to his mother and her homeland.

During his teens in England Seán immersed himself in the centuries old Irish struggle. He was initiated into the world of Irish Republicanism, through links with Irish residents who maintained strong connections with the church and political events back home. All this was about to change temporarily, because at the age of eighteen, he joined the RAF and served his term wearing a British uniform. It is not clear whether he joined up to gain an insight into the workings of a branch of the British military or maybe to win some experience in weaponry. Perhaps he did so as a disillusioned young man looking for adventure, wanting to find his way in the world? Whatever the reasons, there was no doubt that this gave him time to contemplate both his personal and political future. On his demob from the RAF, there is a rather blank period although there are references in his autobiography that throw some light on this issue. During a routine check by police at a road block, a van was stopped and searched and found to contain a small arsenal of weapons. The occupants were arrested, later charged under firearms offences and eventually sentenced to long prison terms. Amongst the arrested party was a young Seán Mac Stiofáin, who was sentenced to twelve years' imprisonment. Ironically, the police checkpoint was not meant to apprehend the Irish activists, but was set up to try and catch two petty thieves who had stolen a few pounds in a raid on a small post office.

Until this event Seán hadn't set foot on Irish soil. However during his term at Wormwood Scrubs, he spent much of his time reading up on Irish history and mastering the Irish language. He also rid himself of his English name, John Stevenson, adopting the Gaelic version. On his release he moved to live in the Republic of Ireland, later meeting his wife Mary before settling down in Navan later.

On many spring evenings, after dusk had fallen, we would take a long walk along some minor roads outside Navan. We would discuss several matters of political nature during these walks. I was amazed at Seán's understanding of the Welsh situation and his knowledge of the names of several individuals. At one stage of his imprisonment in England he came into contact with some of those active in the Welsh republican movement, Cliff Bere being one. I believe Cliff was imprisoned for refusing to serve as a conscript in the British army. Seán had a lot of respect for Bere, who actually stood as a parliamentary candidate for Plaid Cymru following his release. Despite his intellect and astute political mind, Cliff Bere was never allowed to rise in the ranks of Plaid Cymru, who preferred stagnant pacifists bereft of ideas or vision.

It was during my stay at Seán's house that I decided to approach the Irish Home Office department to find out what my legal position was. Following some low key enquiries by one of Seán's friends, I had more or less been assured that I would not be deported. However, I was rather nervous when I finally got round to visiting the department. This time I had to lay my cards on the table. I had to declare that I was Owain Williams and that I had jumped bail and crossed to Ireland to seek refuge. What ensued was a relief: I was told there was no problem as mine was a political offence. However, the official did warn me to 'Keep your head out of politics on this side of the water!' This news was, of course, a great boost for me. Strangely enough, no one even bothered to ask where I was staying or with whom! The only explanation I can think of is that in the early summer of 1968, Provisional Sinn Fein was merely a dream; in a few months, however, it would become known around the globe, its founders including one Seán Mac Stiofáin.

For my security, I decided to still maintain as low a profile as possible, and kept my new identity, Phil McBryde. Through contacts and go betweens, I knew that British agents and Special Branch officers had been sent across to try and arrest me, as I was still regarded as the main threat to disrupt the planned investiture which was now just one year away. Because of my previous convictions as a militant Welsh activist, I was inevitably earmarked as a troublemaker by security forces. There's a misconceived perception that British intelligence agencies do not resort to coercive methods on mainland Britain. But there is ample evidence to the contrary – as I was to find out from direct experience! While it is generally accepted that 'hit squads' were used in Northern Ireland during the height of the 'Troubles', it is difficult to find many people in Wales who would believe that the authorities would resort to such activities against a Welsh citizen.

As a consequence of my visit to the Irish Home Affairs department, it was time for me to move on. During my stay with Seán I had become friends with the whole family; after all, spending several weeks at their home and not making any other human contact brought us quite close together. Mary Mac Stiofáin cooked all the evening meals. I offered to dig the large back garden, which until then had never seen a spade. Since it was covered in knotweed, the surface was very tough. After almost two weeks of backbreaking toil, the task was finally completed. This was one of the rare occasions when

Seán actually smiled. He had planned to turn the disused garden into a cabbage and potato patch. Now, it was ready for planting. Several dozen cabbage plants and a few seed potatoes arrived one evening and I succeeded in completing the planting before leaving.

It was with mixed feelings that I finally left the Mac Stiofáin household. While I was glad to be able to move out and find my own way, I was also feeling that the family needed to have their home back, although I will be eternally grateful for their kindness and hospitality.

I took a bus from Navan to Dublin where I bought a couple of daily newspapers, scanning through the accommodation pages. I noted a rooming house with shared facilities, it seemed reasonably priced for my limited finances. Seán had emphatically refused to accept any money during my stay. The accommodation was on a back street, still not too far from the city centre. It would serve its purpose for a week or two. There were reasons why I chose to stay in Dublin for a short period – a large city provided anonymity. I needed to be somewhere where I could meet up with a contact sent from Wales without being noticed. At this stage it was imperative I was told what the latest developments were regarding my legal defence. I also needed to replenish my dwindling finances.

From a phone box in the centre of O'Connell Street I made a call to a female friend who acted as a go-between. She had never displayed any political leanings, therefore would not warrant special attention from the intelligence services. Catrin was level-headed and responded in exactly the manner I had instructed her before leaving. She was told to cross over from Wales, using the Fishguard to Rosslare ferry. On arriving in Rosslare this contact would complete the journey to Dublin by train. Once in Dublin, she would ring the number of a phone box near Parnell Square at a pre-arranged time.

Catrin was an attractive twenty-two year old with long straight blond hair and a slim figure, married to a friend of mine. After taking her phone call, I asked her to walk up

O'Connell Street, enter the Gresham Hotel, go into the cocktail bar, order a drink and stay there for fifteen minutes. During this time I would observe her entering the hotel from close by, to check that she was not being followed. Once the fifteen minutes were over, Catrin left the hotel and started walking in the direction of St Stephen's Green, as previously instructed. Following at a safe distance, I tried to make a mental note of anyone suspicious who might be tailing her. From time to time I stopped in front of some shop windows to watch the reflection of people walking behind me. Several minutes later, I caught up with Catrin sitting on a park bench not far from Foyle's Bookshop. Having circled the bench once, satisfied we were not being shadowed, I sat down and pretended to read *The Irish Times*. When I was sure it was safe I slid an envelope across the bench towards her and whispered that she should read it, memorise the details then burn it. Nodding her head, she smiled, passing me a long envelope containing bank notes in return. She asked how I was coping and was it very lonely. I replied I was OK, but again emphasised the importance of getting the message contained in the letter to the right person, stating that it was vital to burn the contents immediately after reading and memorising it.

'Don't worry... it's as good as done,' she reassured me.

Just the fact that I had met someone from home was reassuring. What's more, the instructions I had just handed over were of paramount importance. On opening the white envelope, I counted 250 pounds in Irish pound notes. That in itself was a relief as it secured my short term cash problems for the immediate future.

12

Summer in Cork

SINCE MY EARLY youth I had been fascinated by Michael Collins, the Irish soldier and patriot, and I was well informed on his life and times from one of his biographies, *The Big Fellow*, by Frank O'Connor. I decided I had to visit his birthplace in County Cork.

A few days later, on arriving in Cork city, I booked into a small bed and breakfast on a side street leading on to Patrick Street, the city's main thoroughfare. Cork was at the time more relaxed than Dublin, despite being the Republic's second city. It still retained some of the old world tranquillity of a provincial small town. I decided to visit West Cork, including Skibbereen and Clonakilty, which was the area I associated with the early years of Michael Collins. Travelling by bus would not be easy as Cork is the largest county in Ireland. Bus services to the sparsely-populated western ends such as Bantry Bay were few and far between.

Next day I got up early and caught the first bus going west. It was a bright sunny morning, not a cloud in the sky. The roads seemed to get narrower and the pot holes more numerous as we ambled along at a leisurely pace. Depopulation in western Ireland was evident in the form of abandoned smallholdings, often engulfed by poor quality, peaty, heather-clad land. Most of these abandoned houses were hardly more than shacks. Nonetheless, they had once been home to countless families who clung on tenaciously to their few acres, raising sons and daughters to be the lifeblood of the risen nation. From such a smallholding emerged Michael Collins, the youngest of ten children. His father was already in his seventies when he was born. Although I did not have enough documentation with me to identify the exact location of his upbringing, I did manage to locate a small country inn where members of his family still lived. I spoke to a distant relative, probably the son of a second cousin. I was searching for clues as to his past, since some fifty years had elapsed since his death. Many believe it was not a stray sniper's bullet that killed him but rather a planned assassination at the hands of enemies who opposed the peace treaty and the partition of Ireland. Whatever the truth may be, the facts remain a dark secret buried beneath the peaty soil of his beloved County Cork.

My mission to west Cork had taken longer than I expected and I realised the last bus for Cork City had already gone. So I had to hitch a lift, or walk! Walk I did, having tried hitching, standing on the grass verge with my thumb pointing east did not prove fruitful. An old man, heavily wrinkled pointed out a 'short cut', leading over a small mountain range. Being naive, I took his advice. There was one snag; the actual distance was shorter by a few miles, but no car travelled that semi-abandoned road! Twenty one miles I tramped, half ran, trotted and stumbled in the dark before arriving in a small village on the outskirts of the city. For a moment I was blinded by the first street lamp in hours and with a sigh of relief saw a sign stating 'Cork City, 4 miles'!

By the time I reached my room it was well past midnight. Dog tired, I fell on my bed fully clothed and slept for ten hours. If I was to stick in this part of the country I would need a set of wheels, and soon! My financial situation for the short term had been bolstered, but unless I was careful, even frugal, these funds would soon dwindle. My feet were in quite a state after the previous evening's marathon. My right heel was raw, the skin having been stripped bare. Somewhere back in my childhood I remembered my Mam saying the best cure for sore or scalded feet was to walk in the sea. So I painfully made my way to Kinsale, which at that time was a pleasant and even fairly prosperous little town, being a seaside resort and a yachting haven. I noticed several restaurants, shops and two or three hotels, the main street was busy with several members of the boating brigade scurrying along, many in plimsolls and sailor hats.

That summer at the end of the sixties was exceptionally warm and the heatwave lasted for a couple of months. Having limped through the main street, I made my way towards the beach and followed a sign to Charlesfort. A collection of stone walls and the remains of what appeared to be a castle or fortress of some kind, it was surrounded by sand dunes, bushes and long grass. On reaching the hillock where the fort was situated, I was able to gaze out to sea where several small fishing vessels and a few expensive yachts were bobbing about in the calm waters. Several tourists, both local and foreign, had pitched their tents around the fort and the beach. I noticed one with the Union flag stitched on its side. The 'troubles' which erupted a year later had not yet deterred the several British, German and Dutch tourists from flocking to this beautiful part of Ireland. Having walked through the warm clear water of the bay for half an hour I felt surprisingly refreshed and my feet recovered almost miraculously. When I stepped out of the water and walked on the sand, I almost yelled. The sun's warmth had heated it so much that I danced across it gingerly, making my way to a patch of grass which was more bearable. Wearing only a pair of shorts and T-shirt, I decided to lie on the grass to dry my wet clothes. I noticed my legs were very white compared to most of the sun-seekers who obviously had taken advantage of this exceptional summer! Once my clothes had dried I walked back into the town. Feeling thirsty, I visited a newly-built hotel with a friendly-looking bar, which had tables and chairs outside. Passing a mirror in the corridor I almost stopped in my tracks; the beard I had recently grown was now over an inch long! Staring at my reflection I thought 'God! I look like a fugitive!!!!' A friendly young barman served me a pint of lager and as I made my way to an outside table, I caught the sight of an attractive, slim young woman with long straight brown hair. For a fleeting moment our eyes met and she smiled, revealing a set of perfect white teeth. Emblazoned on the top of her black uniform was the word 'Supervisor'.

Next day, feeling refreshed after my walk in the sea and a good night's sleep, I decided to see if I could hire a small car for a few days, since I still wanted to investigate some of Michael Collins' old haunts in West Cork. By a stroke of luck I came across what I wanted at the very last garage in the city, a small black Ford which I hired for a week. I could also use it to look for some kind of job to earn a few pounds while I awaited news from Wales concerning my case. On the following day I drove towards the west of the county, intending to travel as far as Bantry Bay. It was another gloriously sunny day as I drove along the narrow twisting lanes. Farmers were harvesting hay in the small stone-walled fields, some still using a horse and cart and pitchforking the loose hay, others had advanced to using a baler. Through the open windows of my little Ford the sweet aroma of mature, sun-dried hay wafted into my nostrils. This brought pangs of nostalgia – *hiraeth* – as it reminded me of home on the farm when I was a little boy playing on the hay ricks whilst the older members of my family slaved away, bathed in sweat.

On the last day at my lodging house in Cork City, I revisited Kinsale with the idea of trying to get hold of a tent. In those days people just pitched a tent near the beaches or common land, which meant 'rent free!' On the outskirts of the city, driving south, I made out the outline of a hitch-hiker, although dazzled by the bright sun, about to pass, I realised I'd seen this person before. It was the girl who worked as a supervisor at the Trident Hotel in Kinsale. As I pulled up alongside her, she peered over a huge pair of sunglasses, looking hesitant. 'I know you, supervisor at the Trident – am I right?'

'Yes, how do you know that?' she enquired in a lilt I was familiar with. I told her I'd called at the bar for a drink a couple of days ago and passed her on the way out. 'Oh Jaysus,

I remember that face now. Are you going to Kinsale?' she enquired. 'Hop in,' I said.

We had hardly reached Kinsale and I already knew her name was Catherine, that she came from Limerick and was working for the summer as a supervisor in the hotel. She was a very pleasant and friendly person who oozed charm and warmth. I lied and said my name was Phil McBryde! I dropped her off at the front of the hotel, having asked was there a tent shop around. She replied there was one and asked was I planning on staying around for a while. I said I wasn't planning to leave in a hurry!

'Good,' she announced, 'so will I see you around at the hotel, maybe?'

'Now you've talked me into it...'

She flashed a wide smile and laughed. 'I think you're a chancer!' she said, vanishing into the front porch of the hotel and waving.

Later that evening, I found what I was looking for, an Outdoor World mini-market catering for all sorts of camping requirements, tents, caravan awnings, barbeques, bottled gas etc, – the lot. On display outside the store were tents of all shapes and sizes. It didn't take me long to spot one I fancied, not too large, and more important, not too pricey. Once I had placed the folded tent in a carrier bag, I made my way back through town heading down in the direction of the beach near Charlesfort. I surveyed the area, looking for somewhere fairly well-concealed. There was nothing I was taking for granted and at that moment there was no one I could trust. Following a good half hour of pacing up and down around the old fortress, I decided on a spot where there was a small clearing amidst tall thick gorse bushes. Since I had chosen a dark green tent, it would blend in perfectly with this type of foliage. Pleased with myself, I began the task of setting up what was to be my 'home' for the foreseeable future.

It was quiet outside. Apart from the sound of waves breaking on the rocky headland below, a lone lamb bleated forlornly for its mother in the distance. I lay back on the thin inflatable mattress and placed my little revolver under a makeshift pillow. This made me feel more secure. If the worst came to the worst, I was ready! To the sceptic this may sound melodramatic but trust me, many activists or 'radicals' vanish, or become victims of strange accidents within these small islands. Every stranger could be a possible assassin – I had to be vigilant. Bear in mind that I was the number one suspect on Special Branch and MI5's list and as such, I would be chased and harassed almost daily.

Being a hunted fugitive is not a life of romantic fiction; the reality is a lot harsher. Loneliness is never far away; uncertainty, suspicion, even fear are everyday features of being a man on the run. There was no one I could talk to, no one I could trust. That was the reality. Why do it then? I hear people ask. The answer is fairly simple. The gullible public believed I was dangerous because of my past actions. The security services had to come up with an arrest. Information leaked through to us clearly identified me as the 'fall guy' in this episode. This meant I would have been convicted and given a very long sentence to pacify political grovellers within Wales as well as outside. I was, at that time, the only leading activist known to the intelligence services. Only my arrest – or wipeout – would suffice to placate the baying wolves.

During my months on the run, British intelligence agents travelled a fair part of the globe in their search for me. Enquiries were carried out in the Vancouver area of British Columbia, obviously linked to my time living in Canada several years before. Contact was made with police and intelligence services in Columbia, South America, because I could be hiding out there, courtesy of Hywel Hughes, the Welsh millionaire and patriot referred to previously. Since secret agents and undercover squads do not trot around the world without reason, it is logical to believe they 'meant business' in my case.

All of this preyed on my mind and I slept only briefly. Folding my sleeping bag and tidying my few belongings before unzipping the tent, I cautiously opened it a few inches at a

time, peeping outside. All was quiet apart from some teenage
girl campers cooking breakfast on an open fire about fifty yards
away. I stepped out of the tent onto the sandy ground. It was
already warm with the sun burning brightly above. The smell
of frying bacon and sausages wafted across in the soft breeze
as the giggling bikini-clad girls took turns at cooking. Suddenly
I felt hungry but hadn't made provisions for any sort of cooked
breakfast. All I had was a couple of bread rolls, a lump of cheese
and an apple. Ah hell, beggars can't be choosers, so it was
unbuttered rolls packed with Irish cheddar swilled down with
what was left of my bottled water. Dammit, those sausages did
smell good! The girls must have noticed me chomping on the
bread rolls, since two of the most adventurous started moving
across and calling 'Hiya', I limply waved back, at which one
of them, tall and blond with too many curves for comfort,
beckoned me over with her index finger. I decided, definitely
not this morning, Josephine!! Being polite, I shouted 'Thanks,
but I have to go,' and took a detour to bypass them, tossing
my small rucksack over my shoulder, checking my hired car
was OK. Getting into Kinsale meant a half hour walk and not
many people were to be seen. Still, the informal way I was
dressed, complete with sunglasses and a baseball cap plus my
blossoming red beard gave me a feeling of anonymity.

Once I reached town I bought a newspaper, the *Cork
Examiner*, which contained both local and international news.
Finding a small cafe with outside tables, I settled down with
a slice of toast and a mug of coffee, and browsed through the
paper. Without warning I felt a tap on the back of my shoulder.
Instinctively I leapt from my chair and spun around, hand ready
to pluck the revolver from the inside pocket of my jacket!

'Jaysus, you're very nervous this morning. What's with you,
anyways??' It was Catherine on her way to work.

'No no,' I stammered, 'you just surprised me a little. I don't
know anyone here. I wondered who the hell it was!'

Removing her sunglasses she laughed, adding 'Thought you
were going to take a swing at me!'I offered to buy her a coffee

and she accepted, saying that she had half an hour to spare before starting her four-hour shift and she had another four-hour stint in the evening.

Time flew by listening to her. All my worries were put on hold as she told me about her life, her family back home, and her job, which she seemed to enjoy immensely. Catherine had a vibrant personality and an expressive face. She laughed often as she spoke, her large brown eyes sparkled as she recaptured amusing events. What intrigued me was the fact that she could turn the most insignificant happening into a most interesting and absorbing subject. All of a sudden she stopped talking and for a moment, sounded more serious. 'And what about you then?' she enquired, looking me straight in the eyes, 'you haven't talked much about yourself... who are you really? What do you do? Where do you come from?'

These questions made me feel uneasy. I stammered something about she knew my name was Phil McBryde... 'Yeah, yeah, I know your name all right, but NOTHING else! Tell you what, drop by in the bar tonight, I'm working till eleven, maybe we can have a little chat if I'm not too busy!'

'OK, thanks, I'll see you there then,' I answered, glad I had someone to talk to; the bonus was this someone was very attractive and pleasant and I needed female company!

Later that evening I sauntered into the bar at the Trident Hotel, knowing she would be finishing her shift in about an hour. Dressed in jeans and a denim jacket with a Bob-Dylan-style peaked cap covering my unruly hair, I had a quick glance around the bar in search of any suspicious looking faces. It was fairly crowded, mostly with tourists. Quite a few sported English accents; the odd one was wearing a yachting cap (whether or not they owned a yacht or just the cap was pure conjecture!).

As I edged close to the bar I suddenly came face to face with Catherine deep in conversation with half a dozen English tourists. One dressed in white flannels, a navy blazer complete with brass buttons and yachting cap was describing his new 'toy', apparently an £80,000 yacht, moving his hands up and down, obviously well-oiled by the sound of his high-pitched slurred speech. On seeing me she quickly excused herself from the maritime fraternity.

Taking a critical look, arms folded, she remarked, 'God you're a desperate-looking character!' and burst out laughing. Feeling momentarily embarrassed and vulnerable, as several heads in the bar turned in our direction, I aimed for a quieter corner of the bar.

'What's up?' she asked, 'Are you actually blushing?'

'No, no, it's just that I feel like a sore thumb sticking out here – maybe it's the way the others are dressed...'

'Oh fuck them, they're a pack of conceited bastards. It's just I have to pretend to be interested in their pathetic small talk,' she laughed.

'Could I have a large whiskey? Irish not Scotch. Bushmills, if you've got it.'

'Watch it now, I am not a barmaid you know. Hang on till I get Mick to get you one... you can have this one on me!' vanishing behind the bar to tell Mick to pour me a drink.

It was getting noisy in the bar as a coach load of revellers arrived to swell the ranks. I was getting more self-conscious by the minute and concerned at what I was going to tell Catherine about myself later when she quizzed me about my background.

When I was handed a double whiskey, I took a large swig and gulped it down. Catherine brushed past me close and whispered in my ear that she would be finished in half an hour. If I wanted to hang around and wait for her, we could go for a drive or have coffee somewhere. It was a long half hour. She was busy instructing some of the other staff and trying to be pleasant with customers. I felt that the loud-mouthed would-be Hornblower was looking in my direction with uncomfortable regularity. Was it the scruffy gear I was dressed in or could it be he had a problem with Catherine paying too much attention to me? Maybe I was paranoid. Of course I was bloody paranoid!!

Catherine must have sensed my predicament because she glanced across and gave me a sly wink and a smile. Having downed the first glass of whiskey, I got close to the crowded bar and managed to get Mick's attention to order another drink. After a second glass, the world took on a slightly different perspective as my confidence was restored. Soon Catherine emerged from a side door, a small leather handbag over her shoulder. She had changed from her uniform and was wearing a short, striped cotton dress.

'OK, shall we go then?' I followed her through the door. It was a warm evening, the sky clear with a myriad of stars above. 'Where do you want to go?' she enquired.

'Don't mind really – I don't know this place so you choose, OK,' I answered.

'Tell you what, let's have a coffee at Pat's down the road. He's open late. Then we could take a stroll by the quay if you like.'

Over coffee she told me a little more about herself, her ambitions and work etc. Of course, I knew the questions were going to come about me... Who was I really?

Having only met her a couple of days before, I was not feeling confident enough to trust her with my secret, at least not just yet. Since she believed my name was Phil McBryde, I invented an elaborate ploy. I was half-Irish on my father's side and my mother was Welsh; well, at least I was telling half the truth there! Since she wasn't a very political person, I proceeded to concoct a tale of being a Rhodesian citizen on the run from that country's intelligence service for being suspected of collaborating with one of the black nationalist movements set up to overthrow the white minority regime led by Ian Smith. What I had told her in reality was that I was on the run, which was true, but I had exchanged the ones pursuing me from being British to Rhodesian. Catherine was not familiar with the Rhodesian situation – actually it was Southern Rhodesia, later to become Zimbabwe after gaining their independence. I asked her not to question me too much and said that I would eventually explain to her in more detail;

that I had a lawyer working on my case, but it was imperative not to talk to anyone about me since information could get into the wrong hands and that would not be good.

People should understand that at that stage, I trusted nobody. Although I had told Catherine half my story, I wasn't quite sure of her either. Why would she be interested in me? She seemed too good to be true – could she be a plant? Or worse, could undercover agents kidnap me or cause me to have an 'accident'? All this crossed my mind, could this beautiful dark-haired supervisor be a modern day Mata Hari? Where did reality and make-believe cross? As we later shared a bottle of white wine, sitting on a bench outside a small cafe, a combination of the whiskey, wine and Catherine's magnetic personality soon drove away any traces of fears or suspicion of double agents and plotting. Having gone months without any close female contact, desire and human nature soon took over. Holding hands, we walked down to the beach by Charlesfort where I had pitched the tent. We were both merry and giggling. The tent wasn't very large but it was roomy enough for two. My recollection is we didn't do a hell of a lot of sleeping that night!!

The girl from Limerick proved to be not only a very passionate lover but also talkative, amusing and witty. We struck a chord and seemed to get along well. This gave me a sense of security and helped me cope with the loneliness that had engulfed me for the past few weeks. Since she wasn't due at work until noon we had time to talk and enjoy each other's company. That summer was one of the warmest ever in the southern tip of Ireland. In fact during my stay in the tent I could count on one hand the number of times it rained

Since arriving in Cork I had made arrangements to have my mail sent to me at a PO box in the city's main post office. Only something of importance was to be dispatched from Wales. Only one person knew the PO box number and he was in touch with a well-known Republican supporter who lived near Cardiff. Since I had the hire car for only a couple more days, I decided to visit Cork city once more and check for mail. As it happened, I was not really expecting to receive any. It was a pleasant surprise when I was handed a letter addressed to P. McBryde when I enquired at the counter. Returning to the car I quickly opened the plain white envelope and read its contents. My heart started pounding because the friend who sent me the letter urged me to return to Wales as soon as possible. Apparently the republican supporter previously mentioned had been in touch with the solicitor in Swansea who was fighting my case. The republican was also an entrepreneur and proud patriot, willing to pay the cost of my defence. It was imperative I should find a way of crossing from Ireland, undetected. Crossing the channel from Dun Laoghaire to Holyhead was not an option, neither was Rosslare to Fishguard, since there were Special Branch officers at both ports. Airports were also too dangerous. I decided that the safest bet would possibly be by ferry from the port of Dublin into Liverpool. It would still be dangerous, but I had to take some risks

That evening after Catherine had finished work, we took a stroll through town before returning to the tent. From her inquisitive look, I could tell she sensed something was wrong. I was trying to find a way of telling her I had to leave without much warning. It was a difficult situation since she wasn't aware of the full facts. Holding her close, I told her it was to do with a lawyer that I had to see in order to brief him. Looking me straight in the eyes she said, 'You're not coming back, are you? I just need to know the truth'.

I promised her I would return, but wasn't sure when, although if I was captured the situation would be different. She asked me to phone her at the hotel as soon as I had reached the other side. That evening was spent in almost complete silence as neither of us could find words to express our feelings. Next morning, having bid Catherine a sad goodbye and dropping her at the hotel, I took the car back. Then I walked to the city's railway station and caught a train to Dublin. I found that a ferry to Liverpool would be leaving within the hour.

Since I'd left Wales my beard had grown quite substantially, changing my appearance considerably. It was a ginger mass. At a nearby public convenience, I trimmed my beard to look slightly more presentable. I was wearing my Bob Dylan cap and blue denim jacket. I pressed a small stick-on Irish tricolour flag on one of the sleeves, checked in the mirror and hardly recognised myself! With the rucksack on my back and wearing a pair of cheap sunglasses I headed for the ferry. OK, this was do or die.

Deciding on the 'safety in numbers' theory I elbowed my way into the middle of a bunch of noisy teenagers and trudged up the rickety gangway. As we stepped onto the deck I noticed a couple of uniformed crew members on one side and two plain clothes men, complete with long macs and trilby hats. Their darting eyes and bland stares aroused my naturally suspicious mind. I glimpsed two elderly nuns in full regalia struggling with a heavy suitcase. Without a second thought, I sidestepped my way in their direction and grabbed the suitcase muttering 'Let me help you, Ma'am.' The elder and more rotund of the two, wearing very thick-lensed glasses, gave me a broad smile and thanked me in what I took to be a strong County Kerry accent. Making our way through the jostling crowd of passengers, I led them to one of the lounges and found a vacant spot facing the large entrance.

I asked was it all right and they nodded in unison. 'Bless you young man... bless you,' they chorused.

Now, I'm not usually a person to tempt fate... well, not too often! But this was an opportunity I wasn't going to miss, I decided I would stick like glue to these holy ladies, as they could after all be my salvation when I reached the other side. (Maybe I should explain that by 'the other side' I meant Liverpool and not the river Jordan!)

Eventually we set sail and Dublin soon vanished out of sight. The sea was calm as I ferried mugs of coffee to the nuns, despite their protestations that I was 'really too kind'. We must have seemed a strange trio, two elderly nuns wearing black and white habits and a bearded fugitive in denim wearing a nervous frown. Taking into account the actual landing and crossing time it meant almost four hours aboard the creaking vessel. Throughout the voyage I was increasingly concerned about what might or might not occur on reaching Liverpool docks. My plan was to disembark carrying the nuns' bulky suitcase. I didn't feel guilty about this – after all my freedom was at stake and to be apprehended at this stage would mean a ten-year stretch in Her Majesty's institutions!

I desperately needed breathing space and time to consult the new lawyer hired for my defence by Welsh patriot and benefactor Trefor Morgan. Almost five hours and six coffees later, Liverpool's skyline appeared. My heart beat faster. Many of the passengers had already left the lounge and congregated on deck to glimpse the fast approaching city skyline, still visible despite a veil of fog enveloping the dockland. My best policy was to try and mingle with the mass somewhere in the middle. Could I persuade the nuns to leave their seats at the same time? Seizing the initiative, I ventured to tell them someone was waiting to pick me up at the harbour, but could only wait for a short time due to them having a pre-arranged appointment. Stressing I couldn't leave them to struggle alone with their suitcase, I insisted that I should carry their case off the ship, which meant they would have to accompany me. Following a brief exchange of words amongst themselves, they grudgingly agreed with my offer of help. By now I was perspiring with anxiety, knowing my face was prominently splashed on the pages of the *Police Gazette*, which circulated amongst all police officers, both uniformed and plain clothed. Clutching the handle of the suitcase in one hand and trying to assist the wobbling nuns with my other arm plus the cumbersome rucksack on my back proved to be somewhat tricky. Ever so slowly the ragged queue moved closer to the exit, the plumper of the nuns panting and grunting. Occasionally she would remind me, 'We always wait until everyone else has left the boat before we get off,' to which I responded, 'Don't worry, we're almost there now!'

At last we reached the gangway to disembark. I could make out the figures of two officials checking papers and documents, but noticed that only some men were checked. I managed to manoeuvre myself into a position where I was flanked by a nun on each side – although it entailed my 'accidentally' nudging one of them to the side by means of the suitcase. I almost knocked her over in the process, but she managed to steady herself: 'These people have no manners at all, see how I was pushed then.'

Luckily, the officials hardly looked twice in our direction. Had I been alone I would have felt more nervous and conspicuous. Once I had found a taxi for the nuns, I quickly left, but not before they both offered their blessings several times. Hurrying out of the port area, I soon found a bus stop from where I could travel into the city centre. My sense of relief was indescribable. I had managed to cross from Ireland without detection, even though I had only minimal disguise. Mixing with the crowd in the city's busy streets I felt inconspicuous and safe. Now for my next move.

13

Back to Gwynus

My PLAN WAS to head for home at Gwynus in Llŷn. I was homesick and missed my kids and family. Most people's reaction to such a scheme would probably be one of disbelief. After all, I was on the run, police and Special Branch were searching for me far and wide. MI5 had made enquiries as to my whereabouts as far away as Columbia, South America, as well as in the Vancouver area of British Columbia, where I had lived for a couple of years. Since their net was cast so wide, they would hardly dream I would have the audacity to return to my roots in such a situation. So, while returning to Gwynus was probably the safest option open to me, the one obstacle was – how to cross Wales to get there?

Taking a bus to the southern suburbs of Liverpool, I decided to hitch-hike in the direction of Chester. Deep in thought I ambled along, occasionally putting a hand out, thumb raised in anticipation. It took over half an hour before a car pulled up alongside. I still remember it was a dark-coloured Ford Zodiac. A smartly dressed man in his mid forties peered through a half open window. 'Where you going mate?' he enquired.

'I hope to get to Chester,' I replied in my best County Cork accent. 'Hop in' he said, 'I can take you part of the way at least,' as he helped to put my rucksack on the back seat.

The summer of 1968 was relatively quiet on the political front in Ireland, it was after all pre-Bloody Sunday in Derry, and before the emergence of the Provos.

'What brings you over here?' the driver enquired – his name was Mike.

I made up a long story about being a student in Trinity College Dublin and my name was Phil and that I wanted to do a bit of travelling during the summer break. Mike seemed to be a decent enough guy and time passed quickly as we talked. About half an hour after being picked up, the car swung to the left and soon we approached the town of Runcorn. Less than five minutes later, the driver left the main thoroughfare and took another turning. I noticed a large square grey building come into view. My heart sank, scrawled in large black letters on a giant sign was 'CHESHIRE POLICE HEADQUARTERS'.

The driver pulled up just short of the main entrance. 'Sorry, this is as far as I can take you – this is where I work!'

Helping me get my rucksack out of the back, Mike bade me goodbye and wished me luck. I thanked him before inhaling gulps of air. That was truly a close shave. No sooner had I strapped myself into the rucksack than a brown Hillman car spun into the police station's driveway. I noted the number plate, it was JJC. Instinctively I bent down on the pretence of tying the laces on my trainers. JCC and JC were the letters allocated to the old county of Caernarvonshire, before local government reorganisation swallowed it up into the new Gwynedd unit. In all probability the car belonged to the North Wales Police and its occupants would be plain clothes officers of that force. Making my way briskly out of the police parking area, I reflected on my luck. Fate must have been on my side that day! Deciding to stay in Runcorn until nightfall, I made my way towards the town centre, hoping to find a cinema to while away some time. I made a quick phone call to Esyllt. Her father answered and sounded surprised to hear my voice. I said that I wanted a favour; could I be picked up outside Chester railway station later that evening? There was a slight hesitation before he confirmed that he would do so.

The cinema was half-empty but the darkened atmosphere gave me a sense of security and peace of mind. Deciding not to wait until the film was over, since the lights would then be switched on and that would make me self conscious, I waited until there was roughly half an hour of the film left, then I quietly slipped out and made my way to the exit. It was dark – or dark enough. Walking at a brisk pace I aimed for the bus stop which I had left earlier. Luck was with me once more, a bus with CHESTER in bold letters on the front was about to depart. Assuming the journey would take under an hour, it would leave me twenty minutes to walk from the bus station in the city centre to the railway station.

Since I had asked Esyllt's father to meet me at eleven o'clock in our earlier phone call, it would have left him with plenty of time to make the journey from outside Rhuthun. Upon reaching the railway station car park, I circled the area from a distance before venturing to where about a dozen cars and a couple of taxis were stationed, I recognised the Roberts' small dark green Ford. Mr Roberts sat in the driver's seat, sun visor pulled down, wearing a flat cap pulled well down over his forehead. Approaching from the rear, I gently tapped the car's roof with my knuckles before stepping forward parallel with the driver's door as I bent my head to peer through the window. John Roberts spun round, eyes almost popping out of their sockets, his face ashen with fright. It took him a few seconds before he was reassured it was really me.

Slowly he wound down the window, eyeing me up and down before muttering 'God, you look bloody awful, what happened to you?' At first I was taken aback by his comment, though quickly realising he hadn't ever seen me with an unruly ginger beard and hippy-like attire. I laughed and climbed into the passenger seat alongside him. 'You're taking a big risk aren't you?' he commented as we made our way through the thinning lines of traffic on leaving the city centre.

Pausing for a moment before thinking how to respond, I said, 'Yes, I suppose, but then you know me, I've always taken risks and in my situation there's not many options. Besides, this new solicitor needs to see me and that's about the only chance I have of getting back to normal life.'

John Roberts was obviously a very worried and scared man.

He fidgeted as he drove and kept glancing in his rear mirror. He was petrified of being stopped by the police with a fugitive in his car. He kept mopping the cold sweat off his forehead. I reckoned he worked his way through half a box of Kleenex tissues during our comparatively short trip back to his house. Trying to put his mind at rest, I kept repeating that the chances of us being stopped were pretty remote as long as he drove properly and did not exceed the speed limits etc. On arriving at the house, I noticed a light on in one of the upstairs bedrooms as well as the porch light. Entering the house, I was startled by a light suddenly coming on in the lounge. Blinded for a moment, I squinted and shielded my eyes only to realise it was Esyllt, who had been waiting in the dark, and had switched the light on when she heard us enter the room.

She flew across and wrapped her arms around my neck, then suddenly stepped back and cried out, 'God, you look a bloody mess. What in hell have you been doing?'

'Thanks a bunch. That's the second time in an hour that I've heard that compliment!' I retorted.

'Are you going to shave that horrible beard?' she queried almost accusingly. I replied that it wouldn't be a very smart idea right now with half the police in the country on my tail.

Since I had a huge agenda ahead of me during the next few days, I decided to stay just the one night in the Roberts' home, which meant leaving the following day after dusk. Having contemplated all the pros and cons I had come to a decision to cross over from north-east Wales to the far north-west, to reach my parents' farm at Gwynus near Nefyn. While this might have seemed crazy, since most of the Welsh police were looking out for me, my thinking was rather different, since I figured that at my family home at Gwynus was probably the last place the authorities would suspect me of hiding.

It made a pleasant change sleeping in a warm cosy bed with snow white linen sheets as opposed to the previous few months roughing it in a cramped canvas tent, curled up in a crumpled sleeping bag. Sleep came quickly. I had managed to file my immediate problems and anxieties into a compartment of my brain 'for later attention'. I was awoken by the melodious sound of a song thrush perched on an apple tree branch, feet away from my half-open bedroom window. Taking a quick glance at my watch, I saw it was almost ten o'clock. I slid out of bed, washed and dressed before hurrying downstairs. Esyllt and her Mum were sitting in the kitchen. Her father had left earlier to do some shopping in Denbigh, a few miles down the road. Mrs Roberts ushered me to a chair at the kitchen table before placing a large plate in front of me crammed with crispy fried bacon, eggs, sausages and tomatoes, followed by a large mug of steaming tea. There are not many more hospitable people on this planet than Welsh country folk; to call them generous is a gross understatement. Once I had polished off my breakfast to the last crumb, we sat talking, mostly small talk, until Mr Roberts returned an hour later.

There was a small field at the back of the house, surrounded by a mature hedge. When entering this field via the back door, it was impossible for anyone to see who or what lay beyond the hedge. I needed to stretch my legs and get some fresh air. Despite feeling somewhat relaxed and somewhat less tense, having spent a night in a friendly and safe place, I still couldn't quite get away from the feeling of being watched, and even now I wasn't taking any chances. It was a pleasant enough day and the aroma of freshly mown hay wafted into my nostrils. But I couldn't relax entirely – how would I get to Gwynus?

I would be driven by Mr Roberts as far as Abergwyngregyn; there I would switch to a little mini van driven by an acquaintance of mine who worked as an agricultural merchant and who lived a few miles from Gwynus. We decided to leave just before dusk and since the journey would take over an hour, it would mean darkness would have fallen by the time I arrived at my parents.

Abergwyngregyn is no more than a tiny hamlet located on the A55 between Llanfairfechan and Bangor. Having arrived at the hotel car park a few minutes earlier than was planned, there was no sign of Tom or his mini van, but I knew he was meticulous in whatever he undertook and would arrive on time. At exactly the appointed time, we noticed a small vehicle, lights dimmed, enter the car park and drive around the perimeter, before parking a few yards behind us. Although we were the only vehicles there, Tom had been making sure there were no suspicious movements before parking his van. Shaking hands with Mr Roberts and thanking him and his family for all their help and kindness, I picked up my rucksack and hurried across the tarmac towards the minivan.

Tom was a tall, rather bulky figure who could be described as surly, especially by someone who didn't know him. I had known him since he was a law student and I knew he had a heart of gold, despite his smug and sometimes intolerant attitude. We shook hands before he chipped in with an uncouth comment: 'Done a lot of shagging lately?' That was his trouble; you either felt like thumping him or bursting out in uncontrollable laughter. I decided on the latter.

As the miles flew by, he briefed me on the police activities in the Caernarfon area. The investiture of Charles Windsor as the so-called 'prince of Wales' was a little under a year away. This was a controversial event in Wales. Many people disliked the imposition of an English prince on our land. But it had been so since, according to a (believable) legend. Edward I, having been requested for a non-English-speaking prince to follow Llywelyn the Great, whom Edward had killed, had proclaimed his baby son – too young to speak any language – the new 'prince of Wales'. Ever since, the first-born son of the English monarch has been proclaimed 'prince of Wales'. Many of us were prepared to resist this celebration of our colonisation, to be held in Caernarfon's castle.

Apparently, road blocks were a regular event, spot checks were normal on anyone who had the slightest nationalistic leanings. The so-called 'Special Squad' based over the border in Shrewsbury were screening many locals and people were being 'tailed' by murky characters dressed in duffle coats. Telephones were being tapped, mail opened, all the trappings of a nervous state security system confronting a faceless 'enemy'. All of this was, of course, new in Wales. Still, certain sections of the population were openly supportive of the guerrilla war tactics being practised by MAC I asked Tom whether my family were being harassed by the authorities. He wasn't sure. Superficially it didn't seem so. On the other hand it was obvious that there was some form of surveillance because of such close ties with me.

We by-passed Caernarfon via a back road and soon we were heading down the A499 to the turning for Nefyn. With my home less than two miles away, my heart started beating a little faster, doubts started clouding my mind over the wisdom of returning home. Questions, mostly unanswerable, flooded my mind. Was I putting my ageing parents in danger? Could my actions end up in a midnight siege? On top of these doubts and mental conflicts, there was the nostalgia of returning to my roots. Graphic images of my childhood floated before my eyes as we drove up the half mile farm lane. Tom pulled up a few yards short of the kitchen entrance as I had instructed him to do. I was wary of causing unnecessary complications since my brother Ellis was not to know of my return. I have already mentioned how my brother had suffered after his 'kidnap' from a hay meadow as a child of three. Not only would it have been unfair on him to know of my secret visit, it would also be dangerous for my parents should he unwittingly mention to someone that I was home. My line of action was quite simple; apart from my father and mother, only my eldest brother Morris would know the secret.

In order to make sure that Ellis had gone to bed, Tom went up to the kitchen door and knocked. Hiding around the corner, I heard the door being unlocked and a bolt opened, my mother peered into the darkness, squinting her eyes before recognising who had called so late. 'Tom! Goodness me, you called late...'

'Hello, Mrs Williams, sorry to disturb you like this but...'

lowering his voice he enquired, almost in a whisper, 'Is Ellis in bed yet?'

'Oh yes, yes of course, but why do you ask... is anything wrong?'

Tom hesitated a moment before answering: 'Well, no, no, nothing is wrong, but I have a little surprise for you.' Lowering his voice once more, 'I've brought Owain back to see you... but don't you worry now, he won't be staying very long.'

Before she could say anything, I emerged from the shadows and stood beside Tom. *'Helo, Mam, Sut 'd ach chi?'* (How are you?)

Needless to say she was speechless, the shock of seeing me standing on the doorstep must have been awesome. Finally recovering her senses, she blurted, 'Don't stand there, come in, I'll put the kettle on.' Rushing ahead of us she called 'Griffith, you'll never guess who's here...' then lowering her voice she continued 'Owain is back. Tom brought him!'

My father was sitting in front of the Aga which had an extra open fire grate alongside: *'Arglwydd mawr, be da chi'n ddeud?'* (Good God, what are you saying?')

Staring in disbelief, first at Tom then at me, he was confused.'What on earth are you doing?'

Explaining the best I could the motive behind my sudden and unexpected appearance I told them both that it was imperative for me to see the new lawyer who was taking up my case. I also emphasized I would only be staying a short while – maybe a week or ten days. Then the issue of where I would stay and sleep arose. Staying in the house was not an option, it would not be fair on them or Ellis or anyone else. Immediately in front of the house in a parcel of land that was fenced off, where there was a caravan left over by some relatives of ours. It was certainly not a luxury mobile home, but it was habitable. True, it had no running water, no electricity, not even a toilet. But that wasn't a problem since there was a spare toilet close by and a cold water tap, also a Calor gas cylinder outside the door, ample for my needs. After all, I was well-versed in the arts of living rough by now. Mam fished out an old sleeping bag of mine from a bygone era, a couple of towels, a bar of soap, a pot of coffee and a bottle of milk. I would be OK for the night.

After thanking Tom and saying goodbye, I had a few minutes to chat with my parents, who had somewhat recovered from their initial shock. Stumbling across the stony farmyard, I slowly inched my way towards the old caravan. I did not use a flash lamp as this could have attracted attention from any preying eyes that could be surveying the farm from a distance. Gwynus is located fairly high, about four or five hundred feet above sea level, despite the sea itself being less than a mile away – well as the crow flies, though I should add that Welsh crows fly a little erratic at times!

My heart throbbed as I opened the door. Inside was pitch dark; what if someone was waiting? Making sure all the curtains were drawn, I sat down on the bed and tried to listen to sounds coming from outside. There was only the rustle of leaves from the tall sycamore trees that surrounded the gardens of Gwynus. In the distance I could hear the waves crashing on the rocky foreshore of Pistyll beach.

Despite it being high summer, it was still cold in the caravan, because it had been uninhabited for months, if not years. Snuggling into the sleeping bag, I closed my eyes and tried to block the present from my mind – easier said than done.

An alarm clock was never used in Gwynus, as it was never needed. Mam owned a feisty Rhode Island Red cockerel who strutted his stuff about the farmyard, satisfying the needs of almost a hundred randy hens. This feathered version of Errol Flynn also vigorously and loudly proclaimed daybreak with boring and irritating punctuality. So I was rudely awakened from my troubled slumber next morning at precisely a quarter to six!

Gwynus was, even by today's standards, a large livestock farm. As well as the four hundred and fifty acre holding, we also owned a large hill farm several miles away, in addition to renting hundreds of acres of land nearby. At any given time, there would be close to 2,000 sheep and lambs, plus a suckler beef herd of over 100. The whole operation worked like clockwork. By this time my elder brother Morris was in charge of the day to day running, since my second brother John was married and farmed the next holding a short distance away. All the various seasons demanded different projects and skills.

July and August are generally the months when the sheep are shorn, and hay or silage is harvested. At one time we did all the work ourselves. However, with increasing flock numbers and silage harvesting etc, it became an impossible task, so, contractors were called in. Four or five of these semi-professional shearers would easily clip a thousand ewes in one day. The flock had grown so large that eventually the sheep pens were too small to contain them. A makeshift 'pen' was created using the farm lane, which was walled on both sides with gates at both ends to seal it off. At shearing time all the sheep were crammed into this pen. We would then run them off about 200 at a time, into the old pens where Morris had created a sorting corridor which involved a hinged gate at the end of a corridor, operated with a long rope. It was possible to divide the lambs from the ewes without the physical exertion of catching them all individually and hauling them to separate pens. (Alas, today, the old pens are flattened and replaced by a make-do car park for would-be golfers attending our nine hole pay-as-you go golf course! Would I call that progress? No, not really, just a necessity of economic survival since the farm was split three ways following my mother's death in 1991. I think the term used is 'diversification'.)

Bryn Williams was a carpenter by trade and lived in a village nearby. We had been friends for some time, having met when I ran the coffee shop in Pwllheli some years previously. Sitting in the caravan one evening talking to my brother Morris, I mentioned I would like to see Bryn as I wanted to discuss a few matters with him before leaving Gwynus. My brother said he would drop by Bryn's home that evening and ask him to call round to see me. It was a weekend and things were quiet on the farm for a change. Since my arrival I had constructed a sort of hammock between the branches of two oak trees on the farm's ancient woodland less than 200 metres from where the caravan stood. So it was on a warm sunny Saturday afternoon, I was lying on my back on the canvas sheet high above the ground, hidden from the world by a thick cluster of leaves. Nesting crows croaked nearby, wood pigeons cooed and fussed over their newly-hatched young. Suddenly my ears pricked up on hearing a strange sound. It was a low soft whistle, repeated after a few seconds followed by the sound of footsteps treading on broken twigs. I cautiously spread the branches apart and peered down below. The footsteps came nearer, followed by another low whistle. Squinting through the branches I recognised the big mop of unruly hair as belonging to a small-framed person who I immediately knew to be Bryn. Plucking an unripe acorn, I waited until he stood right beneath my hammock, then I dropped the acorn right on top of his head. He stopped in his tracks and raising his head, he peered upwards, but because of the denseness of the foliage, I was invisible!

'Hey, that was a good aim… don't you think?'

Startled, he spun around just as I alighted from the branches like a squirrel. 'Well you bastard – I wondered what the hell hit me on the head!'

We shook hands heartily before he produced a bottle of Guinness from each of his coat pockets, together with a bottle opener. We sat down on the grass and talked while drinking the Guinness. During our chat he mentioned there was to be an anti-investiture rally at the Owain Glyndŵr Parliament House in Machynlleth later that month. Speakers had been invited including the world-renowned Welsh poet R. S. Thomas whom I knew very well. Suddenly an idea dawned on me. If I was to use a tape recorder and tape a short speech to be played at the meeting, it might help raise the spirits of those campaigning.

There was an old recording device in one of the caravan's cupboards. Bryn went to fetch it while I waited, scribbling a

few notes for the speech. It was a strange feeling speaking into
the microphone with the background sound effects of bleating
lambs and a solo crow as accompaniment. I smiled to myself
imagining the reaction of Special Branch officers listening to
the taped address at the meeting. The hours passed very quickly
and I was sad to see Bryn leave, as he was the first friend I had
seen since leaving for Ireland several months previously.

The speech was actually played at the rally in Machynlleth.
Reports circulated that I was to speak at this meeting – naturally
Special Branch had become very interested. To make it all the
more frustrating for them, one of my friends, Neil ap Siencyn,
who chaired the meeting, had announced at the beginning
that 'Owain Williams will speak later on...' According to those
present, no sooner had he announced 'Now Owain Williams
will speak...' there was a lull, before half a dozen burly Special
Branch officers closed in around the speakers' platform.
Without warning my voice filled the room, accompanied by
loud applause as the law officers stumbled amongst the crowd
trying to locate me!!! It was a few minutes before they realised
they had been victims of a hoax... red faces all round!

By the time the above incident was played out, I was far
away from Gwynus, although still on Welsh soil. It is worth
stating that my departure from Gwynus occurred several days
ahead of my planned schedule. There was one incident at the
farm, when a plain clothes policeman called round to see my
family, enquiring if they had heard anything from me. On this
particular day my father, two brothers and a farmhand were
working with the sheep in the makeshift pens on the farm
lane.

As I have explained earlier, when the lane was overfull with
sheep, there was no way of even walking through their midst,
never mind driving a car. I was sitting in the caravan reading
a newspaper brought by my mother, when I heard very loud
and excited shouting, adorned by a few swearwords – mostly
bilingual! It turned out my brother Morris had recognised
the driver as being a local CID member, attached to Special

Branch. That was the cue for Morris to embark on his shrill scream to warn me of the imminent danger approaching the farm. Without delay I gathered a few things together and flung them into my rucksack, locking the door from the inside, I then clambered through a small window at the rear of the caravan, closed it behind me and using a disused farm building for cover, crawled on my stomach, slithered over the farm yard's perimeter block and into a field. Using a hedge of old hawthorn bushes and trees, I made my way into the direction of the small woodland – the very one where I had met Bryn when I'd been in the hammock. Once I was inside the woods, it was almost impossible for anyone to see me with the naked eye. My main worry was, what if whoever that was coming after me were to bring tracker dogs, they would soon pick up my trail and that would be it. Of course this was all conjecture, as I had no way of verifying whether the police were in pursuit. All I knew was that Moi had sounded as if he was giving me a warning.

Once I was deep into the woodland, I felt safer, but still knew I had to get rid of my scent somehow. There was one way of doing this so I headed towards a small stream, more of a ditch in fact, which acted as part of the boundary between our farm and a neighbour's. Without further thought, I leapt into the peaty ditch and began making my way further from the farm. Despite being summer, the filthy water was ice cold and as I stumbled through the mud, it splashed onto my face, and my clothes were saturated, my boots soon full of a slimy combination of mud, twigs, dead reeds and leaves. This ordeal lasted for a quarter of a mile. I was more obsessed with the fear of snakes ending up in my trouser legs than any pursuing cops! I've always had this thing about snakes. I used to dream about treading on them as a kid and would wake up in a sweat, my heart pounding.

Figuring that I had done enough to confuse the most crafty of tracker dogs, I crawled out of the ditch and flopped onto the grassy verge on the other side. Gasping for breath I rolled onto my back as the warmth of the sun began to penetrate my drenched and filthy clothing. Removing my boots I shook them vigorously to drain most of the water and the slime. I took off my soggy socks, squeezed and wrung them before dangling them on a strand of rusty barbed wire to dry. I decided it wouldn't be wise to remove my trousers to dry, since, if there was someone out there in pursuit, I would have to leave in a hurry – and I really did not want to be caught with my pants down!! Then again, I guess it wouldn't have been the first time!

An hour must have passed and there was still no visible sign of anyone following my erratic zig zag path. Checking my boots and socks, I was amazed to find they had become much drier but my trousers and underwear felt sticky and clung uncomfortably to my skin. I was now faced with a dilemma... what next to do? It was far too risky to go back to Gwynus, and by now my family would have no idea where to start looking for me. Deciding to wait a while longer before deciding my next move, I lay back and closed my eyes, puzzling over my next step.

Approximately a mile across the valley from Gwynus was a cluster of about nine or ten small holdings. At one time they were the homes of quarrymen who toiled by day in some of the granite quarries along the north coast of Llŷn. On returning home in the evenings the quarrymen would slave away on the few rocky acres, tending the handful of sheep and the odd cow or two. These smallholdings provided a valuable sideline, supplementing meagre earnings by producing milk, butter, meat, eggs and vegetables. Most of the people living in these cottages were known to me. Some of them had children around my age. We had shared the same schools as well as Sunday school and banged a football against the side of the village post office, and shop, much to the fury of Richard Lewis the postmaster who was also my Sunday school teacher. My second eldest brother John was married to Mary, the daughter of one of these smallholders. Their home was called Llwynysgaw. Somehow I had to find cover for an hour or two before dark, when it would be safer for me to move about. It is probably true to say I could have gone to the door of any of these cottages and I would have been welcomed and nobody would have betrayed me.

For whatever reason, I decided to aim for Llwynysgaw. It was still daylight as I circled my way across small fields, staying close to the banks and hedges to provide cover. Mrs Williams was busy attending to some hens as I approached. Since her back was turned she was unaware of my presence until I called out in Welsh, 'Hello, Mrs Williams. How are you?'

Spinning around, her jaw dropped on seeing my scruffy appearance then she cried out to her husband 'O'r Arglwydd mae 'na hen dramp yn fama!' (Oh my God, there's an old tramp here!)

I realised suddenly that my unkempt appearance had frightened her, my long reddish beard, mud-splattered trousers and filthy wet rucksack would have been enough to scare anyone. I tried to calm her down. 'It's all right Mrs Williams, it's me, Owain from Gwynus...!' On hearing this she let go of a small bucket of chicken food she had been carrying on her arm.

'Owain... Owain Gwynus?' she said in total disbelief. 'Why? What are you doing, where are you going?' I thought to myself, 'This is going to be difficult trying to explain to them.' Recovering her senses quickly her tone changed as she ushered me into the small cottage before putting the kettle on. 'I'll make you a cup of tea, then you can tell us all about it.'

Up to now her husband Ellis had hardly spoken but kept staring at me, eyeing me up and down as if he was unconvinced it was really me. Gulping mouthfuls of strong hot farmhouse tea which warmed me up substantially, I then related to them only part of my story as I didn't wish to involve them more than necessary. I emphasized that I had to get back to Gwynus after nightfall, that I would be grateful to use their telephone to contact my brother John who would come to pick me up and hopefully drive me back to Gwynus. Before my brother arrived with his van, the old man spoke to me for the first time. What he said shook me slightly and made me question the wisdom of going to the house.

What he suggested was that I should consider giving myself up to the authorities... the police... and that I was worrying my parents through my actions of being on the run. It was difficult to try to explain to an elderly couple who had always lived by the law that what I was doing was necessary etc since they would not understand and I did not expect them to. What I did ask them was for them not to mention to anyone that they had spoken to me or even seen me. I must add that they kept their word, God bless them both, and I am eternally grateful for that.

It was with great concern that I made my way back to Gwynus. Later that evening, I managed to contact my other brother Morris who had witnessed all the goings on earlier in the day. Even at the most serious or sombre moments, Morris had the gift of seeing the funny side. He was almost in stitches as he related how the plain clothes officer had to stumble his way through a mass of sheep, trying to get to the farmhouse. Following almost half an hour of struggling, hindered by my brothers' delaying tactics, the cop had eventually knocked on the farmhouse door. He was dishevelled, his posh brown shoes covered in sheep shit. Mam, who answered the door, thought at first that he was an agricultural salesman. When he explained who he was, enquiring whether she had heard anything from me lately, she said she had not and that even if she had, she would hardly tell him. She then shut the door in his face. My brother quipped, 'Don't you worry, he's far enough from here by now – take him a week to clean the sheep shit from his shoes!!'

Back in the small caravan that night, this incident kept cropping up in my mind time and time again. What worried me most of all was that this would be very stressful for my family and that I should move on in the next couple of days. The following evening, my brother drove me in his van to a rural telephone kiosk several miles away. Using back roads we managed to make the trip without incident. Dialling the number of a go-between, I asked him to pass on a message to a third party, who would pick me up at a pre-arranged location and drive me over 100 miles into an area of mid Wales by the Black Mountains.

It was once again time to bid my parents and brothers goodbye, a difficult task at best. Saying goodbye is not my strong point. I usually try to keep it short and sweet as the longer it drags out the more upsetting it gets. During my stay in the caravan, the most stressful situation occurred on a weekend when my two children Iona and Gruff came to stay over with their grandparents. Since they were obviously unaware of my presence in the caravan, I watched them playing outside from behind the curtained windows, almost within touching distance. At this time they were very young; my daughter Iona was ten and Gruff, my son was nine.

Huddled in the back of a small Austin van is probably not the most luxurious way to travel, even for a few miles, never mind over a hundred. Alun the driver was not the most talkative member of the human race. In fact, apart from a half dozen monosyllables uttered through a clenched set of rotting front teeth, made even more undecipherable since there seemed to be a roll-up fag glued to the corner of his bottom lip, he said very little. Unceremoniously we came to an abrupt stop when we had covered roughly half the scheduled distance. After opening the creaking back door of the van, bound tight on the outside with a length of baler twine, Alun removed the soggy remains of the dog end from his mouth before stamping on it vigorously on the muddy ground. 'That's my job done. Dai will take you the rest of the way... and good luck.'

He shook my hand briefly before climbing into the rusty vehicle and disappearing down the farm track. Dai emerged from the front door of the large farmhouse – a more appropriate term would be a manor. A tall figure with dark hair, sporting a well-trimmed moustache, striding across the gravel path with outstretched hand and a wide smile '*Shwmae bachan*, it's good to see you. I've heard such a lot about you and I'm a big fan of yours and admire what you are doing.' I felt rather embarrassed at first but Dai soon put me at ease, inviting me into the house for a coffee before we set off.

We entered a large living room comfortably furnished though not lavish. There were children's toys scattered over the floor. 'Excuse the mess, but we have two kids and they seem to take over the whole house,' he chuckled. 'Judy, the wife, she is just putting them to bed now!'

Within a matter of minutes the kettle was boiled and he placed two large mugs of steaming coffee on the small table, as he began to describe the destination of the last leg of the clandestine journey. I was told it was a hill farm, fairly isolated, its land skirting the Black Mountains not too far from the legendary Llyn y Fan. Time flew by as I talked with Dai. He was a charismatic character with a sharp wit; a horse breeder, who also kept a few cattle and sheep. A large horse transporter was driven from one of the barns with a dozen or so bales of straw inside. My place in the horse box was alongside a massive Hanoverian stallion, Dai reassuring me that he was quite docile and harmless.

'Aye, it's only when the mares are around that he gets excited,' he boomed. The straw bales were used to construct a small makeshift compartment in a corner of the horse carriage.

Well, at least I will have some protection from being trampled by this equine brute, I thought to myself. Once the tailgate was raised, we were ready to move once more. The powerful diesel motor cruised along the farm track and headed south east. Through a small sliding glass panel that separated the cab from the actual container, Dai hollered loud above the noisy engine, 'Are you OK in there, Owain?'

Spitting out a mouthful of straw, I yelled back 'Yes, I'm fine – up to now at least, so long as this bastard doesn't collapse on top of the bales!'

'Don't you worry, I'm driving real tidy, don't want to draw any attention from the cops,' he replied.

It was difficult to make out where we were. I could only tell we were on a fairly narrow, twisted country road and that we were steadily climbing. The constant gear shifting was sufficient clue for that.

We must have been driving for three-quarters of an hour when suddenly the vehicle slowed down to first gear. The road surface sounded very bumpy and we seemed to be climbing a very steep gradient. I imagined we were on a farm track, more than likely a hill farm. By sheer guesswork I figured we had travelled about one mile of farm track before the lorry came to a halt. 'OK, Owain we've arrived!' observed Dai through the sliding glass panel, after switching off the engine. 'Let you out now,' he added.

14

Meeting with Solicitor

STAGGERING UP FROM my crouched position in the back of the horse box, throwing aside the bales of straw which had hemmed me in, I inched my way towards the open tailgate. Outside was pitch dark with the exception of a faint yellow glow which shone above the entrance porch of what appeared to be an old stone farmhouse. At first glance, it seemed to be a traditional Welsh hill farmhouse, sturdy thick walls, small wooden-framed windows. Shaking my head vigorously to dislodge the loose straw which clung to my hair and beard, I heard Dafydd shouting out loud as I spat the chaff from my mouth – 'Jesus, man, you've got enough straw in your hair to feed a bloody stallion for a week!' he chuckled.

Before I could respond, the door of the house opened and a stocky young man stepped outside. He had a dark beard and was wearing green overalls. He held an oil-fired storm lantern in one hand, 'Shwmae, Edwin – I've brought you the cargo,' Dafydd greeted the stranger. We moved across the cobbled farmyard in his direction.

Edwin met us with outstretched hand. 'Owain, isn't it? I'm so glad you came here and you're very welcome.' He seemed a very jovial and sincere person who made me feel at ease in his presence. 'Right then, don't just stand there, come inside. Gwen's made some tea and a bite to eat,' he added, ushering us inside. I noticed the large porch had a low ceiling and great slabs of Welsh slate covered the floor. On entering the kitchen, sparsely furnished with what seemed a homemade wooden table, two similar chairs and a settle, in one corner stood a traditional Welsh dresser cluttered with ancient looking willow-pattern plates and other items of crockery.

Gwen was a homely-looking young woman with straight blonde hair tied at the back with a ribbon. Hurriedly wiping baking flour from her hands on her apron, she greeted me warmly with a broad smile. I noticed she was in mid-pregnancy. Edwin smiled, pointing towards the bulge – 'it's our first,' he proudly beamed. 'Aye, the first of many, I hope.'

'Wales could do with a few extra hundred of bona fide patriots,' Dafydd quipped.

'Few hundred? *Myn uffern i*. Give us a break man – half a dozen wouldn't be bad now, would it?'

At this Gwen chipped in; 'Half a dozen? Huh… well, I tell you something. Unless they all arrive together, you'll have to bring them to this world yourself! This one's caused me enough problems as it is!' she laughed.

Over supper I was given the exact location of the farm. We were pretty high up. The farmhouse itself was over 800 feet and the land rose to over 1,000 feet on the edge of the Brecon Beacons. There was a small town or village called Trecastell a few miles away and two or three miles in another direction there was a small rural pub.

'Mind you, Owain, don't think you'll be spending many evenings down there, not with all the cops in the country hot on your tail!' said Dafydd, adding, 'Oh don't worry man, you're completely safe up here. Only the bloody postman calls and he turns up about twice a week.' The evening passed quickly,

Dafydd looking at an old chapel clock ticking loudly on the wall, leapt to his feet. 'Good god, it's half past midnight, must be on my way.' After handshakes and hurried goodbyes, he left.

'Well, we'd better turn in as well, got a hard day tomorrow and I'm sure you must be tired after all that travelling,' said Edwin. 'I'll show you to your room. There's only one little snag – Gwen and me have to go through your room to get to our bedroom.'

It was a fairly small room with a low ceiling, complete with an old dormer window that had seen better days. I noticed that the bed had clean sheets and pillows. There was also a neatly folded woollen blanket at the foot of the bed.

Early next morning I was woken by the sound of tip-toeing footsteps hurrying past my bed. It was Edwin on his way downstairs. Checking my watch, I saw it was only half past six. A few minutes later, Gwen passed quickly through the room, taking care not to wake me. I sat up quickly saying it was OK, that I was awake anyway.

'Did Ed wake you, then? Clumsy donkey, I told him not to make a racket!' She sounded annoyed.

'No, no, it's all right,' I lied,' I was going to get up early anyway.' I was still feeling knackered after the previous day's events. Deciding I would give Ed a hand – I was told not to call him Edwin – I donned a pair of old denim jeans, complete with holes in both knees, and a T-shirt, and walked down the rickety stairs into the kitchen. Ed was already working his way through a king-sized bowl of porridge and the kettle was boiling on an old blackened kitchen range.

'Morning, Owain... tea? Why did you get up so early?' Ed seemed to be in a hurry because he spoke while shovelling porridge into his mouth.

'*Bore da*,' I responded. 'Thought you could do with a hand on the farm'

Ed explained that he and Gwen had only bought the farm in the last few months. It had been left in disrepair, the house had deteriorated and much of the land had gone back to nature. Large areas were covered in bracken, gorse and rushes. Ed wasn't complaining, thought it was an ideal place to start farming on his own and raise a family. The price had been within his reach owing to the rundown condition, as not many people would have the urge or the stomach to tackle such a challenge. Explaining that he was in the process of clearing some gorse and removing some tree stumps from an area of land half a mile from the house, he asked if I could drive a tractor.

Smiling, I replied, 'Of course, used to drive an old Fordson for my father when I was about ten years old.'

He laughed. 'I forgot, you are a farm boy too, aren't you?'

It was hard, gruelling work, lugging old stumps and roots, not to mention the large boulders that dotted the peaty barren tract of land. Lunch hour brought a welcome break from the toil so we returned to the farmhouse, Ed driving and me clinging on to what remained of the rusting mudguard of the creaking Fordson Major. It wasn't so much that the track from the fields was rough and bumpy, but the myriad of potholes meant I was tossed up and down like a yo-yo. Once we had scavenged platefuls of homemade fries, bacon and eggs, it was back to the fields again. By the time we returned drizzle was falling and the nearby mountain, Y Fan, was shrouded in an eerie mist. Bit by bit one field was cleared, before we moved on to the next, and then the next. Ed's plan was to plough, cultivate and re-seed all these fields with fresh grass. Before this could take place, ditches needed to be opened and new land-drains would be needed in the wettest patches of land. Without proper drainage the land would quickly return to being a bog and all the hard labour would have been in vain.

Following about a week of field clearance, Ed decided it was time to shear his flock of Welsh Mountain and cross Kerry sheep. Traditionally sheep shearing can start anytime from mid May to late June in the lowland farms. In the hill country, it occurs much later, mid July to late August is normal. At this particular time, many hill farms had not resorted to using shearing contractors or even electric shearing machines. Instead the centuries-old tradition was the neighbours to help out, where they would gather a crowd of up to twenty men, moving from farm to farm until the whole neighbourhood was done. As it happened, shearing by hand, using manual shears, was an art I had inherited from my father and my eldest brother Morris. I remember as a young boy, just left school, holding my first pair of hand-shears my father had bought me. Shearing is a skill that can be acquired but more often than not it is something you either inherit or have a natural capability to carry out. My father, for instance, had once managed to shear over 140 in a day; Morris had managed over 120. I tried to match these figures, but it took a few years to catch up with my brother, who was very fit and strong.

Shearing day finally arrived at Trwyn y Fan (not its real name). A motley crowd had gathered, young and old, short and tall, who all spoke Welsh with an accent peculiar to the area. Both Ed and myself had previously discussed the problem of my north-west Wales accent. Although I had the knack of switching into various accents when speaking English, I was not as competent when using Welsh. It was decided I would speak English amongst the shearing crowd, but would camouflage my northern accent by adopting a sort-of semi-mid-Atlantic accent. I wouldn't have a big problem with that because of my years in Canada. Stripped to my vest, wearing a battered old Australian bush hat and a pair of faded denim shoes, I quickly set about removing the fleeces off the sheep and noticed I was managing at least two for every one of the others. The others talked a lot, mostly small talk or farm talk... Who had a new tractor? How had the lambing gone? Some of the younger ones talked about lighter issues.How many pints had they managed last Saturday? Who was screwing the village bike at the last count?

Wool was beginning to pile up where I was shearing since a very young lad, a bit overwhelmed, was trying to wrap it and put it into extra large sacks in the corner. Above the noise of the clicking shears I began to hear drifts of conversation, much of it half whispered as some of the older shearers made remarks about my prowess as a shearer. Since they all spoke in Welsh and their understanding was that I was a London Welshman, I gathered from what was being said that they were rather baffled as to how a city chap – London Welsh – could shear sheep with such speed and skill. Now here I was at an advantage. While they talked about me, thinking I couldn't understand a word, I on the other hand understood every word spoken, which gave me time to think of an answer to their questions.

Following a couple of hours of shearing, it was time to take a short break for cool drinks and a sandwich which Gwen brought down to the shearing shed. Sitting on top of a bulging wool sack, I felt a bit uneasy and isolated, not being able to participate in the conversation.

Suddenly, one old farmer with a white bushy moustache ventured to speak to me, in English. 'How did you learn to shear so good and you from the middle of London?' he queried.

Of course, I'd been given ample time to think of an answer to the question. 'Oh, well, you see, I've got an uncle who runs a sheep station in Australia, in New South Wales in fact. I spent a couple of years down there, good place to learn.'

The old man swallowed the story and turning to the others, repeated in Welsh what I'd told him. One of the younger ones commented, 'So that's where he had the hat from, ha, ha!'

At this the older man who had talked to me rebuked him. 'Hat or no bloody hat, he can sure as hell shear. Maybe you should borrow his hat!' The others laughed.

Ed, who was standing close by gathering loose bits of wool, winked at me with a smile of satisfaction on his face. The rest of the day passed without incident as I decided to speak as little as possible, so as not to give away my accent. We were just about to pack up our kit, when one of the younger helpers suddenly asked, 'Has anyone heard anything about that bloody mad north Walian, on the run from the cops, wanted for blowing something up in mid Wales? They say there were roadblocks down by Lampeter the other night, reckon he's not far away!'

I almost choked on the ham sandwich I was eating. Luckily no-one took the matter any further and soon everyone left in different directions.

After they'd gone, Ed came over to me with a wicked smile on his face. 'Thought you were a goner, then!'

'You're telling me!' I said. 'Didn't know where to look when that thickhead mentioned a mad north Walian – cheeky bastard!!'

A few days after, we had been slogging away getting rid of the remaining tree stumps and the last of the boulders when Ed suggested we pay a visit to a small local a couple of miles down the road. I believe it was called either the New Inn or Cross Inn – I can't remember. However, when Ed made the suggestion I had deep suspicions about the wisdom of taking such a risk despite his reassuring words that only a few locals frequented the inn. After much persuasion, I reluctantly agreed to accompany him. This was more to do with the fact that I didn't want to let him down than really wanting to spend a few hours away from the comparative safety of a remote farm.

At the pub there were only three or four customers present, two elderly farmers deep in conversation at a corner table and one scruffily dressed character leaning on the bar, a pint of Guinness in one hand and a cigarette butt dangling from the corner of his lower lip. The barmaid, a well endowed blonde with a low-cut colourful blouse, lazily made her way across to us.

'*Shwmae*, Ed? Usual, is it?'

'Aye, a pint of Buckley's please, Susan. What would you like, Phil?'

For a moment I thought he was going to say Owain.

'A Jameson – with a dash of lemonade please.'

'Who's your friend then, Ed? Not seen him here before. Local?' Evidently the barmaid was nosy.

'Well sort of... a relative... second cousin... lives near London now,' Ed lied.

'Oh, I see. Sais bach, is he?'

I'd had a chat with Ed in the car on the way down and we decided that we would pursue the same policy as we'd done with the shearers. I would speak as little as possible, and not in Welsh because my north Wales accent would give me away. Ed talked to the barmaid, who every now and then would glance in my direction.

'He's a quiet one, isn't he? What's the matter love, lost your tongue?' She was goading me.

Ed saved the day again.'He's been working in the fields all day and he's tired.'

We'd been there for a couple of hours when a tall, well built man walked in, suited, colourful tie, well-groomed. He ordered a scotch and soda and then turned towards us. '*Shwmae*, Ed... how's things... getting that farm of yours into shape yet?'

'*Shwmae, John bachan*... aye, it's coming along. Hard graft, mind, but as they say, Rome wasn't built in a day now was it?'

There was something about this stranger that made me feel uneasy. True, Ed seemed to know him, but...???

While they chatted, I pretended to be immersed in the *Western Mail* crossword, but somehow I felt that this well-dressed newcomer was eyeing me with more than a passing interest.

'Half past ten – last orders.' We quickly downed our drinks and left.

In the fresh air, I felt slightly giddy and realised I hadn't done much drinking recently, It was of course pre-breathalyser days; with today's more stringent laws Ed would have been doomed. As we drove home, Ed stunned me by revealing that 'John' was a detective inspector attached to Special Branch and one of the leading figures in the hunt for saboteurs and nationalist activists – which meant he was assigned to the squad looking for me!

Then and there, despite Ed's protestations, I decided I would have to leave as quickly as possible. I had been instructed that there was a farmer living less than a mile away who had volunteered to offer me shelter should Ed's farm come under suspicion. His name was Merfyn and we'd already met. But I couldn't leave Wales again until I'd met up with a new solicitor – Geoff Thomas. This had been arranged through intermediaries and paid for by well-known Welsh patriot and entrepreneur Trefor Morgan. Trefor had visited my parents' farm at Gwynus while I was in Ireland. He had outlined plans for my defence which included hiring the services of a private detective from the Denbigh area to investigate some shady and improper activities by certain members of the police and Special Branch.

Two days following our visit to the pub, I was driven by Merfyn to a remote area outside Ammanford in Dyfed. I was taken to the car park of an isolated pub on the foothills of a bleak mountain range. Waiting for me in a small white saloon were Trefor Morgan and Geoff Thomas, the solicitor. We warmly shook hands before going into the detail of what lay ahead. It was obvious from the start that Geoff Thomas knew exactly what he was dealing with and I went through all aspects of the case as he vigorously scribbled every detail down in a notebook. I was told that an extra few weeks were required so as to gather enough evidence to counteract what the police were striving to claim. The wily solicitor warned me that if I were to be arrested at this stage I would face at least ten years' imprisonment – and he needed time in order to build my case and secure a not guilty verdict.

Early next morning, Ed drove me from the farm – after I had said an emotional farewell to his wife Gwen, who vowed they would name their unborn baby Owain in my honour. I was deeply touched. I was dropped off outside Cardiff and caught a bus heading towards Bristol. After debating the pros and cons of several airports, I decided that Bristol would be the best choice for a flight back to Cork city.

Since I had a few hours to spare before catching my plane, I opted to do a little sightseeing once I crossed over into England. The West Country was unknown territory to me, most villages and towns being until now just spots on a map. For some reason, Clevedon held a fascination for me. Maybe it was the name or maybe I had heard somewhere of its famous suspension footbridge, which I wanted to see. The town was quaint and very English, with a small quiet tavern in the suburbs. The public bar had a very low ceiling. It was completely dark inside and apart from myself there were two elderly gentlemen drinking the rough cider. The barman asked me, 'What'll it be, sir?' in as broad a West Country accent as one would ever hear.

Eyeing the trembling old man alongside, I said 'A pint of rough cider please.'

The old fellow put his tankard down and croaked: 'And believe me, son, it is bloody rough today!'

So that was that, another hour spent idling away the time until I had to catch a bus to Bristol, then the airport. I went out to sit on a park bench, re-reading the newspaper. Time dragged. Searching in my pockets, I found a rather battered packet of cheese and onion crisps and ate them as slowly as it was reasonably possible. God, I thought, what people will do to try and pass the time!

Tension was building up and my stomach was beginning to churn – but not because of the rough cider and crisps!! I took my place in the bus queue. Once the city bus arrived everyone scrambled on board. I was the last and as there were no vacant seats I hung on tenaciously to the grab rail above as the vehicle sped erratically, veering from side to side along a narrow road. By the time we arrived at the city centre my right arm was aching from the effect of being half-suspended through the journey. I grabbed my rucksack and set out to get the bus to the airport.

For some reason I felt more conspicuous in the busy city streets than in a small town. Subconsciously I found myself glancing over my shoulder at almost every street corner, or even worse, stopping in shop windows to stare at the reflections of passers-by. Putting my hand on my brow, I felt the sweat gathering and running down my cheeks; I thought, 'Williams! No, no, no, McBryde... get a grip or you'll blow it!'

Instinctively my pace quickened as I entered what seemed to be the city's busiest shopping streets. Side-stepping and making my way with a deftness that would surely be the envy of any would-be Welsh fly-half, I eventually found the airport coach stop. I took my place in the queue, noting that amongst the couples there was a rather forlorn-looking single female. She was peering at the timetable over large rimless spectacles – she looked foreign. Edging nearer as she backed away from the notice board, I 'accidentally' bumped into her.

'Oh please forgive me, I'm terribly sorry... Ma'am !' I gulped.

'No, no, eets alright,' she said haltingly in a strong Dutch accent. She had a large travelling bag and a suitcase labelled 'Aer Lingus, Cork.'

I asked casually where she was going and when she replied 'Cork!' I explained that I too was heading in that direction.

'Oh, that iss gutt!' explaining she was travelling alone and she was a student going to Ireland as a nanny over the summer holidays. I breathed a sigh of relief. If I stuck with her, I would be carrying the large travelling holdall as well as my rucksack – the bag-carrying lark was beginning to get monotonous! But hopefully we'd pass through security as a 'couple', much less conspicuously than going solo. Soon I knew most of her family history; her name was Sonja and she was twenty-one years old, studying politics and Celtic history, hence her choice of Ireland for a summer job. She turned out to be a most pleasant, attractive young woman – once she removed her glasses.

Who was I? Well I was Phil McBryde who was doing a tour of Ireland. I thought, 'This is brilliant. I'll just fly through that fucking airport, I feel it!' As it happened my passage though that airport was so easy, just chatting to Sonja – that is when I had a chance as she rambled on non-stop. I couldn't understand half of what she was saying so I just nodded and smiled, occasionally chipping in with a 'yeah,' or 'No!' or 'A-hah!' and it seemed to work. Then we were up in the air and heading for Cork. We had scarcely left Bristol when the captain's voice announced that there was to be an unscheduled stop in Cardiff Airport. Had information filtered through that there was a fugitive on board? When the plane touched down at Cardiff, would I be arrested? Sonja was trying to say something while my head was in overdrive trying to fathom the ins and outs; she repeated: 'Why we go to Kaa... diff?'

Trying to be cool, I said, 'Probably a minor matter... perhaps they have to pick up some bigwig at a moment's notice.'

She looked perplexed. 'Beek week?'

I told her it would be only a minor delay, but by now my stomach mustles were tightening as I imagined all sorts of scenarios. Ten minutes later we were losing height as the pilot began preparing to land. Once we had landed, we were told to remain in our seats and were grounded for almost half and hour. I waited with bated breath as the clock moved ever so slowly. Sonja chatted away as before, but I could not act normally as the stress and fear of the unknown played havoc with my nerves.

Eventually the doors opened and after what seemed to be an eternity, a solitary figure wearing a long grey scarf wound round his neck entered. I breathed a sigh of relief. The plane hadn't been stormed by gun-toting police after all!! Strange to say, I never got to know the reason for the unscheduled stop or the identity of the extra passenger.

Sonja proved a very valuable asset since we got through Cork airport without any complications or hassles. Once out of the terminal, I found her a taxi, she left me an address and a contact telephone number, and we said goodbye.

15

Back in Ireland

I MADE MY way to the nearest phone kiosk and rang Catherine at the hotel in Kinsale. She seemed pleased to hear my voice and we arranged to meet later that evening after she finished work, which would be almost midnight since she was on the late night shift.

I slung the rucksack on my back and headed for Kinsale. The road network in South County Cork left a lot to be desired. Most of the way it was grass verges and loose gravel. I was half blinded by undimmed car headlights. Stumbling along, one hand raised to shield my eyes from the glare, I could swear that many vehicles were just inches away. It was several miles to my destination and the chances of my having a lift were pretty slim. Just as I was starting to think I would have to leg it all the way. I spotted a parked car at a make-do lay-by. As I approached, a figure emerged from the shadows, zipping up his flies hurriedly.

'Excuse me, you going towards Kinsale by any chance?'

He looked me up and down and then said, 'Yeah, ok, hop in.'

Although there were only three or four miles to go, I was relieved, since my whole body was aching after spending the day travelling with the cumbersome rucksack strapped to my back.

Kinsale was a fairly busy seaside resort and far from dead when I arrived late at night. Most bars were still open and loud juke box music could be heard through the open doors of a couple of cafes. Catherine wouldn't be finishing her shift at the hotel until midnight so I went to the Blue Shark, a small cosy bar that I knew, and ordered a strong coffee. Bearing in mind the enormous stress I had been through during the past few weeks, I felt quite relaxed, and released from the habit of looking over my shoulder at intervals. I was back in Ireland, more or less free to move wherever I wished without fear of being recognised and hunted down – that was a welcome change.

As I sipped my coffee and considered all the recent events, from the corner of my eye, I noticed a face that seemed strangely familiar. Racking my brains, I shut my eyes as images from the not too distant past flashed across my mind. BINGO! I knew that face. Before I left Ireland for Wales, I had noticed this character in this very bar! He had been sitting at a bar stool with a copy of *The Times* in front of him, diligently solving the crossword – not *The Irish Times* but the English version. He was middle aged, slightly rotund, greying and had rimless glasses drooping on the bridge of his Roman nose. Since I'd been on the run, scanning, surveying and recalling faces had become an instinct. I'd become particularly sensitive to anyone who, for whatever reason, came across as being 'different.' This particular man had occupied a seat bang in the centre of the bar. There was a long mirror stretching the whole length of the bar and he was able to observe anyone who entered or left the premises. I'd had a feeling then that his eyes were observing me via this mirror, but as my eyes came into contact with his, he'd quickly returned to his crossword.

Deciding to test if my memory was correct and to see how he would react, I got up from where I was sitting and walked directly behind his seat on my way to the bar. I deliberately turned my back on him and ordered a single shot of Bushmills whiskey. The bar maid apologized. 'Sorry, we're out of Bushmills. Would a Jameson do?'

'That'll be fine,' I replied, glancing sideways into the mirror. Sure as hell *The Times* crossword man's shifty eyes were glued on me. My brain clicked into overdrive – I was being watched!

I returned to the seat I'd previously occupied. Who the hell was he? Special Branch, MI5, MI6? There were several English residents as well as holiday makers in Southern Ireland at that time. But this specimen didn't 'fit'. He had none of the trappings or trademarks of the maritime fraternity, the yachting cap and plimsoll brigade who frequented the watering holes of this quaint harbour town. He was overdressed, in a suit and tie, wearing brogues.

A gentle tap on the back of the head brought me back to reality. Catherine had finished work a few minutes early...

'God, you were really miles away then... what's on your mind now – or are you not telling me?'

'Oh, nothing – just thinking about back home, that's all.'

'Oh yeah? Sure it's not one of those Welsh chicks you saw over there?'

'C'mon! You're not jealous, are you?'

'No, but if you were seeing someone else I'd like you to tell me just the same!'

We left the bar. The mystery man was still observing me via the mirror as we stepped outside.

I walked quickly away. Catherine had to half-trot to keep up.

'Jaysus, what's the hurry?'

I wanted to get round the street corner before Mr Mystery could come out of the bar to see which direction we were taking.

Catherine was no fool. 'What the fuck is going on? Is someone following you or am I being paranoid?'

'No, no, I felt a bit chilly, not wearing a jacket. Trying to warm up, that's all!'

'Don't you worry about that – I'll soon have you warmed up when we get inside that tent,' she laughed.

The camp site was dark but my tent was outlined by the flames from the next pitch's barbeque. Catherine had thoughtfully brought a bottle of wine, some buttered rolls and a block of Irish cheddar. It tasted better than a slap-up meal in a top restaurant. As we ate and drank, she broached the subject of my true identity. I found myself embarrassed and guilty for not being able to tell her who I really was. I still felt vulnerable and could not fully trust anyone, not even her, with all the details.

'Look,' I started,' I'll get round to it, eventually... it's just bloody difficult at the moment...'

She cut across me. 'Listen, Phil, I don't want to press you... if you can't trust me enough, that's fine – but it's very hard for me to deal with. I mean, you could be an escaped robber or even a fucking murderer, for God's sake!'

'It's not that that I don't trust you,' I lied, 'but I need time and besides – I don't want to involve you too much!'

'For crying out loud, whoever you are, whatever you've done... I'm with you NOW! You can trust me!'

Although I'd only just crossed back to Ireland, I knew that when I got a message from my solicitor, I would have to leave again. So I told her I'd have to go back to Wales in a few weeks. This only made her more confused and insecure. Out of the blue she asked 'Can I come with you next time?'

I was lost for words. 'Hold on, now, I don't think that's a very smart idea... you know I could get arrested and where would that leave you?' I stammered.

'I don't frigging care, don't worry, I'd make my way around. Please,' she pleaded.

'I don't know... I'll have to give it some thought, OK? It's... a pretty serious step, you know.'

Eventually, after a spell of emotional and physical cuddling. I fell into an uneasy sleep.

Over the next few days, I kept more or less to the same routine, though I tended to frequent the Blue Shark bar less often. There was a payphone there which I had once used to ring a friend in a telephone kiosk in Wales. Could there be a bug on this number? And worse, had my last call been intercepted? About a week afterwards, I decided to visit it late in the evening. Sure enough, there he was, apparently glued to the same bar stool which gave him a clear view of who came and went via the long mirror. I brushed past his seat on my way to the bar, ordering my usual Bushmills. Again I glanced at the mirror – no mistake, over his rimless specs his darting eyes were working overtime. I found myself a seat where I could observe him. No sooner was I seated than he got up and made his way to the small recess where the payphone was. Although his back was turned I could tell by his movements that he was dialling a number. For a split second he glanced over his shoulder in my direction, before swiftly turning back to the phone. My heart sank. This was not my imagination playing up. This man was British Intelligence and I was being tailed.

Many things went through my mind at that moment. What was the game plan? Were they intending to watch me low key in Ireland to see if I would make a move to cross back home?

Was it paranoia on my part to think a hit squad would target me on Irish soil? If they wanted to eliminate me, my staying in a tent at an isolated spot would give them an ideal opportunity.

The more I thought about this, the more anxious I became. If MI5 or whoever knew of my whereabouts in Ireland, then there would be others watching me, not just the Mystery Man at the Blue Shark. Who had he been phoning? Panic began to creep in. I was so vulnerable right now. I began to sweat. I had to be more vigilant! I had to make sure no-one found out about my tent!

Following his phone call, Mystery Man went to the wash rooms. It was my cue to disappear – fast. Leaving my glass of Bushmills hardly touched – ah, such sacrifices – I legged it and vanished round the first corner, my heart throbbing uncontrollably. What the fuck to do next? The bastard had me in a right panic. I would have to sort myself out and try to bring some calm into the situation. But how?

Aware that Catherine was intent on coming to meet me at the Blue Shark, somehow I needed to tell her there had been a change of plan. Either I could lie low for another half hour and meet her on the road or I could go to the Trident Hotel, where she worked and risk leading whoever was following me to her. I decided on the first option. I walked down a poorly lit street and found a bench in a small park. It was the longest half hour of my life. I checked my watch every three or four minutes. When I finally met her, I had to 'come clean'.

I explained I was a member of a Welsh underground movement and I had been linked to acts of sabotage and all kinds of conspiracies. I told her I'd been involved in sabotaging the Tryweryn dam and had served a prison sentence, which made me a prime suspect for pre-investiture nationalist activities. I did not tell her my real name. I decided to stick to Phil McBryde for the simple reason that if she were to be caught, she could say she had no idea who I was. Therefore it would be hard for any authority to charge her with conspiracy to aid a fugitive from justice. If I were to be completely truthful, however hard I tried, I still couldn't bring myself to tell her the full 100 per cent – a small margin kept me away from total trust.

Over the next few days, we developed a routine of never meeting in public and taking long detours when returning to the tent. I steered clear of the Blue Shark and the Mystery Man. What worried me most was that he had already alerted others within whichever organisation he worked for. Although I had decided against carrying my revolver with me to town since my return from Wales, I now changed my mind and took it with me everywhere, hidden in an inside jacket pocket. Some will accuse me of over-reacting, but at that time and in that situation I couldn't take chances. If it was a case of them or me, it certainly wasn't going to be me!

The time had come for me to contact a go-between in Wales. This entailed finding a coin phone box and ringing a pre-arranged call box at home. It had been agreed we would speak on the second Sunday following my return to Ireland at exactly seven o'clock in the evening.

Making sure I wasn't being followed, I took a bus to Cork

City and carefully made my way to Patrick Street. The cathedral clock struck seven as I walked into a kiosk and dialled a number. A female voice answered,' What's the weather like in County Cork?'

'It's getting very, very warm – in fact it's hot!' I replied.

'OK!' said the female voice, 'Just be careful you don't get burnt!', which meant that she had understood my coded message that someone was closing in on me.

'Can you make it to the wedding next Thursday? After all, you're supposed to be the best man! It's at two o'clock, same church as last time,' she added.

'I'll be there,' I said and hung up. There was no wedding or best man and the church was to be the railway station at Wrexham.

On the bus back to Kinsale my mind was in turmoil. The message meant I was needed back home as my solicitor was now in a position to finalise my defence argument. This excited me, but there was the risk and stress of trying to cross again to Wales less than two weeks after returning. Once back in Kinsale I made my way to McGuire's, a quaint old waterfront bar. Ordering a strong coffee, I sat facing the door, pretending to read a copy of the *Cork Examiner* that I'd bought in the city. I'd have to tell Catherine that evening. Sitting alone, as I had been doing for the last couple of weeks, there was too much time to think. I was very apprehensive about the fourth journey home. I considered the options – train to Dublin, ferry to Liverpool? Fly from Dublin? Fly from Cork to Birmingham? Taking the Rosslare to Fishguard ferry would be suicidal, since both harbours would be teeming with Special Branch.

I made my decision. I would risk flying from Cork to Birmingham and be damned. My picture had been widely circulated for several months, featuring in a prominent spot in the *Police Gazette*.

Catherine arrived bang on time. I watched her approach from a hidden position. She walked briskly, turning her head occasionally to glance over her shoulder. Ah well, she was learning to be careful! This was not the right moment to tell her about the need to journey back to Wales. I saw she had a bottle of Jameson's in her bag; maybe a few swigs later I'd have enough courage to break the news. We ate a pizza, sat outside the tent to watch the sunset and opened the bottle. Briefly escaping from reality, I relaxed a little. But there was no getting away from the undercurrent of insecurity and doubt. Finally Catherine said to me, 'Phil, I can sense that something's happened today. Since this morning you've been acting differently. What in hell's going on?'

This was it. She had to be told. 'Well... I've had some news. My solicitor wants to see me again... urgently. He's come up with some good news but I have to sit down with him to check that every detail is correct. He needs to make my case as watertight as possible, so I have to cross over to Wales again... some way or another, and that means next week...'

'What? You mean you're leaving in the next few days? Just like that? And where do I fit in?' I'd never seen Catherine lose her temper or even get angry... but she was – and she was hurt.

Before I could say anything, she said, 'Right, Phil, this time I'm coming with you. Christ, I care for you and I need to be with you and see this through! Can you not understand that?' She spoke with passion and I know she meant every word.

'Whatever, OK,' I replied, 'But remember, it could be dangerous for you as well.'

Her reaction took me by surprise. She flung herself at me and kissed me passionately. My unruly beard usually made her skin break out in a rash. Passion and drink made me agree to shave my beard off then and there! This momentary lapse was enough to strip me of my strongest disguise. On the other hand we had one hell of a night!

It was well into next morning when I realised the extent of my folly. I didn't blame Catherine because I was old enough to know better. I felt naked. Once my head had cleared, I realised that on no account could I be seen in town – the Mystery Man should not become aware that I was now beardless.

We decided that I'd confine myself to the area near the tent and the old fort and beach. Catherine would bring food and other provisions when she returned from work in the evening. I managed to book plane reservations for both of us using a nearby telephone kiosk and Catherine went into Cork to pay for the tickets. As we made our plans, we decided to leave the tent in its well-hidden location where I also buried some items I wouldn't be taking with me – the revolver, which I buried in a wooden box, a transistor radio, binoculars and a wooden cross I'd been given by a female friend for luck.

Our last night in the tent was Wednesday and Catherine arrived breathless and excited. I'd asked her to check if the Mystery Man was still around. She had indeed taken a peep in the bar and had seen him sat on the same stool as usual. 'Sure he's a creepy looking bastard. I think he's glued to that fucking stool,' she blurted, taking a swig from a can of lager.

'You sure you weren't followed?' I was nervous. She cut across me, hurt. 'Holy mother, what do you take me for? I'm not bloody stupid! I doubled back a couple of times, just like you showed me!'

'OK, calm down. Come here, give me a hug.' I approached her with open arms. She smiled and wrapped her arms around my neck, holding me tight. 'I'm getting really fond of you, Phil... but I'm not sure how much I mean to you.'

God, the last thing I needed right now was to get emotionally tied at such an insecure time in my life. Tomorrow I could be captured, who knows – or even dead!

'Listen Catherine, I think the world of you. I love being in your company and I appreciate your kindness and all the help you've given me. But at this time I can't promise any commitments. It wouldn't be fair on you... after all I'm on the run and my future, if any, is pretty dicey!'

Listening intently to every word, her smile vanished. That was the trouble, one moment her face glowed, her eyes would sparkle and the next, she'd sink into a bottomless pit of despair.

We were up early the next day after an almost sleepless night. A flock of wild geese flew high above and a curlew's call broke the morning silence. Although I was trying to hide the tension that gripped my stomach muscles, Catherine, on the other hand, was as excited as a child waiting to embark on a Sunday school trip, rather than an insecure clandestine excursion into the unknown. Once we were satisfied that the remaining belongings were stacked away and the tent zipped up and padlocked, off we went. Catherine carried a small shoulder bag and I had my well-worn rucksack. We gave the town of Kinsale a miss and followed a small footpath that took us to the Cork city road beyond the town. Once we arrived in the city centre, we had time for coffee and toast before catching the airport bus. Conversation had worn a bit thin; my stomach was churning and my mind was busy elsewhere. Even Catherine's chatter fell on deaf ears. I could also feel a headache developing.

I had a gut instinct that something would go wrong. At the back of my mind was an image of the Mystery Man, etched deep and everlasting. The airport bus wasn't very full – a German couple, a loud Irish-American, a couple of girls on their way to England to find work... But Catherine was still thrilled at the prospect of flying out of Ireland. Despite my earlier concerns about having her with me, I began to be glad of her company, as without her it would have been even more of a nightmare. Entering the airport departure building was not easy. I cursed myself for the stupidity of shaving off my beard. Surely I'd stick out like a sore thumb? Up until now, I had been positive, confident and composed but now, it was a different ball game. My hand felt sweaty as we walked towards the departure desk. Despite a short pause as an official thumbed through our passports, we were handed our boarding passes. Since we only had hand luggage, there wasn't the hassle of weighing and labelling any bulk and there would be no wait at luggage control on the other side.

The flight to Birmingham was scheduled to leave at 10.00 am and was to arrive about an hour later. Once we were settled in our seats, I couldn't see anything to arouse my suspicious mind. As we took off, I knew it was far too early for a sigh of relief as this was only the first stage. The next stage would be trickier and riskier. I was not a wanted man on the Irish side, but the English side would be an entirely different matter. A pleasant stewardess served us coffee, biscuits and small packs of Irish Cheddar cheese halfway through the flight. Despite Catherine's protestations, I had insisted we consume no alcohol. I needed my faculties in running order.

My ears buzzed as the noisy engines roared and we landed rather bumpily at Birmingham airport. My heart raced. What would await us when the doors opened?

16

Arrest Again, and Trial

EVEN AS THE Air Lingus jet swayed to an unsteady halt, out of the corner of my eye, I noticed the chief stewardess pick up a phone. A brief exchange of words followed before she replaced the receiver. One might say that was quite a normal procedure when a plane arrives at its destination. That may well be so, but what raised my suspicions was the fact that, as she replaced the receiver, her head turned and she gazed directly at where I was sitting. Since I was continually on my guard because of my situation, this incident served to set my pulse racing. Had someone from airport security been made aware there was a wanted fugitive on board? Could they then have radioed the cabin crew who in turn had alerted the stewardess? Was I just being too suspicious and paranoid? Maybe, just maybe, it was purely coincidental that she looked in my direction?

My naïve thinking on the last point was immediately scuppered when the stewardess calmly announced that certain rows of seats were to disembark first. Surely there couldn't be another coincidence in the fact that our seats were amongst the few that were announced. Not for the first time that day, my heart sank.

'Something's not right here...!' I whispered in Catherine's ear. Naturally she was quite unaware of any irregularity for the simple reason she wasn't looking for any. Sensing danger, I carefully removed a crumpled and well-thumbed notebook from an inner jacket pocket and pressed it into Catherine's hand, whispering again 'Stick that up your jumper... Keep it safe!' I nodded in the direction of her already well-stocked bra.

For one moment I thought her eyes would pop out of their sockets... 'Jayeessssus... what the hell is it?' Keeping my voice to a whisper I told her it was a little address book, but it was all in a code that only I understood. Basically, it contained several telephone kiosk numbers across Wales and some in Ireland, plus a few addresses. Slowly, we moved towards the exit, a nervous Catherine sticking close to me. A quick calculation revealed there were fewer than two dozen on their feet heading in the same direction. Following what seemed to be an eternity, the exit door opened and we filed out in a ragged queue.

I made sure we were bang in the middle for obvious reasons. So as not to cause any unwanted delays, we had all the documents to hand, passports etc. I knew there would be some form of check, but I still hoped that would be purely routine. As we rounded a corner with the customs counter in view, we noticed several uniformed police officers standing in a row. Had I had any hopes previously about walking through undetected, they soon vanished. I had walked into a trap.

Suddenly we were right at the front of what had been a queue. For some mysterious reason, the rest had been 'delayed' behind us. There was no way of getting out of this one, so, putting on a brave face, we strode up to the customs desk to be met by a sullen plain clothes official who greeted us offhandedly, 'Anything to declare?'

I threw my rucksack onto the desk, Catherine doing likewise with her shoulder bag. The customs officer emptied Catherine's half-empty bag, which contained merely two toothbrushes, a half empty toothpaste tube, a bar of soap, two towels, some items of underwear and a short nightie. The official raised his eyebrows 'Hm, travelling light aren't we?' he half scoffed.

'Sure, we are just going to a conference...' she began, when a gruff voice cut across her.

'Yes, that's right, you're coming to a conference with us. Mr Williams, I presume... Owain Williams?'

I whirled around to see where the voice came from; it continued, 'I'm Detective Inspector so-and-so, and this is Detective Sergeant so-and-so... I have a warrant for your arrest!' Unceremoniously I was then flung against a wall, hands above my head, legs kicked apart as they frisked me for weapons or whatever.

Catherine stood gaping. 'What the fuck's going on?' She never received an answer.

As we were marched towards a side exit, our fellow passengers were kept waiting until we were well clear. There were two unmarked police cars waiting, engines running, with uniformed police officers in the driving seats. I was put in the back of one car, Catherine in the other. We were driven the few miles to Ladywood police station in the suburbs of Birmingham, where we were to be detained. Whenever two people are arrested, it is police policy to split them up and keep them completely separated, as this weakens their resolve and causes confusion, since one has no knowledge of what the other has told the police under questioning. Since I was wanted by the Gwynedd constabulary which covered north-west Wales, the Birmingham force had no real interest in me, apart for holding me in custody and waiting for the Welsh police to pick me up later. Catherine's case was different inasmuch as she was a citizen of the Irish Republic and not wanted for questioning. For that reason she was only cursorily searched, so my notebook was safe.

Once the mundane task of filling forms and routine questioning was over, I was put in a cell and the doors slammed. After what seemed hours, a uniformed constable brought me some lukewarm tea. When I enquired about Catherine's fate, I was greeted with silence and a blank stare. Luckily, before boarding the plane in Cork, anticipating the possibility of such a scenario, I had written down my parents' address and telephone number and told her should anything go awry, to travel by train to Wales and stay with them. Despite my appeals and concerns over her safety and whether she had been released or was still being held, I was totally ignored. As it happened, one of the Birmingham-based detectives had explained to me earlier that they had been given instructions by the Welsh police that I was NOT to be given any information, nor was I to be given a meal.

There followed one sleepless night at Ladywood Police Station before the Welsh 'cavalry' rode into town next day to collect me. Throughout the night I was in turmoil at the thought of facing a very long prison sentence, should I be found guilty at a later trial. What had become of Catherine? If she had been released, how would she cope in a strange country? What would she do once she arrived at the end of the line – Caernarfon station? Once off the train she would have to find the right bus route to take her towards my parents' farm, the snag being there were only a couple of services a day for the last three or four miles. On the other hand, Catherine had plenty of resolve and ingenuity and I assumed she would telephone my parents, and, most likely, my elder brother Morris would fetch her by car.

Because I was held in a police cell at Ladywood rather than being taken to a prison, it was uniformed police constables who brought over my breakfast next morning. The 'feast' arrived on a battered tin tray, two thin slices of stale bread, a cylindrical wafer-thin slice of an anaemic margarine plus a minute dollop of a watery substance posing as strawberry jam. Yes, by then I was hungry, but, not that bloody hungry! Oh for a slice of blackened toast coated with creamy Irish butter...

Heavy footsteps marching along the tiled corridors of the police station heralded the arrival of the Welsh entourage. Two detective inspectors, two detective sergeants and two or three detective constables had been assigned to escort me back to Wales. Since I had already crossed the path of most of these gentlemen in the past, their faces were familiar. For example, Det. Inspector Gwyn Owen had been merely a sergeant months earlier, when I had jumped bail. Ironically, DI Gwyn Owen had been involved with investigations during the Tryweryn dam campaign when he was merely a detective constable.

Three unmarked police cars were brought down to Birmingham to fetch me. Eventually I was placed in the back of one of these cars, handcuffed and seated between a constable and the other DI. I believe his surname was Vaughan. They were all Welsh speakers. When the small convoy eventually set off, there was one car in front of us and the other behind. I allowed myself a wry smile on reflecting that although I weighed just under eleven stone, and at a stretch reached five feet eight inches in height, they reckoned on sending seven men in three separate cars to escort me back! Actually it wasn't that simple; the truth was there was tremendous support, not only for me personally, but also for the campaign against the proposed investiture at Caernarfon castle, a mere ten months away. The authorities, including the government, took us seriously because there was genuine fear that my supporters would attempt to prevent me appearing in court. Primarily this was also the cause of such secrecy surrounding my capture, since the authorities did not want the public or media to know about it until a time of their own choosing.

As a matter of fact, although at the time I had no way of knowing, the press had been alerted by my mother. It was more than a day later I learned that Catherine had been released from Ladywood police station a few hours following our arrest. She had then taken a train to Caernarfon, travelled by bus to within a few miles of the farm before eventually arriving at my parents' house. Since my parents had no knowledge of Catherine's existence even, it was quite a shock when she landed on their doorstep and told them the news of my capture. My mother, well aware I could be in physical danger when on the run, had immediately rung a local BBC Wales reporter and told him what had happened. She believed, rightly, that once the press were aware of the story, then the chances of my having an 'accident' were pretty slim.

Of course, I was completely ignorant of all this as we cruised along the motorway in the direction of the Welsh border. Inside the car, the atmosphere was rather tense, hardly a word being spoken. I well recall when this silence was briefly broken when the DI who was handcuffed to me on my right suddenly spoke in Welsh.

'*Felly rwyt ti wedi penderfynu gwynebu be sy'n dy ddisgwyl?* So you've decided to face what's coming to you?' Funnily enough, he did repeat the question in English, which I found rather strange at the time. In fact, he repeated this question another three or four times.

Since I did not have a great deal of faith in this certain cop, I remember thinking out my reply carefully, saying simply, 'I didn't say that, you said it.' This I repeated each time he spoke.

Apart from this question, the only comment he made was, 'What have you been doing with yourself all this time?'

For that one I kept my reply short: 'Oh, just this and that,' which seemed to shut him up temporarily.

Crossing the border into Wales, off the A55 at Chirk, the convoy pulled up a narrow side street and parked behind what looked to be a small transport cafe. All of the officers stepped out of the vehicle and walked towards the cafe with the exception of one detective constable who remained with me in the car. It was at this stage that something strange occurred, that took me completely by surprise.

The DC said, 'This is between you and me, so don't mention it to anyone else...' He pulled out what seemed to be a small newsletter from his pocket. 'Could you autograph this for me?' he asked.

I was gobsmacked; it was a copy of the *Police Gazette* which circulated amongst all members of police forces throughout Britain and Northern Ireland. On one page, staring at me was a photo of myself, with the word WANTED in large letters!

Since it happened so quickly and unexpectedly, I was lost for words... not knowing whether to laugh or what. Surely he was taking the piss?

'You're not being serious?' I managed.

'Yes, I'm serious... you don't have to believe me, but there's a few like me in the force who admire you!'

Eventually I complied, although not quite sure of his motives. This certain detective was quite young, about my age and had been brought up locally. Pocketing the autographed copy he repeated, 'You won't mention this to anyone will you?' At which I smiled and reassured him. After all, I could do with friends at that time. Eventually, the others returned, bringing me a mug of tea, sugared... ah well, beggars can't be choosers!

Arriving at the wet and ancient walled citadel of Caernarfon, the convoy pulled up alongside the police station in the shadow of Edward I's massive castle. My heart skipped a beat as the back door flew open and I was led, still handcuffed, up the granite steps and into the Victorian interior. There was only one naked bulb hanging from the decaying ceiling as we entered. One of the officers flicked some switches and I was half blinded as a dozen lights came on simultaneously. The cop with whom I shared a bracelet half dragged me into a room, where the solitary figure of Detective Superintendent John Hughes, head of Gwynedd CID, sat at a table. There was no mistaking his pillar box red face and cropped snow white hair. He wore an immaculate grey pinstripe suit and his apparently permanent scowl had been replaced with an aura of smug self-satisfaction.

'*Aaah, Owain bach, croeso'n nol ata ni fachgan!*' (Welcome back to our midst lad! or words to that effect). He kept speaking Welsh: 'So, where have you been for so long? Led us a merry chase and wasted a lot of police time... Well, never mind... You must be hungry by now, so we've made provision and there's a nice dinner just arrived for you. Bet those English cops in Birmingham didn't feed you?'

No, you old bastard, you made sure of that by telling then

not to give me food! I thought to myself. No, definitely not, I'm not falling for that one!

A heaped plate of steaming roast dinner was placed on the table in front of me, beef, potatoes, cauliflower, carrots, gravy, the lot. 'What's the bastard up to?' I thought. 'Obviously trying to soften me up.'

'Tell you what, we'll leave the room now and let you eat your meal in peace, then we can have a little chat.'

At that they all walked out, closed the door, and left me with an old clock ticking loudly on the grey wall. Obviously suspicious of the cops' strange behaviour, I scanned the ceiling, the walls, even under the table for concealed microphones or even a camera, but could see nothing. The hot dinner stared at me... So what the hell, I ate it anyway! By now, of course, I was starving, so I grabbed the knife and fork and attacked the plate with gusto. No sooner had I finished than the tall figure of Superintendant Hughes reappeared through the doorway.

'I see you managed to polish it all off... Don't you worry, Owain bach, we'll look after you here,' he boomed. 'You see Owain, you help us and we'll help you...' he began.

'Now, where did I hear those words last?' I reminisced. 'Damn, right here in this same bloody station six months or more ago.' At this, he unclipped a brown attache case he had brought in with him and dug out a large file of documents.

Picking out two or three pages pinned together, he sat in a chair alongside me and said 'I'd like you to read these couple of pages and just sign here at the bottom.' He indicated with his finger. 'Take your time,' he added. While he talked two members of the CID stood, arms folded, one each side of the door.

Did the stupid idiots think I was going to try and 'leg it' – again?!

I pretended to read the printed material. It was basically a 'confession' on my part to the three original charges relating to possession and handling of explosives. Looking up from the document, I turned to him and said, 'You know I'm not signing that, it's a confession of something I didn't do!'

The false smile he had been wearing starting to fade and his whole attitude changed as he glared across the small table at me.

'All right, Williams, we've had enough playing games. If you don't want to cooperate then I can make it very difficult for you. Do you think we don't know where you've been for the past six months?' his voice raising with each sentence uttered.

'Damned right, you old bastard, you have no idea,' I thought to myself.

He continued, 'We can pin most of the jobs that took place after you jumped bail on you... and we know you've been plotting to take over Caernarfon Castle using guns...' he sounded menacing now as he thrust his crimson face in my direction: 'What's more, we have evidence that shows there is a clear link in all these incidents that have taken place. You'll be going down for a very long time when I'm through with you.'

Obviously aware that his 'softly softly' approach was not working, he was now reverting to threats and intimidation! The grilling continued well into the night; at times things got rather personal.

'I wonder what your little bit of skirt is up to now?' I was of course aware that they knew of Catherine's existence since the Birmingham lot had passed over all the details connected to my arrest. 'Won't be long till she finds some young randy buck... nothing you can do since you'll be doing fifteen to twenty years. She won't waste her time on you... nice bit of stuff, from what I hear,' he goaded. Previous experience had taught me the best policy was to ignore these comments. Of course I had become very fond of Catherine; after all, she had been my closest companion as well as friend and lover during the past few weeks. I wouldn't go as far as to say I was 'in love' with her – that would and can mean many, many things.

On a personal level, for what it's worth, I can truly state that I have been in love on several occasions. Whether 'love' is the correct word, I really don't know, to be honest. What I do know, at the time I sincerely believed it to be love. My very first love was the girl who became my first wife. I truly believed it was for eternity. A few years, later when it all blew apart, I genuinely thought it was the end of my world. At the time I had no desire to carry on living and contemplated ending it all. I was still in my twenties and we had three children. It took me a very long time to recover. I was deeply hurt and felt bitter at the time. Roughly one year later I decided to rejoin the human race and started to get out into the big world again.

Through my numerous contacts in the nationalist and republican movements, I met people from all corners of our nation of which a fair proportion were females, many of whom were young and attractive. Eventually, I believed I had married at too young an age, when I was not mature enough to handle responsibilities. Having drawn the above conclusions, I decided that I was not in a state of mind to take on another long-term or permanent relationship with any member of the fair sex – at least, not yet! This did not imply 'playing the field'… although it seemed like it at times! What it entailed was a series of passionate and sometimes deep relationships which would last for several months. I cared deeply for most of them. Unfortunately it would end up with suggestions, some veiled, about 'commitments' for the future etc. Now I quite understood this was a perfectly natural progression in any normal relationship, but the problem was, at this time (the mid 60s) I was dragged into the more militant republican nationalist cause as a kind of standard bearer, because of my actions and imprisonment.

17

Trial 1968

BACK AT THE police station in Caernarfon in 1968, Chief Inspector John Hughes was a tired and angry man. Despite the shouting, table-thumping, chair-kicking and threats, he had been left empty handed since I refused to sign any of the papers stuck under my nose. It must have been well past midnight when I was finally bundled into a cell. Ironically it was the very same cell that I had occupied almost eight months earlier when I was arrested in early January. Next morning I was hauled before the magistrates' court, since a person cannot be remanded to a prison without the rigmarole of a magistrate's hearing. When dawn finally broke, I was given a small breakfast which included the proverbial mug of lukewarm anaemic tea. By now my family were aware I was in custody at Caernarfon and my father and elder brother Morris came to visit me in my cell before the court hearing. Again it proved to be a difficult and even awkward reunion. My father was grave – and the pain in his eyes was visible. Ten minutes was all we were allowed during which I tried to put on a brave face saying I would win the case and would soon be home.

Geoff Thomas, my new solicitor, had been alerted and had travelled up from his Swansea chambers to interview me before the court met. Geoff was a charismatic man, early forties, of stocky build with greying short-cropped hair and a mischievous smile. He took me through all the formal procedures and informed me he was in touch with a well-known barrister called Andrew Rankin QC who had a reputation as a robust and even aggressive counsel.

213

Shortly before ten o'clock I was led into the court, where there were three magistrates, two men and a woman. It was all a formality that lasted less than ten minutes. They remanded me in custody for seven days. The remand prison turned out to be Risley near Warrington. Incidentally, Catherine, who was staying at my parents' farm, had travelled with my father and brother but was not allowed to see or speak to me. During the short hearing, I had turned my head around to see if she was there. Sure enough she sat amongst my family and small band of supporters at the rear of the court. She had smiled broadly, blown me a kiss and raised a defiant thumb.

Risley on the best of days was not Beverly Hills. On this certain day it looked even gloomier as its outline emerged through a thick fog. At least it was not new to me since I had been held here before jumping bail. Amongst a bevy of infamous occupants at this time was Myra Hindley, who, together with Ian Brady had carried out the horrible crimes which became known as the Moors Murders. Thankfully I only ever set my eyes on her once, at a prison church service on Sunday morning where males and females mixed for the half-hour service. Here I have a confession to make; I attended that particular service to get out of my cell for half an hour. Normally on a Sunday, I was not even taken out for the half-hour 'exercise' – due to staff shortages, or so I was told. During the nine or ten weeks I was held here, I was confined to my cell even during daytime, apart from weekdays for the 'exercise' stint.

Time dragged by ever so slowly. The regimented routine was boring and frustrating and my pending trial weighed heavily on my mind. Apart from the weekly journey to court in Caernarfon on Mondays, the only other break was when my lawyer, Geoff Thomas would visit me to discuss aspects of the case and also to dig for information concerning four of the witnesses we had lined up. Roughly four weeks following my arrest, a committal hearing was held at Caernarfon which lasted all day. It was at this hearing that the police prosecution outlined the case against me.

By then, the charges had been whittled down to three counts of possessing and handling 'explosive substances'. Their main witness was John Gwilym Jones from Anglesey, who I have referred to earlier; also Edward Wilkinson and Robert G. Jones from the Penygroes area near Caernarfon. These were the same three who had been arrested at the beginning of the year and had made the *Evening Standard* headlines. We were also informed that forensic evidence would be produced to prove I had handled explosive substances, traces of which had been 'found' in my father's car. Amongst the hearsay 'evidence' the police presented were 'statements' by one of the three that I was plotting to take over Caernarfon castle days before the investiture. Strangely enough, the latter was used for a story in the local weekly *Herald*, under a glaring headline: 'The Fantastic Mind of Owain Williams!'

At the end of the committal hearing, it was announced I would be sent for trial at the next Caernarfon Assizes. The case would open on November Ist and end on 5 November! Yes, you've got it, Guy Fawkes' day! Complete with Gunpowder Plot!

For some mysterious reason, the authorities kept refusing permission for me to be transferred to a Welsh prison, either Cardiff or Swansea. My lawyer, who lived in Swansea, argued that his journeys to Warrington placed a strain on him and disadvantaged me, since he could not see me as often as he wished. Finally, following weeks of campaigning, the authorities agreed I would be transferred, although they refused to reveal to where!

Early one morning I was rudely awoken before five o'clock, given minutes to gather my few belongings together and marched down to the reception area. A large white prison van appeared. I was bundled inside, handcuffed between two prison officers. Outside the prison gates, two police cars were deployed for 'escort' – one was ahead of the van and one at the rear. In addition to the two prison officers who shared a 'bracelet' with me, two more sat in the back of the van, with another two at the front. The police car in front contained two police officers, as did the one behind. In all, ten men had been deployed to 'escort' me to wherever I was being taken. We sped along the motorway heading south at speed, sometimes with blue lights flashing and sirens blaring. Despite my enquiring several times, 'Where are you taking me?' I was met with blank expressions and silence.

At one point I was starting to get worried, until one of the officers finally answered, 'We have no idea, mate, it's a mystery to us as well!'

Shortly after, a message came over the police radio saying I was being taken to Tewkesbury police station. Since I had never heard of Tewkesbury before, never mind knowing where it was, I wasn't much the wiser. What I did deduce was that on arrival at Tewkesbury, a message would be radioed or telephoned from the Home Office stating which prison I was being transferred to. Well, I thought, they are taking me seriously at least, or why resort to such cloak and dagger tactics? In fact, later that day I learnt that the Home Office, after consultations with Special Branch, had come to a decision. Whether their intelligence-gathering was factual or reliable, I have no way of telling, but apparently they believed an attempt would be made to hijack the prison van carrying me by militant nationalists who opposed the investiture. That revelation went some way in explaining the covert nature of the operation to transport me from one part of England to another.

It was Geoff Thomas, my solicitor, who explained to me a few days later how he had bombarded the authorities to have me transferred to a Welsh prison, which would be nearer to his offices in Swansea. As a matter of fact, when instructions from the Home Office eventually reached Tewkesbury police station, it was specified that I was to be driven to Bristol prison, which I then was.

Even the dumbest student of geography would tell you Bristol is not in Wales! However, from Swansea to Bristol was a helluva lot easier than to Shrewsbury or Risley. When Geoff

216

Thomas eventually arrived at Bristol to discuss the forthcoming court case, he said that the Home Office had insisted I was not to be transferred to either Swansea or Cardiff prisons. They feared demonstrations would be held outside either of these prisons. I fully realise that these revelations have never before been made public. Since Geoff Thomas sadly died a few years ago, he is not here to confirm the above. The whole truth lies somewhere in secret files at the Home Office or some other records office and whether they will ever be released is another matter. Since I have never spoken about these incidents in public before, the news does demonstrate that the intelligence services – all the way up to the Home Office – took us seriously. Against all expectations, a small dedicated group of patriots had taken on the might of the British state and forced them to employ thousands upon thousands of police, intelligence services and even the military itself at a cost of millions.

During his second visit to see me at Bristol, Geoff told me a little more about the pending Assizes court. A member of a well-known Welsh academic family had been plucked out of semi-retirement to head the prosecution. Alun Talfan Davies QC was well entrenched in the Welsh hierarchy and intelligentsia where respectability was, and is, paramount; Geoff Thomas' task was to gather as much information as possible to 'feed' Andrew Rankin QC, my barrister.

Although I have explained that Bristol was more accessible for my legal needs, it was on the other hand very remote from my family and most of my friends. During my time in that most Victorian of prisons, I received just one visit from home. I well recall the day that my second eldest brother John drove all the way down from Llŷn to see me. John never was what you would call a globetrotter. He always preferred to live in his 'square mile,' so it was a pleasant surprise when he arrived unexpectedly one weekend. My mother had sent a change of clothing and a couple of items I had asked for. Since I had not had an opportunity to speak my native tongue for some weeks, it was most welcome to speak with him in Welsh. There wasn't much news from home; he told me my parents were coping and my two eldest children Iona and Gruff seemed to be managing and visited my parents at weekends.

We didn't see eye to eye on many subjects, because John was not into politics or current affairs. His life revolved around farming and rural matters, with the little village chapel at Pistyll very high on his agenda. Despite apathy and lack of support, despite the peeling paint and dwindling congregation, the chapel doors were still open, and for that thanks were due mainly to John and his wife's efforts, plus two or three other individuals. (Sadly, the doors closed for the last time three or four years ago.) As I said, we had our differences, but we were still brothers and blood is thicker than water! In a flash, his visit was over and I was marched back to my cell and the metal door slammed shut.

Because of my political situation I was more or less in complete isolation throughout my comparatively short stay at Bristol prison. My solicitor paid me one final visit to ensure he had every scrap of detail essential to fight my corner. There was one worrying factor. The prosecution had come up with allegations that evidence of an 'explosive substance' had been found in my father's Vauxhall car. According to their 'evidence', swabs on several parts of the car had tested positive for nitro-glycerine which is the key component of gelignite. Since I was absolutely sure I had never carried explosives in that particular car, it was rather obvious that 'some person or persons' had found a way of planting the damning evidence on it. For instance, they alleged traces were found on all the door handles and window controls, on the handle of the boot as well as on the steering wheel, gear lever, light switch – but strangely enough there was none on the indicator switch!

This actually caused a dilemma for my defence team. If the prosecution came up with 'evidence' about the nitro-glycerine traces, it would be futile for us to say 'No, it's not true,' since who would believe us against the police and forensics? During the rest of my time on remand I got hold of all kinds of books dealing with nitro-glycerine, nitric acid and so on. I researched items that would show traces of the same substances and the results were quite revealing. I had known all along that certain artificial fertilizers contained nitric acid, but now I discovered that cellulose paint used to spray cars could show positive in tests for nitro-glycerine. Luckily for me, my father's car had one of its doors sprayed after a minor accident a few weeks prior to the car being confiscated by police. By another stroke of luck, the garage owner was well known to my family and he provided the receipt showing that he had actually sprayed the car. What my defence was looking for was just enough evidence to show that the forensic swabs could be flawed and there was an element of doubt as to the origins of these 'traces'.

Although my scientific knowledge is pretty limited to say the least, through my studying this particular subject I got to learn that traces of nitric substance in cellulose paint used for spraying cars etc, would show for a matter of days, rather than weeks. So, in order to show that the car had been sprayed but a few days before the police's forensic tests, the date on the receipt was brought forward a couple of weeks or so. It is up to the reader to form his own conclusions as to the ethics of that little bit of 'biro juggling'. After all, whoever planted the traces of explosives on my father's car surely had a helluva lot more to answer for!

Little by little, my defence case was gaining more and more information. We succeeded in getting hold of one of the three originally charged with handling the explosives. Robert Gruffudd Jones had been an acquaintance of mine for some time. Robin, as we called him, was quite a character. Having spent most of his life as a lorry driver employed locally, he lived not far from Penygroes, which is some six or seven miles from Caernarfon. Although the prosecution had tried to have Robin testify against me, he had flatly refused. Instead he had come forward voluntarily to be a witness for me. Of the other two involved, Eddie Wilkinson and John Gwilym Jones, the latter had decided to turn 'Queen's Evidence' and therefore was exempt from prosecution. There was general concern amongst my defence team that his evidence could be damning. Later at the actual trial in November, all three were called to give evidence, but it was only John Gwilym Jones' testimony that sided with the prosecution. It was crucial therefore that the forensic 'evidence' produced by the police prosecution was scientifically challenged and proved to be unreliable. If the prosecution were able to call on a witness testifying on oath that he had seen me handling the explosives, together with so-called 'forensic evidence' to substantiate that claim, it would have meant curtains for me.

The opening day of my trial arrived: the first day of November 1968. A large crowd had gathered outside the Assizes court in Caernarfon, as well as around the castle walls nearby, while inside the court itself was packed with my supporters. Amongst the crowd were my father and elder brother. Catherine had travelled up from London, where she had found a job at the Hilton. During the case she stayed at my parent's farm, as did a dozen or so of my loyal supporters, mainly from south-east and mid Wales. Before being escorted to the dock, I had one final visit from Geoff Thomas, my lawyer, together with my senior barrister, Andrew Rankin QC, whom I met for the first time. We went over the case in detail. My defence had a list of the prosecution's witnesses, plus certain details of what their evidence comprised. Andrew Rankin was meticulous, with a sharp mind and a loud booming voice. He was twice my size, at over twenty stone in comparison to my eleven! Bearing this in mind it was no overstatement when he was described as a heavyweight, both physically as well as in the legal profession.

The hearing opened and the charges were read, to which I pleaded NOT GUILTY. Following all the formalities, it was time for the prosecution's senior barrister to make his opening speech. Alun Talfan Davies QC was a well-known figure in the legal circuits in Wales. He was, from the start, intent on portraying me as a most dangerous terrorist. Opposition to the forthcoming investiture at Caernarfon Castle, less than a stone's throw away, was prominent in his address to the jury members. Although the three original charges of possessing explosives had been whittled down to one single count, it was still pretty serious stuff. There was no mistaking the line he was taking, which was to convince the jury that I was the instigator of much of the campaign that had been taking place. It was asserted that I was involved in the plot to take over Caernarfon castle, days before the investiture.

The one charge still standing against me concerned the bombing of the Snowdonia Country Hotel at Penisa'r-waun, a small village outside Caernarfon, ten months previously. Police evidence on this charge was twofold: dubious forensic 'evidence', which was claimed to have been found in my father's car plus verbal evidence from their key witness, John Gwilym Jones. Originally charged with the explosives offences, he had decided to turn 'Queen's Evidence' in exchange for all charges against him being dropped.

When the latter was brought to the witness stand, it seemed obvious he had been briefed by the prosecution on what to say and what not. He referred to an occasion when he met me at a lay-by on Anglesey, described how I had opened my car boot and produced a timing device. He said I had just come off the Irish Ferry, the insinuation being that I had collected the device from Ireland. As well as implicating me, he also alleged that the other two who were charged with him were links in the chain that had procured the said explosives.

Under cross-examination from Andrew Rankin, John Gwilym Jones seemed to falter and was extremely nervous. Pressurised by Rankin, he seemed unsure and fell into a couple of traps. By the time he had finished giving his evidence, his brow was covered in sweat.

One incident occurred on the very first day of the trial, after the jury had been selected. During lunch break, two elderly ladies who were jury members had visited the public toilets on the Maes, opposite the castle. Catherine, who sat at the back of the court had also visited the same toilets. As she entered, the two jury members were on their way out, so they met face to face. Catherine immediately recognized them and quite innocently remarked, 'Don't you be too hard on him now!' This had apparently upset the two ladies no end and on returning to the court after the recess they had told the chairman of the jury about it. The judge was not amused and ordered the two ladies be freed from their duties. As for poor Catherine, she was publicly castigated by the judge for 'interfering ' with members of the jury and was banned from attending the court forthwith.

Two new members were selected and took their seats on the benches. As it happened, these two were from the Meirionnydd area, both Welsh-speakers, as opposed to the two that had departed, who were non Welsh-speakers from the anglicised Llandudno area. Would this change the jury's final verdict? I don't really believe so, but thought the incident was worth mentioning!

When the time came for Robert G Jones to take the witness stand, the case stood on a knife's edge. Robin was a well-known and colourful character who lived with his family at Groeslon, a village between Penygroes and Caernarfon. He was a straight-talking no-nonsense sort of guy, likeable and very blunt, who called a spade a spade. Since Eddie and Robin had already been 'dealt with' by an earlier court, and had both been given suspended sentences, it wouldn't make a difference to them what they would decide to say. It was fairly warm inside the court and Robin was perspiring as he faced Alun Talfan Davies. The latter was attempting to lead Robin into saying or even insinuating something he had no wish to. Robin was no mug and stood his ground even when things got a little difficult for him. Since an earlier witness had already stated that Robin had handed a third person a 'package' which was said to contain par-ammo gelignite, he could not very well deny it as there were no other witnesses.

Talfan Davies pressed him for an answer... had Robin

handed a package to Owain Williams? There was a hushed silence in the packed courtroom. Minutes ticked away. 'Come now, Mr Jones... is it yes or no?' asked the impatient QC.

Slowly and deliberately Robin said, 'Yes. I did hand him a package...' Talfan's joy at the reply was evident, but the smile froze on his face when Robin added, turning to the judge, 'But you see, my Lord, it wasn't explosives in that package, no, it was a gun!' This was followed by gasps echoing around the courtroom, then loud clapping and cheering and shouts of support.

'Silence in court... silence... silence,' bellowed a pompous-looking court official, as he bounced to his feet.

At first I was flabbergasted at Robin's unexpected response. 'Oh my God,' I thought 'You've dropped me in the shit now!' thinking that I would now be charged with possession of firearms on top of the explosives rap. Of course, after deep reflection, I realised that what Robin had done was to unravel the prosecution's case! Since there was no mention of a gun in the charges, the prosecution was left with egg on their faces.

Not only were cracks appearing in the prosecution's witness statements, but also their much publicised forensic evidence was beginning to lose credibility, thanks mainly to the hard work of my lawyers. The so-called swabs containing nitro-glycerine were now questionable, since evidence was produced claiming my father's car had recently been sprayed, leaving traces of a substance similar to nitro-glycerine.

When the final day of the trial arrived, I was feeling pretty shattered as I still had no clear idea of how it would end despite some positive developments. Both barristers addressed the jury on the last day, and I was tense and nervous, and suffering from an acute migraine. Andrew Rankin in his thunderous voice rammed home his message to the jury that they could not and should not find me guilty, since the evidence against me was unreliable and dangerous. Once the speeches were delivered, the jury left to consider their verdict. I was escorted by two prison officers back to my cell, which had been my 'home' for the last five days.

While I was held in the police station at Caernarfon, I was under the supervision of prison warders and not police officers. In order for this to happen, the entire police station at the rear of the building was commandeered by the prison service. It was quite an elaborate exercise. If my memory serves me right, there were eight warders allocated to guard and watch over me. Every morning I was taken out to 'exercise' in the back yard of the police station, normally accompanied by four or five guards. I am not quite sure what they expected me to do, but there was one guard in each corner beneath the massive stone walls which framed the compound. I believe these were part of the old town walls, some of which go back to Roman times when the town was called Segontium.

During the first day or two walking around the yard, one of the 'screws' suddenly said to me, 'Why don't you try and make a break now?' That day, there was a long sturdy wooden plank, like a scaffolding board, leaning against the wall. I could in fact have taken a run and scrambled up this board to reach the top of the wall. I didn't fall for that one as I didn't think I'd get very far. Mind you, at that desperate time it probably crossed my mind!

My father and Morris came to see me in my cell and Catherine was allowed a few minutes, despite her minor transgression, while I waited for the jury to return. It seemed they were deliberating for hours and the stress of waiting was quite harrowing.

Geoff Thomas came to see me. He was in a sombre mood, saying, 'Things have gone pretty well on the whole... but one can never be sure in such a situation. I feel we've won it, but just in case things go wrong... you should be ready for quite a long stretch... I would guess no more than twelve years and no less than ten!'

I was truly gutted, although I had always been prepared to face a stiff sentence. Nonetheless, when the actual crunch time arrived, it was hard to stomach. Needless to say worrying and speculating wouldn't help matters, and as my family were ushered out of my cell, I was left to contemplate in solitude. Soon the jingling of keys and clattering of the cell door brought me back to earth – it was destiny time!

During the couple of hours spent in the cell waiting for the jury's verdict, I had heard much singing and shouting outside the court building. The strains of *Hen Wlad Fy Nhadau* could be heard clearly, sung by what sounded like 200 people. Obviously there was only room for a few dozen inside the courtroom, but many more supporters had congregated outside, singing, which helped to prop up my spirits. Standing once again in court between the two screws, I waited full of tension for the judge and jury's return. Once again a gowned official called out 'Court'; everyone stood up – the jury filed in followed by the judge and as he took his seat, the people in the public gallery also sat down.

When faced with difficult situations, I always try to remain focused and this time was no different. Although knowing full well my family and supporters were seated right behind me, I refrained from turning around to look at them, since this would distract me and weaken my resolve and spirit.

Once the feet shuffling and nervous coughing had subsided, the judge spoke. 'Ladies and gentlemen of the jury, have you formed a verdict?' All eyes turned towards the jury benches in anticipation; the foreman of the jury rose to his feet.

'Yes, my lord, we have,' he replied. The silence in the courtroom was overbearing, the tension was immense.

'And what is your verdict – guilty or not guilty?' enquired the judge.

It seemed like an age as the jury foreman gazed down at a slip of paper, before answering in a nervous tone: 'Not guilty' came the reply.

All hell broke loose, the shouting, even screaming, reaching a crescendo.

'*Cymru am Byth!*' yelled a loud voice. '*Hwrê!*', then the strains of the Welsh national anthem broke out again. The crimson-robed English judge looked on bemused and even produced a weak smile. It was a futile act on behalf of the court official to shout 'Order!' since no one took the slightest notice.

How did I feel when I heard the verdict? Ecstatic is the only word I can bring to mind that describes my feelings at that moment. Both the prison officers who had flanked me for five days vanished like the morning mist, leaving me temporarily in a quandary as the fact of my new-found freedom began to sink in.

People clambered over benches and pushed and shoved to get at me, much back-slapping and handshakes followed. My father's face at that moment will forever haunt me. His relief was indescribable and my brother Moi was all smiles, giving me a knowing wink and a thumbs up sign. Catherine was determinedly fighting her way through the crowd to give me a hug and a big kiss. My brother left to find a phone box to give my mother the good news. We all knew she would have been sick with worry.

Outside the large crowd of even more supporters from all parts of Wales had gathered in anticipation of the verdict. My solicitor told me there were calls for me to make a speech on the steps of the court. After some soul-searching I decided against this. I was exhausted.

Andrew Rankin, and Geoff Thomas, my hard-working and loyal solicitor, had invited me to the hotel they were staying in for a little celebration drink and a snack. 'The Royal Hotel' as it was then known has since been renamed to the 'Celtic Royal Hotel' and is an impressive building. Once at the hotel I was ushered into one of the rooms where a large bottle of champagne was produced. Andrew Rankin himself did the pouring and offered me a toast. I was truly flattered. For the first time I had the opportunity to thank them for all their efforts and hard work.

Throughout the case and even before, one person more than any stands out, because without his support and generosity I could well have spent twelve years incarcerated. Trefor Morgan, as I have previously mentioned, volunteered to take over my case, hired and paid for my solicitor, and also hired a private detective to investigate certain police and Special Branch covert activities throughout my case. At the end of the day it was a team effort and the support given me by the general public in Wales was tremendous. I will be forever grateful to all those who helped me throughout those very hard and difficult times, family, friends from near and far. This obviously includes the support I received from the good people of Ireland.

One quick observation: after the not guilty verdict was delivered, in the middle of the euphoria one could not fail to notice the dejected faces amongst the prosecution. The image that stands out most in my mind was the expression of anger on the face of Det. Supt. John Hughes, then head of Gwynedd CID. I well recall the glare he gave me as our eyes met across the courtroom amid the pandemonium.

Back at the hotel, once we had savoured our victory celebration drink, it was time for my lawyer and barrister to leave. They had stayed a week at the hotel and were now returning to their families. During this time the press hawks had gathered in a separate lounge for a press conference. It was after all a top story, not just in local terms, but at a national level. Many Fleet Street papers were represented, including the big selling *Daily Mirror*. When I entered the room, I was temporarily blinded by all the flashing press cameras; there were television cameras, too, both BBC and ITV. Most of the reporters just wanted a story, I don't think many of them worried whether I won the case or lost it.

Most questions thrown at me were predictable. What were my immediate plans? Was I looking forward to seeing my family? Would I still be leading protests against the investiture? Did I have any future plans of a romantic nature regarding the 'mystery girl' from Ireland? To all this I made a brief but polite statement that I was returning home to be with my family, especially my children whom I hadn't seen for almost a year and that I hadn't any political plans for the near future. I was of course aware that I had to manage my words very carefully since some of the press are notorious for misquoting and misinterpreting what someone tells them. All in all the result in the next day's papers wasn't that bad, apart from one of the tabloids referring to me as 'The Welsh Bomber!'

As for the 'mystery girl', Catherine, who had been so supportive: last I heard she was still working at the Hilton. I did go to London for two days to meet her, shortly after my trial ended – but just the once.

Being driven home to my parents' house later was an altogether strange feeling. It was hard to believe I was now really free, with no need to look over my shoulder for a shadowy figure in pursuit. However, this temporary feeling of freedom and well-being would be short-lived, for over the next seven or eight months I would be subjected to an intense form of surveillance never before witnessed in Wales!

18

Pre- and Post-investiture

'OVERJOYED' IS THE only suitable word to describe my feelings as I tasted freedom for the first time in almost a year. One irony which surprisingly evaded the attention of the media, was the fact that I had been acquitted on November the fifth!! That should have rung a bell since it was Guy Fawkes' day which commemorated the former 'gunpowder plot' and my case was referred to as the explosives case! My first few days with my family were precious and unforgettable; seeing my two children, Iona and Gruff gave me great joy. They had grown so much in a year! At our first reunion things were pretty tense, because they had of course been put under a lot of pressure while I was away. Other children had made unkind remarks about me, probably reflecting their parents' views. So, they were frequently told 'your Dad's a bomber' or 'your Dad's a nutcase'.

At this time my youngest child, Teleri, was still in Heswall Children's Hospital in the Wirral. Her condition had not changed and would not, since it was incurable.

It was difficult trying to get back to a 'normal' routine although I attempted to take part in general farm work at home. My old bedroom was there waiting for me on my return and at weekends, Iona and Gruff invariably came to stay. Although politically the situation did not seem as volatile as it had been earlier, there were still rumblings of discontent under the surface.

My solicitor, Geoff Thomas' departing words to me on my acquittal, rang strongly in my ears: 'Well, Owain… there you go, you can get away with almost anything now. If you break speed limits or whatever, they won't touch you… because they've got much bigger things in store for you!' He then added, 'Be very careful how you go!' and shook my hand warmly.

By Christmas, there were just six months to go before the investiture at Caernarfon Castle. During the winter, a couple of explosions rocked some government buildings in Cardiff and elsewhere. All the bombings were attributed to MAC and the security services were no nearer finding the perpetrators than they had been over a year ago. It was early in the New Year that I first noticed strange cars parked on the roadside not far from our farm. For the most part they were normally Ford Zodiacs or Zephyrs, usually dark, metallic, with muddied or blackened number plates.

One day we noticed the County Council workmen excavating the side of the main road, the B4417, opposite our farm gate entrance, about twenty paces from the gate. At first we did not pay too much attention to this, since we believed they were making room to store salt to use on icy patches on the steep hill past our entrance. However, one morning as I drove my red Volvo through the farm gate, I noticed a mud-splattered Ford Zodiac parked in this new 'lay-by', the driver's face hidden behind a sun visor. Alarm bells rang. Since by now I was familiar with the methods used by the security services, I decided to ignore them completely. Once I had shut the gate, I climbed back into the driving seat and continued up the hill towards the village of Llithfaen to fetch my mother a loaf of bread and a newspaper. No sooner had I passed the new 'lay-by', the driver of the Zodiac pulled out and followed me up the hill and into the village. I pulled up outside the shop; he parked some thirty yards behind. When I finished my shopping, I returned to my car and drove back towards home. When I stopped at the entrance to open the gate, he returned to the newly created lay-by. When I got back to the house, I told them about the man in the lay-by. I don't think anyone believed me at first, thinking it was another example of my vivid imagination. However, as other members of my family drove out of the farm entrance, they were also followed in the same manner – even my parents when they visited Pwllheli market every Wednesday! Later we discovered that around eight to twelve men had been assigned to carry out surveillance on me and us, and that meant there were also eight separate vehicles involved.

During the following week I learnt that six of the men were actually staying a mile away at Plas Pistyll Hotel, which has since been demolished. Of the other six, two were in Nefyn and the other four spread around Llŷn. Despite some naive people believing there was an element of 'Keystone Cops' in all this, it should be remembered that all the undercover agents were seasoned veterans who had experiences of counter-terrorism in Cyprus and Aden. They were all armed with hand guns. What's more, they were not playing hide and seek with me!

Throughout the ensuing months these shadowy figures remained so close even our local postman used to comment on their presence. One of the postmen came up to me while delivering our mail and said, 'Don't think I'm being nosey… but there's a strange car parked over by the back road over there', pointing across the small valley, 'and there's a guy sitting in it with binoculars – he seems to be watching this place… big, ugly, nasty looking bastard, wears a dark duffle coat!' We eventually got to learn there were actually four cars at any given time watching our farm at different locations, all parked at vantage points, although the new lay-by was occupied around the clock. It seems that the eight watchers took turns, four at a time while the other four rested.

One day an incident took place which I won't forget in a hurry. My brother Morris had been angry for some time about these faceless people. With the intention of trying to 'chase them off' he asked me to accompany him in his car to the farm gate. Once there, we parked and got out. It was then I noticed Morris was carrying a hefty pick axe handle. He strode

231

towards the car in the lay-by, banged on the driver's window and shouted, 'Why don't you bugger off right now... or else step outside.' As he spoke, he waved the wooden handle menacingly up and down.

No doubt about it, the driver was caught by surprise, but quickly, he picked up a small hand receiver and spoke urgently to a fellow agent. In less than three minutes, a dark grey Ford Zephyr raced to the spot. Brakes screeching and dust flying, it came to a halt a couple of feet from where we stood. A tall man wearing a brown duffle coat leapt out to face us. 'Do we have a problem here?' he enquired cockily.

My brother squared up to him 'Bloody right... you are the problem mate!' Morris wasn't one to shy away in such situations and could be relied on to hold his ground.

Calmly, the tall stranger let his unpegged duffle coat unfold, revealing a hip holster which contained a revolver. 'Now don't start anything silly, Mr Williams...!' nodding towards the holster, 'We are only carrying out our duties...!'

I believe the sight of the revolver took my brother by surprise, since before he had assumed these people were not to be taken too seriously, but now... Still feeling angry, he stormed: 'Duties? Bloody hell, have you really got nothing better to do...' and spun round, pushing the duffle coated gunslinger aside as we returned to his car.

Apart from the normal front entrance, there was a separate back road to Gwynus. Basically it was no more than a horse and cart track and had once been used to transport farm goods such as animal foods, fencing posts and wires. Although it ran over fields with hardly any hardcore base in places, in summer when it was dry it was still negotiable. Since I was unable to move freely anywhere because I was tailed by these shadowy figures, I decided to try an 'experiment'. One evening there was a half moon, not too light but light enough to see where I was going. Once the sun had set I walked over to my car and with no lights switched on, I carefully drove towards the old track, which meant opening and shutting three metal gates before entering the little used back road that could take me to Pwllheli – or anywhere for that matter. My eyes soon got accustomed to the semi-darkness as I gingerly inched my way over the grass track, scaring the odd rabbit on the way. Once I reached the main road, just checking there were no approaching car headlamps in sight, I continued to drive with my lights switched off for another half mile before venturing to switch them on. Feeling pleased with myself, I decided to stop at a roadside telephone kiosk and ring my friend Bryn, asking did he fancy joining me for a little drink at the Crown Hotel in Pwllheli.

So as not to draw attention to the car, I parked at the rear of the hotel using a narrow back street. Bryn soon arrived. There were also a couple of other friends whom I used to meet occasionally when in town. Bryn laughed uncontrollably when told of my moonlit drive and how MI5 agents had been hoodwinked – temporarily at least!

Wales was politically dormant at this time. There still was no clear leadership on the investiture issue. Plaid Cymru once again had shown a complete lack of moral courage, sitting on never-ending fences. Their stance on the investiture had not shifted an inch... they issued boring statements, at pains to point out they were 'not for the investiture and not against it either'. With such spineless drivel, no wonder their stock was low.

The colonialist symbolism was unmissable. The investiture was to be in the English King Edward I's castle, built to control and intimidate the Welsh people who he had invaded and conquered, having betrayed and beaten our true Prince of Wales, Llywelyn.

The electorate were fairly split down the middle on the issue, but in the predominantly Welsh-speaking heartland a substantial majority opposed the forthcoming circus. Unfortunately another opportunity was wasted. For the sake of political correctness, principles and the moral high ground were abandoned. One or two selfish dilettantes put greed before national salvation. Courage and true vision were forsaken. Personal ambition and political self-enhancement took precedence over national pride and integrity. The political cowardice was unpardonable and words fail me in my attempts to condemn the actions of those responsible. Unfortunately the small band of patriots who stood up to be counted were left to fight a lone battle with the odds stacked against them, shunned by many of their fellow countrymen, and hunted like animals by those supporting the status quo.

Meanwhile my occasional travels along our muddy back lane continued at regular intervals. I was able to borrow my father's car from time to time. This helped immensely since a metallic coloured Vauxhall was far less conspicuous than a brilliant red Volvo sports model. A pattern eventually emerged; I deliberately used my Volvo to drive out through our front entrance, in full view of my 'minders', who naturally would tail me wherever I went. At night time, if I wished to get away unobserved, I took the mud track at the back using my father's car. This tactic seemed to work.

Not only could I visit Pwllheli from time to time, I was also able to travel much further unhindered, even as far as Cardiff. All this worked quite simply. I would switch my father's car with a friend, continuing on my journey in either a Land Rover or an old Austin van. As time passed, I became more confident and soon I was embroiled in clandestine meetings with other activists. Plans were afoot to try and block all roads heading to Caernarfon a day before the investiture. The idea was to have several dozen protestors to stage 'sit-ins' on these roads. I had calculated we could mobilise at least 200 people to participate in such a peaceful form of protest. Many would have been members of Cymdeithas yr Iaith Gymraeg (the Welsh Language Society), which mostly consisted of young people who were students at either Bangor or Aberystwyth Universities. They were already well versed in such protests, having participated at earlier language rallies. Feelers were sent out via contacts we had amongst students to see what their reactions would be.

Pre- and Post-investiture

Despite my reservations about the practicality of this idea, I was willing to give it a try, even though I knew that many in the Society's hierarchy were either middle class, from extremely pacifist backgrounds, or were Plaid Cymru members and sympathisers who considered people like myself too radical. Whatever the reason, the response we received was negative and any such plans had to be shelved.

MAC continued to be active during the spring and summer. More water pipes to England and government buildings were bombed. Police and army were deployed to guard water mains from Wales at strategic locations. There was growing panic at Westminster where Cledwyn Hughes, Labour MP for Anglesey, had been moved by prime minister Harold Wilson from his position as Secretary of State for Wales, being replaced by George Thomas, MP for one of the Cardiff seats. Cledwyn Hughes could be described as a 'patriotic' Welsh Labour Parliamentarian, while on the other hand George Thomas was the complete opposite. George was a 'true Brit' and was regarded by most as being anti-Welsh, a fanatical royalist who regarded the coming investiture as his baby. Harold Wilson was under much pressure from many sides to call off the investiture. In fact he had at one time decided that was the best option. The regular bombings were creating mammoth problems and the cost of the security involved was increasing daily. It was at the insistence of George Thomas that Harold Wilson changed his mind and allowed plans for the ceremony to proceed.

If I had imagined for one moment that my 'guardian angels' from MI5 were satisfied they were succeeding in their role of controlling my movements, I had a rude awakening one midsummer day. Less than a mile from our farm in the small village of Pistyll, there lived an out of work mechanic. Ironically his name was Gordon Thatcher – no relation whatsoever to the Iron Lady! My Volvo's suspension was playing up, and since it was capable of almost 120 mph, good suspension was paramount. One day I called past Gordon's home. Since he was out I left a message with his wife for him to call at the farm.

235

Next morning Gordon arrived early. He took the car for a drive along the farm lane and back and on his return he told me it was probably a snapped wishbone. Since I was busy with work on the farm, I think we were carrying bales of hay into the barn, I left him to it as he unpacked a large tool box, jack etc. We had only just finished unloading a large trailer load of small bales, the sweat was streaming down my face and chest when suddenly I heard frantic shouts, despite the noisy tractor engine: 'Now... Now... come here for fucks sake!' ('Now' is what my friends call me.) Switching off the tractor I jumped down and hurried to meet him, thinking he had injured himself or something:

'What the hell's the matter, Gordon?'

'You won't fucking believe this, but some bastard's been sawing your brake pipe with a hacksaw...!!' he answered in excited tone.

'Don't be bloody stupid... no one would do such a thing...' I answered.

'Well, I'm fucking telling you... come and see for yourself'.

Harvesting the hay was my priority that day. However, more to please him than anything else, I hurried past the farmhouse to an old corrugated shed, which housed my Volvo. I noticed the front wheel on the driver's side had already been removed, as had the broken wishbone. Gordon sounded very excitable in his strong Lancashire accent, which was even more pronounced at that moment. 'If you bend down on your knee, and look just there, just beside where the wheel axle meets the drum... see there...? There's a lot of mud and dirt covering the brake pipes, but if you look carefully where the pipe bends, you'll see where the hacksaw's hacked the pipe, it's not gone all the way through – but there's only a tiny margin remaining!' I squinted until my eyes fell on the almost severed part of the brake pipe.

'Well, I'll be damned!' was all I could manage. Straightening myself up, I stared at Gordon in disbelief. 'What bastard would do that?' I said, not really expecting an answer.

'Well, Now,' he replied. 'For my bet, it must be some of those

Cartref Plas y Bryn
Bontnewydd
Caernarfon
Gwynedd

To whom it may concern

My name is Gordon Thatcher. In the summer of 1968/1969 I lived in Pistyll Terrace, Pistyll, Pwllheli, Gwynedd.

During the early summer of 1969 I was called by Owain Williams of Gwynus, Pistyll to carry out repairs on his car. The car was a red Volvo P1800 Coupe. It was garaged in an outside shed that had no door. On inspecting the car which had problems with the suspension, I had to remove the front wheel on the passenger side. There was a problem with the wishbone in this area of the car which needed replacing. During my inspection of the vehicle, I noticed that someone had tampered with the brake pipe - it seemed to me that a hacksaw had been used to saw across the brake pipe, although the pipe had not been severed there was substantial damage. On discovering this I immediately left the car and went to search for Owain Williams around the farmyard. I found him unloading a load of baled hay in the barn. When I told him what I had discovered, he did not believe me. Afterwards he accompanied me back to the car. On kneeling down he saw the damaged break pipe and was obviously very shocked and disturbed to find out what had occurred.

At that time it was just a few weeks before the investiture at Caernarfon Castle and I knew that Owain Williams and the farm at Gwynus was under constant surveillance by undercover police and Special Branch officers. It was common knowledge in the village and the surrounding area that Gwynus was under round the clock observation, for instant, a special lay by had been built opposite the farm entrance where a vehicle belonging to the surveillance team was constantly parked.

I testify that the above is a true account of what I witnessed.

Yours Truly,

Gordon Thatcher

Testimony from Gordon Thatcher

wankers parked outside your gate!' Then, in a more serious tone: 'Tell you what, the way you fucking drive, you'd have no chance, mate, you'd be a goner!'

This particular incident shook me no end. Although I had honestly believed my life was in danger while on the run in Ireland, I had naively assumed that the worst fate in store for me was to be watched 24/7 until the investiture was over. Obviously I was mistaken. Before returning to join the others in the hayfield, I had a brief chat with Gordon. I asked him to promise not to mention this incident to no one else. I was concerned lest my parents would hear about it as it would cause them more grief and pain. As far as I am aware, Gordon kept his word.

Strangely enough there was another incident which took place shortly after the above, proving it was not just my paranoia that made me suspicious. Bryn Williams, whom I have mentioned before (the very one who brought me the bottle of Guinness to the hammock in the woods at Gwynus where I was hiding) was working as a carpenter doing maintenance work at a comprehensive school in Botwnnog in Llŷn. One day he was on the roof when one of his co-workers called him and said he was wanted by someone. Scuttling down the scaffolding to ground level, he rounded a corner and saw a tall stranger leaning against the school wall, puffing a cigarette.

'You Bryn Williams?' enquired the stranger. At first glance, Bryn imagined it was someone from 'health and safety' or somebody who had come to discuss his life insurance policy. Hesitating a few seconds before responding, since his first language was Welsh and he did not feel at ease speaking English, he replied: *'Ia, Bryn ydw i... pwy sy'n gofyn?'* (Yes, I'm Bryn... who's asking?')

Before his sentence was finished, the stranger abruptly cut across him 'English mate. Speak English!' It was more an order than a request. Bryn was taken aback by this rude and unexpected comment. He was protesting that he didn't like his attitude when the stranger cut in once more: 'I've got something to show you... won't take a couple of minutes... my car's around the corner' beckoning with a nod of the head.

Parked close to the school wall was a gleaming black Mercedes. Opening the passenger door, the stranger ushered Bryn inside, saying 'We need a little chat!'. Slamming the door shut, the tall stranger strode across to the driver's side and to Bryn's surprise he started the engine and sped off. Grabbing the passenger door handle and twisting vigorously up and down, Bryn realised, too late, that the door was locked.

Because we were close friends, Bryn was well aware I was being closely watched by the secret services and within minutes had come to the conclusion that his abduction in broad daylight must be connected with me. Once he had deduced this, he thought he was being driven to Pwllheli police station for questioning. However, the car passed through that town and headed towards Porthmadog. When the car sped out of that town, Bryn really began to panic. When he tried to ask the stranger where he was being taken, there was no reply.

To Bryn's surprise, as they crossed the English border at Chirk, the driver broke his silence 'OK, my friend, seems you've been keeping the wrong company and now you're in deep trouble! You know damn well what I'm talking about... and if you don't, you sure as hell will when we arrive in Shrewsbury and you meet my gaffer!'

That's when it dawned on Bryn where he was being taken. The special surveillance squad, made up of Special Branch who were liaising with MI5 and military intelligence, were based at Shrewsbury. Bryn's first reaction on hearing this news was one of relief. At least he knew where he was being driven and had an idea who his 'kidnapper' was. On the other hand, he was concerned what his fate would be... for instance, would they trump up a charge against him?

We had often discussed such scenarios when talking about the covert activities of secret agents and intelligence services, not only in Britain but far beyond. I had already mentioned to Bryn, following my court acquittal, what my solicitor Geoff Thomas had said, 'You're free to do as you please for now, but they have greater things in store for you!' Which meant they couldn't afford to arrest me a second time – but they would get at me through others. When the car finally came to a halt outside the 'citadel' in Shrewsbury, Bryn naturally felt nervous and isolated.

Once inside the police station, he was led up a flight of stairs and into a sparsely furnished room containing a long timber table, a dozen chairs, and large metal filing cabinet. There were eight men waiting for him in the room – the driver vanished.

'So what have we here, then?' asked Det. Chief Supt Bob Booth, head of West Mercia's plain clothes section. (It should be explained that a major water mains supplying Birmingham from the Elan Valley reservoirs in mid Wales had been targeted by MAC two days previously and had been shattered, cutting off supplies to that city.) Chief Superintendant Booth was far from being a happy man, leaping from his chair, rolling up his sleeves as he spoke. 'Why don't you stay in those fucking Welsh hills!' he hollered.

Bryn, taken a little by surprise, replied: 'I was perfectly happy in my Welsh hills till you took me from there.'

Bob Booth glared at him menacingly, then suddenly turning to the others said 'I'm sure you gentlemen would like to go for a walk, grab a drink or something... just leave Bryn with me here, you can come back later!'

Once the other seven had departed, Booth, who was a big man, tried to intimidate the small-framed Bryn.

'You keep your fucking war on your side of the border! Cross over to my territory and all hell will break loose!' he yelled.

Suddenly he grabbed Bryn by the lapels with both hands, slammed him against the brick wall, then he reached behind with his free hand and produced a sharp looking stiletto, used for opening mail. Thrusting the pointed knife at Bryn's throat, actually touching his skin, his face now red with rage: 'I'm warning you, I won't simply crucify you, I'll nail you to the fucking wall!' he yelled. 'You know what you are, don't you? You're a sly, spineless yellow Welsh bastard... and so's your mate, that fucking Owain Williams!'

Bryn, obviously shaken by not just the physical manhandling but the verbal abuse and insults, decided not to retaliate which would only serve to aggravate this idiot further. The harassment and cross-examining and innuendos lasted for several hours, from the time he was picked up at 8.30 in the morning till he was brought back at 8 in the evening.

Shortly after, Booth picked up a phone, spoke briefly and within seconds the other seven returned. Amongst the team of eight in the room was Detective Chief Supt Jock Wilson, ex Scotland Yard, who had been commissioned to lead the Special Squad in overall charge of investiture security. Out of the eight there was but one Welshman, Detective Chief Inspector Gwyn Owen, whom I have mentioned earlier. It was becoming evident that the authorities – that is the Home Office – did not trust the Welsh police with political security or 'counter terrorism', hence the so called Shewsbury squad, consisting solely of top English policemen led by a Scot. There was no question that MAC had succeeded in planting the seeds of doubt and mistrust in the higher echelons of power.

Throughout the hours of grilling, Detective Chief Inspector Gwyn Owen hardly spoke. Apart from asking Bryn how he was on his arrival, it was obvious he was there to supply any 'local knowledge' which the others didn't seem to possess in large quantities.

One of the other police chiefs was also taking an interest in Bryn. Detective Superintendent Dixie Dean, who I believe was a leading light in the Cheshire CID, was next to have a go. 'You know, don't you, we have evidence about you and we know you're involved in several of these bombings... We have photographs of you taken at lots of rallies and demonstrations with Welsh extremists!' At this he dragged a chair and parked himself till he was facing Bryn eyeball to eyeball.

'What are you trying to do, turn Wales into another Cyprus?' Then sinking to new levels, he bellowed, 'Your wife just had a new baby hasn't she? Well, it can be easily arranged when she visits the shop a bomb could be planted... how would you fucking like that then?'

Bryn could hardly believe he had heard right. How could anyone stoop so low? As it happened, Bryn's wife had given birth to Iwan their first child only about two months earlier.

Now it was the turn of the Cheshire CID chief to have Bryn all to himself as the others all filed out. Again, similar to what occurred with Detective Chief Superintendant Booth, once alone he began to rant and scream. 'I don't give a bollock if you blow up Birmingham water supply... in fact I don't care if you blow bloody Birmingham itself up! But you cross over into Cheshire once more with your bombs and I'm telling you, I'll be

241

dragging you out of your bed before dawn... and that fucking Owain Williams, I'm telling you when I'm finished with you lot you'll go down and the fucking key will be thrown away!'

After several hours of bullying and threatening the mood suddenly became more mellow. Bryn sensed he was coming to the end of his shocking ordeal.

Rolling down his sleeves and putting his jacket back on, Booth turned to Bryn, laying a 'fatherly' hand on his shoulder, his voice patronisingly soft: 'I think you're a smart lad, Bryn... you will listen to reason and turn a new leaf. But, that other one Williams, Owain Williams, he won't listen to reason, never... until he's six foot under. Believe you me, if he is within fifty miles of Caernarfon on the day of the investiture, he's going to have a little accident!'

With those sobering words ringing in his ears, Bryn was led to the same car that brought him in the first place and driven back to his home village of Llanaelhaearn near Pwllheli.

It was early on the following morning that I received a short telephone message from Bryn, – I noticed from the tone of his voice he sounded on edge. He was aware there was a tap on my parent's phone since I moved back to live there a couple of years earlier, so we kept conversations to a minimum. Since I was only calling at the Crown pub in Pwllheli, I drove through our front entrance and, of course, one of my minders was waiting in the new lay-by. As soon as I closed the farm gate and got back in the car, he started his engine and followed me, down through Nefyn and on to Pwllheli. Having parked the car on the High Street I entered the Crown.

Bryn was already at the bar, a large tankard of bitter in his hands. On seeing me he put his beer down then, glancing nervously over his shoulder, he said, 'Were you followed?'

I looked at him with a puzzled gaze. 'Followed? Of course I was bloody followed. I'm always followed, you know that. What is it with you anyway? You're looking bloody nervous... and you sounded odd on the phone!'

Edging closer, dragging his pint along the bar, he whispered in my ear, 'I've got something to tell you... it's important... can't talk in here, wait till we're outside, OK'.

'Yes, OK, OK, calm down for God's sake... nothing's going to happen in here!' I replied.

Raising his eyebrows, a slight look of disbelief on his face, he added 'I'm not so fucking sure about that!'

Once we stepped outside into the cold January air, I saw that my shadow was still in his car reading his paper. Naturally with eight agents 'watching over' me, it wasn't usually the car driver that was involved – he would alert others and they would visit any premises I had entered, mixing in with the crowd, although I had learnt the knack of spotting them by now. Anyway, as we walked down the High Street, Bryn retold the tale of his abduction the previous day, almost word for word. It was obvious he was badly shaken by the events. What had shaken him the most was when he had been more or less warned that his family would suffer, even to the extent of threatening the lives or his wife and young baby son. One thing was obvious, Bryn had been taken to Shrewsbury with the sole intention of scaring him into keeping clear of me. It wasn't a veiled innuendo but rather an open threat.

Had I not known Bryn as well as I did, then possibly I would have difficulty in believing his story, but of course it all tallied, – the elaborate surveillances on myself, an earlier attempt to tamper with the brake pipes of my car. One thing I certainly didn't wish to happen was for someone innocent to be subjected to harassment, or even suffer physical harm purely because of their association with me. Although we were close friends and enjoyed a drink and a laugh together, I felt it unfair he and his family should be targeted in this way. With this in mind, I told him maybe we shouldn't meet as often in future. I was also aware that some members of his family felt that he should steer clear of me, for his own good.

Bryn was adamant. 'No bloody way! I won't let any of those bastards decide who I'm friends with!' He sounded hurt that I had even broached the subject. If anything, Bryn was more concerned about my safety, feeling 'those bastards' were gunning for me and sincerely believed my life was in danger. 'Don't forget what they did to your car… I'm telling you, those bastards are ruthless'.

Even as we chatted on our way down the street, my shadow was following about fifty yards behind. When we stopped for a few minutes, he also came to a halt, pretending to gaze at shop windows. Analysing the events of the past few weeks, even days, it was becoming even more obvious that the authorities were deeply rattled at the apparent ease with which MAC were carrying out their attacks, selecting targets almost at random.

At this juncture it is worth remembering that the security services had decided to carry out early morning raids on the homes of nine members of the Free Wales Army, mostly in west Wales. Amongst those arrested and detained was Julian Cayo Evans (known as Cayo), self-styled leader and commandant, a colourful and charismatic horse breeder from south Ceredigion. Of the other eight, Dennis Coslett, Dai Bonner Davies, Gethin ap Gruffydd, Glyn Rowlands and two brothers, Vernon and Eddie Griffiths, were the most well known. Coslett, who had lost one eye in an accident, was easily recognisable from his eye patch. Membership of the FWA was no secret since its members openly paraded at rallies and national memorials wearing their green uniform emblazoned with the emblem, the white eagle of Snowdonia. Of the nine it was undoubtedly Cayo who symbolised the FWA, regularly appearing on TV news programmes, on radio and in the press, including the Fleet Street papers. Cayo was a born propagandist, flamboyant and witty with a vivid, at times wild, imagination.

Because the FWA was not a secretive organisation, it was very easily penetrated by Special Branch or MI5 agents on several occasions. One example of how naive some FWA members were occurred at a weekend training camp held in a mid Wales forest. Apparently a stranger turned up. No-one had seen him before and he did not know the password when asked, 'Which way to Abbey Cwm Hir?' The answer was supposed to be 'Llywelyn rests in peace' but the stranger had no clue what to say in reply. Dai Bonner, a little more astute than some of the others immediately tagged on; 'He's a bloody infiltrator... a cop... or worse, get rid of him.' Suddenly, hearing the commotion Cayo arrived and asked what was the problem, to which Caio responded, 'Ah, let him go men, he's one of Gethin's boys from the south'.

There were several examples of lax security and naivety which contributed to the authorities piling up evidence of conspiracy against the FWA leadership at the ongoing trials. It is ironic that one of the main witnesses against them was the particular stranger I have just mentioned, who was in fact a detective sergeant attached to Special Branch. It may well all be history by now, but it is worth recording that the nine were held in captivity from early January until the eve of the investiture on 1 July. At the end of one of the most lengthy and costly trials, Caio, Cosslet and one of the others were given hefty prison sentences. Basically they had not committed any crime or even detonated a single bomb but, because the intelligence service could not capture any MAC members, the FWA were made to be 'fall guys' and paid the penalty.

Meanwhile at my parents' farm, surveillance on myself and members of my family continued around the clock. Different tactics emerged. One example was a decision taken to replace a couple of the Ford Zephyr cars with battered mud-splattered Ford vans. Presumably these vehicles seemed more like the transport used by the local farming fraternity. There was a joke circulating in the area that the two sheep being daily transported across the county were the most travelled sheep in Wales. Despite wearing tweed flat caps and green leggings the two detectives didn't quite mix in with the weather-beaten farmers and were referred to as Cop One and Cop Two!

Apart from that, the situation was far from being amusing. In fact, the pressure was immense and at times I lived in genuine fear. An example of this was when I would go out for an evening and on returning by car, I would be met at the farm gate by one or two of my shadows wearing duffle coats, hood pulled well over their heads. Obviously I had to get out of my car to open and shut the gate. Never once did they speak, just stood alongside, still and silent. Sometimes when it was misty, or drizzling, they would appear as silhouetted eerie figures in the car's headlights – and they were big bastards. When I reached the farmhouse, it was dark apart from one dim light in the kitchen. There were no outside lights, so anyone could have lurked in the shadows.

With the military build-up around Caernarfon increasing daily, there would be in the region of 9,000 soldiers based around the town by the end of June. In addition to this there were the uniformed police officers, including several dozen Special Branch and MI5 agents totalling another 1,500-2,000. At a rough estimate, there were around 12,000 troops and police around and inside the town by investiture day. Considering the population of Caernarfon was less than 11,000, it gives you an idea of the massive security operation.

By this time I had come to a painful decision. Since it was now futile to contemplate any mass protest or any other kind of protest on the actual day, I decided to leave my country two days before the actual investiture. Taking a ferry from Holyhead, I headed for Dublin accompanied by a female friend from Blackwood in Gwent. I hasten to add our relationship was purely platonic. We were of the same mind, that staying in Wales throughout that royal circus was unpalatable. Later I was told that the authorities breathed a sigh of relief on learning of my voluntary short-term exile.

Moving around Ireland by train and less occasionally thumbing a lift, we travelled as far as Galway City, down the west coast to Limerick and Kerry, finally arriving in Cork City the day after the investiture. We had deliberately evaded all contact with TV sets or radio during our brief stay. But in Cork City, as we walked down the main street in search of a cafe, we passed a newspaper stand selling the *Cork Examiner*. On a billboard alongside in large capitals was the headline 'TWO KILLED IN

WALES EXPLOSION'. Not knowing what to expect, I bought the paper. Glaring headlines read, 'TWO WELSH PATRIOTS KILLED IN AN EXPLOSION AT ABERGELE ON THE EVE OF THE INVESTITURE'. Since the article was brief I quickly read the remainder of the item. At the very end it stated that as a sign of respect, the Irish Tricolor would be flown at half mast on the Thomas Ashe Hall for the next two days.

I was gutted. The two men were named as Alwyn Jones and George Taylor. The latter was in his thirties and the father of three young children, while Alwyn Jones was barely twenty-two, married to a young Jamaican girl, with a baby daughter just three months old. My body shook with grief and sadness. I knew Alwyn – he was a member of the Patriotic Front and a true patriot. Obviously he had been recruited into MAC, together with his friend George Taylor. Because that organisation was run on a cell basis, no one would have been aware they were members, apart from whoever recruited them or a director of operations. Although I had never met George Taylor, I was aware that Alwyn's mother was a widow and he was an only child; they were very close.

I broke down and wept like a child, sobbing uncontrollably. Some people stared, one or two even stopped, before walking past. Words fail me in trying to explain my feelings on that tragic day. It is far too personal and emotional for me to even try. Every nation has its martyrs and heroes; when conflict occurs, people get hurt and some die. For centuries, Wales had not experienced a national divide such as that caused by the investiture. People who have been subjected to oppression or neo-colonialist aggression, no matter whether it be physical or mental, whether it be by territorial eviction or cultural and linguistic exclusion, frequently lose or disown their identity.

Undoubtedly many will still see Alwyn Jones and George Taylor's untimely deaths as something of their own doing: in one way that could be the case. However, the events leading up to the investiture, the vast amount of money and resources, including British military might, that went into this royalist and establishment propaganda exercise, might lead us to question its real purpose. A great number of Welsh people, particularly young ones, consider Alwyn Jones and George Taylor to be true martyrs, who died so that Wales could live.

Two days following the royal circus in Caernarfon, we returned by ferry from Cork, arriving at Swansea in the early afternoon. If I had been saddened by news of the two deaths the previous day, then the sights that greeted me on my return to Wales turned my stomach. Union flags and royalist bunting cluttered the streets right across the city and the remains of street parties to mark the occasion were still visible. My female companion was angered by the sight while I was momentarily too depressed and weak even to contemplate anger. All the way back north, which would have been in excess of 160 miles, there were more flags and signs of 'celebrations' worthy of any nation of grovellers and hypocrites. Even at Aberystwyth, which houses a proud university famous for teaching Welsh students through their native tongue and specialising in the history of our country, union flags were still visible, despite attempts here and there to take them down.

The British establishment had seized their chance to undermine the 'Welshness' of that university by sending Charles there to study for a few weeks before his investiture. It had been claimed by the royalist propaganda machine that he, Charles would become a 'fluent Welsh speaker' in a matter of weeks. This was of course never the case. Days after leaving the university, during his investiture at Caernarfon Castle, he clearly fluffed the few lines written for him and he must have been an embarrassment to his tutors. Needles to say not a word of Welsh has crossed his lips in the last forty-three years, except perhaps an odd 'diolch' at a garden fete or some exclusive function.

On crossing into my native county of Caernarvonshire at Porthmadog, here and there I saw the odd union flags limply draped on lamp poles, but nothing like Swansea or some of the towns on the way north. Eventually, I drove up to the farm gate. Across the road written in white paint was 'WELCOME BACK OWAIN!' I knew immediately it was the work of my 'shadows'... cheeky bastards.

Apart from the flippant painted slogan, the one thing that was ominous was the gaping vacuum in the parking space across the road. Obviously now that the royalist circus was over, there was no more need for the secret services to strut their stuff. Eventually, a few weeks later, council workmen arrived to fill it in with soil! Despite the departure of my 'shadows' from outside the farm gate, I had been conscious for the last forty miles, from just outside Dolgellau, that I was being followed. When one has been subjected to constant 'shadowing' for months on end, there is a gut instinct about such things. And since my car had been fitted with a homing device for some time, I knew that someone didn't have to sit on my tail to know my movements.

My parents were glad to see me home safe and well once more. They were naturally aware of the tragic deaths in Abergele. They also told me that a soldier had died outside the walls of Caernarfon castle when his jeep burst into flames, leaving him trapped inside. It was believed this incident was an accident, although not much has been documented on this tragedy.

Since I was tired out, both mentally and physically, I decided on an early night although sleep was difficult to come by because my mind was in turmoil.

Very early next morning, I was suddenly awoken by loud shouting and hammering on both back and front doors. Leaping out of bed, I climbed into my clothes and raced downstairs, two at a time. 'OK, OK... what the hell is going on?' I hollered, unlocking the kitchen door as I spoke. An incredible sight greeted me. The courtyard outside was packed with plain clothes policemen. I found out later there were fourteen of them and they had arrived in eight cars. A tall middle-aged man wearing a light coloured raincoat and a brown trilby hat greeted me: 'I'm Detective Superintendent A. A. Clarke and I have a warrant to search the premises.'

'But what for?' I enquired. My question was ignored.

19

Still Harassed

NO SOONER HAD six or seven of the plain clothes mob streamed into the house than they were churning out drawers and emptying cupboards onto the lino-clad kitchen floor. Once the kitchen was done, leaving potatoes, farming accounts and Mam's private correspondence scattered all over the place, they moved on to the front room. Even my mother's sacred Welsh dresser suffered the same indignities as they peered into all the jugs and shifted the plates around.

My Mam was still in bed, having been unwell for several days. Realising that nowhere was safe from their searching, I leapt up the dozen or so creaking steps to my mother's room. She was half up with a concerned look on her face.

'What's all that commotion I hear downstairs?' she asked. I knew my mother well enough that to lie or mislead her would be futile, so I explained the police had arrived in numbers, but it was a routine visit, in view of what had occurred the night before the investiture, when two local men were killed after a bomb exploded prematurely.

Looking me straight in the eye, in a shaky voice, she asked 'Tell me the truth, did you have anything to do with that event?'

'Mam, you know I was in Ireland when that happened... remember, I had been warned not to be within 50 miles of Caernarfon two days before the ceremony, or I would have an accident,' I replied.

No sooner had I spoken when heavy footsteps could be heard on the stairs. Two of the men entered Mam's bedroom. 'Have you no respect whatsoever?' I yelled angrily.

They both stepped back out of the door. 'All right, but we'll have to search the room later – we'll be back in twenty minutes,' insisted the taller of the two.

My mother's condition meant she could not be moved at such short notice. She had been suffering from angina. At this stage, my elder brother Moi ran upstairs to see what was going on. Explaining to him that they intended to search Mam's bedroom later on, we were discussing what to do next when a local home help who had been helping out over the last few days arrived. This gave my brother and me an opportunity to hurry downstairs to check what the police were up to. By now all the cupboards and drawers etc were emptied and lay on the floor in scattered piles. Private papers, farm business documents, animal records – all had been tossed on the floor at random.

We stepped out of the kitchen into the small courtyard, where three or four of the most senior officers were talking in hushed voices. It was obvious they were contemplating their next move, as they huddled at the top of stone steps that led down to our cellar. These days the cold damp cellar was hardly in use. Once it had been a hive of activity when we used to churn the cream into butter which my mother sold locally. The old wooden churn stood in a corner, a reminder of my former school days when one of my many chores was to turn the handle round and round until specks of butter would appear on the small cylindrical window in the churn's lid. Much to my annoyance, that was a job I had to do twice weekly!

My brother was getting angry and I could tell by his expression we were heading for a showdown with the law. I can't remember exactly what happened next, but all of a sudden one of the more bulky officers lost his footing on top of the stairs and fell in a heap on his arse.

'That was a very silly thing to do, Mr Williams!' It was the voice of the then Det. Chief Superintendent A. A. Clarke, addressing Moi.

'Silly? Silly, did you say? Well, we'll see about that... so get your bloody hat and get lost... NOW... before I start punching!'

came my brother's angry retort, as he squared up to the top cop.

Before the situation could develop, the voice of one of the most junior officers was heard from the farmyard. He rushed up, breathless with excitement, holding a piece of paper in one hand.

'Chief, I've found something here! It was in his caravan!'

Obviously, he'd been meticulously searching the battered old caravan that I had used occasionally in the past. My heart throbbed uncontrollably and I was momentarily gripped by panic. What had he found? Was there something I had missed or forgotten?

Their voices lowered to almost a whisper, as they examined the crumpled piece of notepaper. My brother looked at me with curiosity for a second or two before asking 'Jesus, what's up? You've turned as white as a ghost!' I was by now trembling like a leaf, at first thinking they had planted something in the caravan that would incriminate me. Not just a bit of paper; it could be anything, detonators, a firearm or maybe some explosives. After all, these fellows had been allowed to rifle through my caravan unaccompanied, so who would question whatever they 'found'?

Several minutes later, I was told that the scrap of paper contained the name of a woman I had met in a bar in Builth Wells the previous year. I recalled the time when a crowd of republicans were travelling to Cilmeri nearby where the monument to Llywelyn – the last true Prince of Wales – stands. We were attending an annual rally to commemorate his death on 11 December 1282. The girl in question was a native of the Isle of Skye in Scotland and could speak Scots Gaelic. As it happened, I had never met a person who spoke that language before, nor had I heard it spoken. She must have scribbled her name and address on this piece of paper, hence the sudden interest amongst the lawmen. The questions that followed were endless; who was she? Was she a member of a secret pro-Celtic organisation? Was she an old girlfriend?

'Mind your own business!'

Eventually, after what seemed an age, the whole mob vanished in their fleet of cars. As a matter of interest, that was my final police raid at Gwynus. I did not experience their presence again until over ten years later, at the height of the *Meibion Glyndŵr* (sons of Glyndŵr) fire-bombing campaign at the end of the seventies and early eighties, when uninhabited holiday homes in Wales owned by outsiders were burned.

It would be several weeks later that John Jenkins and Ernest Alders were arrested and charged with several of the unsolved bombings that had occurred across Wales over a three year period. Both men were serving members of the British Army and were based at Saighton Barracks not far from Chester. Eventually, following a lengthy trial, John Jenkins was sentenced to ten years imprisonment for his part in the bombings leading up to the investiture.

As it happened, his accomplice, Alders, was treated far more leniently after turning 'Queen's Evidence' against his comrade. During the trial it became clear that John Jenkins had been extremely clever in planning and carrying out many of the bombings in those eventful days. It is worth noting that John Jenkins, throughout his trial and consequent long prison sentence, never betrayed any of his comrades within MAC, despite all kind of pressures from the authorities. He was incarcerated in quite inhumane circumstances, most of the time as a category A prisoner at Albany prison on the Isle of Wight. During his many years in prison he studied and wrote, publishing a book titled *Prison Letters*. John's sacrifice for his country cost him dearly, including the breakup of his marriage, but he took it all with extreme dignity and to this day he is ever active at patriotic events where his fife and drum band is most popular.

People often ask me do I have any regrets? In all honesty, that is not an easy question to answer. I have consistently told the press and media, that I have no regrets and politically, that is true. On the personal side, yes, there are instances where I possibly might have handled situations in a different way. On the other hand, I am a person who does things on the spur of the moment. In other words, I hate wasting time contemplating ifs and buts that can lead to inaction.

This 'act first, think after' approach led me to a difficult period in my life, which occurred prior to and immediately followed the investiture. At the end of 1969 and the early part of 1970, the condition of my then youngest daughter, Teleri, deteriorated. The final weeks of her life were very painful and traumatic.

I had been on the run from the police and intelligence agencies and gone through a strenuous court case, which left me feeling depressed and sometimes isolated. During this time that I was to become close to Gillianne, who was at the time still married to Julian Cayo Evans. For some unexplained reason we were drawn together, since she was also going through a difficult patch and offered me sympathy and solace in my time of grief and troubled emotions. I responded in like manner and our mutual sympathy developed into an affair. Her marriage was all but over when we embarked on the affair and during the summer of 1970, we moved in together and settled in a small hill farm in Gwynedd called Erw Wen. In the past, Gillianne has been wrongfully characterised by some sections of the nationalist fraternity as a sort of 'scarlet woman'. Nothing could be further from the truth. Gillianne was and is a most sincere, honest and kind person who does not deserve these criticisms. These people can criticise me all they want, because if any blame should be apportioned to anybody, it should be to me.

To cut a long story short, our relationship lasted less than two years. About a year after we set up home, I suffered a very serious horse riding accident which resulted in the fracture of the upper arm or humerus into several fragments. This accident caused me severe physical pain and I was confined to a chair for ten months, dependent on painkillers for almost a year. At the best of times, I am not the ideal patient, nor am I good at dealing with frustration. Gillianne, who had been under a great deal of mental pressure because of family matters and our affair, couldn't handle the added pressure of a semi-invalid partner. Sadly, we split up less than a year later, but not before our daughter, Alwen Eryri, was born in February of that year. I am glad she eventually grew up to be almost a complete replica of Gillianne: gentle, unselfish, generous and attractive.

Following that break-up, it took me a couple of years to recuperate from the riding accident and I was not romantically involved with anyone, apart from a couple of casual encounters. At this stage of my life, I was busy trying to reclaim some derelict land at the back of the farm. Erw Wen is a small hillside farm, fairly isolated, just over 90 acres. Much of it is very steep, and cultivating it involved patience as well as risk-taking. All in all, it was a challenge I relished – after all, my life has been a series of challenges. Seeing lush pasture replace bracken and reed was most fulfilling. Six days a week I worked on my parents' farm at Gwynus, travelling there daily, while at evenings and weekends, I toiled and struggled with the land reclamation at Erw Wen.

Amongst my very first tasks on purchasing the farm was tree planting. When I moved in, the farm lay on a windswept hillside overlooking Caernarfon Bay. Despite this, it was sheltered from the cold easterly winds by the hillside, most of which had a south-facing aspect. In all, I planted over 1,000 trees, starting with larches and a couple of dozen Norway spruce and a few other conifers. Once it had created enough shelter as a windbreak, I went on to grow many deciduous trees, such as silver birch, mountain ash, oak, alder, a few chestnuts, and beeches. It took a few decades for these trees to mature and grow, but the results were worth waiting for.

During the summer of 1976, one of the warmest summers I can remember, I was to meet a girl who influenced my life a great deal. Monika was a native of Darmstadt, not far from

Frankfurt in central Germany. At the time she was a student in her final year at Frankfurt University, studying languages and philosophy. Monika was in her mid twenties, with long, straight blond hair, blue eyed, slim and attractive and also highly intelligent. When we first met, she was already aware that Wales was a nation with its own language, culture and history. Around the time we met, my little daughter Alwen came to stay with me during school holiday time, when she was five years old. Soon after, Monika offered to care for Alwen during her stay that summer, and moved into Erw Wen to live with us.

Following our first meeting we became very close and a strong relationship developed. Although we were from very contrasting backgrounds, there was a mutual attraction and we seemed to care for the same causes. As I have previously mentioned, Monika was a linguist and a very competent one. Soon she stated a desire to learn Welsh, which she accomplished in a very short period of time. I can truly say she was able to speak, read and write Welsh in less than six months, including mastering the complicated mutations. Our relationship proved to be a very calming and stabilising influence on my life. For her part, I believe she found the rural lifestyle a huge contrast to the bustling highly charged urban life of a cosmopolitan city.

During the period leading up to the 1980s, our farming consisted of breeding lambs which were housed in corrugated sheds I had built. By wintering the sheep indoors, it was possible to have lambs born early in January, as opposed to the normal Welsh lambing season of March. Once the lambs reached ten to twelve days old, we would turn them out onto a sheltered parcel of land in a small valley below the farmyard. We could feed the sheep bales of hay and around a pound each of concentrated meal. Monika took to farm life like a duck to water. She learnt to recognise most of the ewes individually, and even had names for many of them. There was a particular one, an orphan she found half-dead outside, which she had raised with a bottle. Wrapping him in an old piece of blanket, she stuck him in the bottom oven of the Aga cooker to warm his body, before giving him a few drops of colostrum to help his recovery. Almost miraculously his limp body revived and within a couple of days he could stand on his four legs. During this time, Helmut Schmitt was the German Chancellor. Jokingly she baptised him 'Helmut'. Amazingly, the animal lived to be eighteen years of age – that is an incredible age for a sheep, especially considering that 'Helmut' was born with serious complications as he was blind in one eye from birth. After he grew to full size, he responded to 'Helmut', just like a dog does, and would follow us around the farmyard, head on one side as he tried to see where he was going with his one good eye. On sheep farms male lambs are normally sent for slaughter, usually for export, but Helmut was the exception.

Monika and I eventually parted. She returned to Germany because her mother had developed Parkinson's disease and she wished to be close to her. She also didn't think there was much future for her in Wales since, at that time, I was unsure of myself and I didn't feel I was ready to marry for a second time. We remained good friends and I would occasionally fly to Frankfurt and spend time with her at her apartment near Ingelheim am Rhein, not far from Mainz. During these visits I decided to try and learn the German language and succeeded in being able to hold a limited conversation.

Several years after Monika and I parted company, on a cold winter's day, old Helmut passed away. He was buried alongside a small lake I had created beside the farm track. My two youngest children Rhys and Enlli helped shape a little wooden cross on his grave. His grave still exists, or did, between that of an old sheepdog called Rex and two Rhode Island Red hens that my children insisted on having a full ceremonial funeral.

At this stage of my life, my mother's health began to deteriorate and she felt lonely, so my other brothers and I took turns to spend the night at Gwynus to keep her company. It was towards the end of the eighties that I bumped into an old acquaintance in Pwllheli. Her name was Doran and I had known her since I kept the cafe there years ago. It was Christmas time and my cousin Owen Penant from Australia had come to stay with me. Since we hadn't met for over thirty years I decided we'd have a party in the farmhouse and invited a few friends to join us. Doran and her sister Peta came and we had a great time.

From that day, things moved pretty fast and Doran and I started dating. We were married the following March and lived at Erw Wen for around twenty-five years. We have two children, Rhys Fychan, twenty-four, and his sister Enlli Fychan, who is twenty-two. I revived the old name Fychan since the anglicised Vaughan was already in use by several of my family members.

Doran took a teaching course after the two children started school and eventually gained a degree at Bangor University. It took some time to find a job, before getting a part-time and temporary post at a local secondary school, specialising in teaching Welsh as a second language. This meant having to travel wider afield to secure employment. Around ten years after, she took on a full time post at Ysgol Emrys ap Iwan in Abergele.

Towards winter's end in 2013, we decided to sell Erw Wen and move back to my former family home at Gwynus, Pistyll, near Nefyn in Llŷn, where we now temporarily live in a chalet while renovating the old farmhouse. Because the house is a Grade Two listed building, it means lots of rules and regulations on how we do things, what materials we use etc. There is of course a plus side to moving back, since our tourism business is located here and it is convenient to operate and manage whilst on site. Apart from a nine-hole golf course that I had built in 2002, there is also a caravan and camping park with both static and touring vans.

My mother started the caravan park over 60 years ago and when I inherited that part of the farm she had six static vans on it. At present we have ten static vans and almost sixty tourers as well as several tent pitches. Over the years, we have spent heavily on building a new shower and toilet block with facilities for the disabled, two play areas, a launderette and a small shop doubling as a reception office.

During the development stages, a great deal of effort has gone into tree planting and landscaping. The trees and bushes I planted are maturing and have transformed to a great extent what was a fairly bare, windswept plateau into a more sheltered and leafy spot. I believe that it is not an overstatement to say that more trees have been planted on this corner of land during the last twelve years than during the whole of the last three centuries. Of course there were already many large trees in place previously, mostly sycamores and ash. We had lost dozens of ancient elms around forty years before when Dutch Elm Disease struck. On that subject, I was overjoyed when I discovered three smaller survivor elms hidden amongst brambles and hawthorn, which are now miraculously thriving.

Most of my close friends and family are aware of my great fondness for trees. Nothing gives me greater satisfaction than planting them and seeing them grow and thrive in later years. I suppose it's my way of giving something back to this wonderful planet which has mostly given me great joy and love of life – along with the pain. During the last two or three decades, time has flown by and this only serves to remind me of the importance of being grateful for each passing day and to make the most of what time I have remaining.

And 'making the most' includes having a go at politcs.

20

Politics – Legal this Time!

SOME TWENTY-SIX YEARS ago, I decided, against my better judgment, to stand for election to the local council. At that time, the present Gwynedd County Council was divided into three districts. Clynnog Ward was in the Dwyfor area and there were three candidates. The sitting member was Gethin Evans of Plaid Cymru, but also standing was John Partington Jones, a local garage owner who stood as an Independent.

I decided to stand as Independent Nationalist. I would not have felt comfortable standing under an 'independent' only banner, because it could mean I would be 'all things to all men'! On the evening of the election, there was quite a bit of excitement and Clynnog village hall was well packed. When the result was announced, I was declared the winner having taken exactly half the votes, while the other two shared the remaining 50 per cent. All my supporters were jubilant and there was much shouting, cheering and hand-shaking.

Having decided to take the 'democratic path,' I set about trying to get policies implemented which would, I hoped, benefit local interests and the community I represented. Local government however, proved to be slow and cumbersome and despite my enthusiastic efforts, it became obvious that no wind of change would be allowed to blow soon! Amongst the newly-elected members, there were three or four who shared my feelings and aspirations to improve the economic situation in Dwyfor. Two of these members were under the Plaid Cymru banner and the other was an 'Independent'.

One way of trying to get things moving was by proposing a 'Motion to Council'. If that attempt were successful, it would mean the council going through the motion of securing its implementation. It was through this procedure that I was able to introduce several motions and ideas which were later implemented. Some of these may be worth mentioning. There was a 'Special Crisis Conference' called, whereby eight or nine of the District Councils on the north and west coast of Wales were invited to send delegates to Pwllheli to discuss such matters as lack of employment, a need for locals to have priority over incomers on council housing waiting lists, and the need to strengthen the base of the Welsh language

Despite our local council officers and certain elected members putting in a great effort, our plans received the full backing of only one other council. That, I must add, was the first of several disappointments I experienced as a councillor.

There were several successes later on, particularly after the three District Councils were merged to create the new Gwynedd County Council in the mid 1990s. At a local level I succeeded in getting support from the new council to find grants to construct improvements to the A499 which links Caernarfon to Pwllheli, including a new by-pass for the village of Clynnog Fawr. Another 'Motion to Council' to bear fruit was the one I proposed to celebrate the 600th anniversary of Owain Glyndŵr's War of Independence from England. Because of this, all school children in Gwynedd were given a book documenting the life and struggles of Glyndŵr.

The motion also called for the council to implement a policy whereby all schools in Gwynedd would erect a mast and the national flag would be flown every day outside our schools. This part was only half successful, since it was decided each school would have to exercise its own discretion on whether to fly our flag. I think fewer than thirty schools opted for this clause. It gave me great pride to see our local primary school at Brynaerau being the first to display our flag. Our local *Caernarfon Herald* displayed a photo of four of the senior pupils raising the flag for the first time. Amongst the four was my young son Rhys Fychan, together with Caio, Ali and Kirsten.

In that motion, I also called for a worthy statue to be erected on Y Maes in Caernarfon town centre, to commemorate Owain Glyndŵr. Other councillors rejected this and only a handful of Plaid Cymru members supported me. That was the last straw. As I already had doubts about that Party's total commitment to reviving our identity and national consciousness, this latest pathetic inaction proved me right. Since I was still under the label of 'Independent Nationalist' on the council, I was now joined by Cllr Evie Hall Griffith, which meant we were a 'group'. I was still searching for ways to set up an alternative national party to oppose Plaid's lukewarm variety.

An opportunity arose with the announcement that the 2001 census would not have a 'tick box' to record one's Welsh identity. One day towards the end of 2000 I received a call from John Humphries in Gwent, who was the first person to inform me of this anomaly. John told me the Scots and Irish were to be given the opportunity to announce their ethnicity with special tick boxes. Further to this, John also revealed that in a recent USA census, Welsh Americans had a box to indicate their ethnic origins; there are two million of them. We met up to discuss how we could get the Office of National Statistics to change their minds.

John Humphries had only just retired as editor of the *Western Mail* and had recently become active in Welsh Nationalist issues. During our first meeting he told me of his background in a working class area of Newport in Gwent. He told me that In his childhood and early youth, he wasn't even aware that Newport was in Wales – and as for our language, he had never heard a word of Welsh spoken. It was later on in life that one of his sons met a Welsh-speaking girl from Rhuthun in Clwyd, and they had a son named Rhys. John related to me how he came to realise that little Rhys could speak only Welsh and that he couldn't communicate with him. From then on, he became enraptured with all things Welsh. Strange as it sounds, although we come from very different backgrounds, we struck a chord and remain close friends to this day.

During the earlier stages of our 'tick box' campaign we decided to set up a new movement called Cymru Annibynnol, or 'Independent Wales', meeting at Glyndŵr's old Parliament House in Machynlleth. Amongst the many dedicated patriots who attended and even addressed meetings was world-famous poet R. S. Thomas. Despite John's continuous letters and dialogue with ONS, they would not budge from their original unreasonable stance. John came up with an idea. Cymru Annibynnol could organise a makeshift coffin to travel across Wales and Welsh people would be invited to place their census forms in this coffin, rather than return them to the ONS. When the story hit the national news, TV, radio and press, we expected several hundred would agree to leave their forms in our coffin. As it turned out, surprisingly, almost 9,000 people deposited their forms in the coffin, culminating in the authorities threatening John and me with arrest and imprisonment. However, the attitude of the ONS only succeeded in hardening our resolve to stand up to their bullying tactics. In particular, the *Western Mail* committed itself to supporting our campaign, even commenting in their editorial column.

A TV reporter interviewed me shortly after the census: 'What has become of the coffin? Do you have any idea of its whereabouts?'

I replied very seriously, 'Strange you should ask me that, but one minute it was there, and the next minute it had disappeared… Just like Owain Glyndŵr 600 years ago!'

Before I end this small but hugely important story, I must comment on the sad and sorry part played by Plaid Cymru in this incident. They point blank refused to take part or support us in the campaign. Rather than confront the ONS head on, they decided to print little stickers with 'WELSH' on one side, urging their members to paste them onto the appropriate box that queried nationality. When this sticker was placed over the particular box, and a cross inserted next to it, they had overlooked the fact that the forms were electronically checked. Since the box underneath the sticker had 'British' as the question, each box where 'Welsh' stickers had been attached counted as 'British'! That incompetent act stupidly hoodwinked several thousand of their members into unwittingly stating that they were 'British'!

There is no question in anyone's mind today that the turnaround in attitude by the ONS for the 2011 census in which Welsh people could declare their Welsh identity was due in the main to the 'Independent Wales' coffin campaign.

Cymru Annibynnol had served its purpose and was wound up the following year. Gwynedd Council has been run by Plaid Cymru for several years now. It is only partially true that their large majority on the council is responsible for their U-turns on several issues. Unquestionably, the most controversial shift was that in relation to rural schools and small schools in general. Sometime before the 2008 council elections, they revealed policies that would mean the closure of scores of Gwynedd's primary schools. These proposals caused uproar and outrage, and there were harsh letters in the local papers calling for the hierarchy to listen to the people.

It was this more than anything else that resulted in the formation of a new nationalist party, Llais Gwynedd – The Voice of Gwynedd. Having read an article in the local *Caernarfon Herald*, in which one Aeron Maldwyn Jones spoke of forming an opposition party, I decided to contact him and we met to set down ideas and put up several candidates in the forthcoming May elections. The enthusiastic response to this meant that we fielded two dozen candidates and had thirteen of our members returned. Our success meant that Plaid Cymru were one or two short of an overall majority, relying on one or two Independent, Labour and Lib Dems to keep them in power.

Shock waves from that election reverberated across the county and beyond. Plaid had to try and change tactics to carry on with their mission to close small schools. Instead of implementing the closures en bloc across the county, they decided to pursue a policy of concentrating on catchment areas one by one. Up to a point, this policy of 'divide and rule' worked. Instead of close to 1,000 protesters congregating outside the council offices, as had previously occurred, now there would be around 100 instead.

Llais Gwynedd has stood steadfastly against school closures and also led the campaign against the closure of nursing homes and homes for the elderly. Some leading Plaid politicians were professing the demise of Llais Gwynedd after the 2012 elections, and called us a 'damp squib' and worse. Nonetheless, we were returned this time with fourteen members, an increase of one. In the Dwyfor area we have ten members as opposed to Plaid's six. Before Llais Gwynedd was formed, several dozen Plaid councillors were regularly returned unopposed. Now they have to fight for their seats, and that's the way it should be. It's called democracy.

Our successes in breaking the mould and halting Plaid's ambition of turning Gwynedd into a 'one party state' has resulted in several of that party's leading lights turning their anger and frustration into downright hatred. Many of the distorted lies published in local newspapers over the last five years in letters demonstrate the venom and bitterness that simmers below the surface. On reflection, it speaks volumes that Plaid Cymru, which professes to be 'The Party of Wales', spends more time attacking Llais Gwynedd than it does trying to address the true enemies of our country, that is, most of the London-based political parties.

There is only one logical conclusion to this assertion. Could it be that Plaid are running scared at the thought of a truly alternative Welsh political party emerging to challenge them? While it is true that Llais only operates within Gwynedd at present, there is evidence of genuine discontent across the nation. After all, it's only a few years ago that a new party sprang up in Blaenau Gwent and succeeded in booting the ruling Labour party out of its stronghold. That party was aptly titled 'Voice of the People'. Although that party has more or less disappeared, it still served as a warning to any of the major traditional parties to take heed.

After being involved in my country's politics for several decades, at the deep end, I truly believe that the few who dared challenge the status quo with all their might deserve a little praise and recognition. After all, some paid with their very lives! Furthermore, it is recognised today that but for the protest movement in Wales during the 1960s, 70s and 80s, we would not today have achieved even the small crumbs we have of recognition of our identity – and Plaid Cymru would be even weaker than it is now.

It is worth remembering that even forty years ago, Plaid Cymru had three MPs. Today they have… three!! Whether their supporters will admit or not, it is blatantly obvious that in its eighty-four years of existence, Plaid has become static. I will offer one reason why this is: it has failed to strike a chord with ordinary people. The party members are still regarded in many quarters as elitist. There is still suspicion about some of their motives. One of their main problems is the linguistic division that exists in some areas of Wales, for instance in Cardiff itself, or parts of it at least.

21

Rallying Cry

So BACK TO the question: why did I act? A combination of factors provides the answer: political influences during my youth; the 'winds of change' blowing in other countries. But in Wales there was so much apathy. I knew it would take a drastic step to stir the required reaction. An explosion was needed that would halt the building of the dam and possibly save the doomed valley. I hoped it would rock the nation and disturb its status quo of respectability; I hoped, more importantly, that it would awaken ordinary people, the very core of our society, because without their support it would all be futile.

My vision was firstly to demonstrate the will to resist oppression and kick authority in the teeth; secondly to send shock waves throughout the nation and hopefully kick some arses along the way. Maybe all this does not answer the question fully. It has taken decades for the effects of the ripple of that first explosion to achieve a fraction of what it was meant to. True, it can be argued we have at least some small trappings of nationhood, such as the Assembly, though that is still far from being equal with the Scots and their Parliament. Minor law making powers are being allowed, but a nation needs far more powers than the right to charge five pence for a plastic carrier bag to prove its nationhood!

Many of those voted into Parliament or the Assembly suffer from a common political dichotomy. They have a problem distinguishing between being Welsh or British. They fail to understand that you simply cannot be both. It has to be one or the other. There are of course some encouraging signs. In the last census, many more people declared themselves to be Welsh rather than British, in contrast to previous censuses. I have already referred to the struggle that took place before the 2001 census to secure the right for Welsh people to register their identity on the census forms.

What lies ahead? For those of us who believe in the day when an independent Welsh state will be established, the long hard struggle will continue. One serious issue which could have an effect on that struggle is the fragile state of the Welsh economy, compared to Scotland and various regions in England.

There are no easy solutions on the horizon. Within the Welsh-speaking heartlands, the answer has to be small businesses and increasingly, tourism. The latter does not come without its detrimental side-effects and should be designed to fit in with and benefit local communities. Large-scale developments and massive foreign-owned caravan parks do not provide the answer, since a vast percentage of their incomes vanish over the border into the pockets of developers and shareholders. Small, locally-owned tourist ventures, on the other hand, spend their money locally, sustaining local communities and employing local labour. This helps indigenous young people by providing opportunities for them to remain where they are needed, and where they belong.

Above all else, the health of our economy dictates whether we survive as a people, therefore it is imperative that officialdom does not impede the efforts of local business and entrepreneurs to create opportunities for growth and jobs on a sustainable scale. At present too much red tape and paltry rules and regulations are killing the very essence of what they purport to 'defend'. Every time a young person is forced to move away from Llŷn or other areas, it leaves a vacuum because eventually their homes will go on the market, more than likely to be purchased by someone who does not speak our language and probably couldn't care less about it.

Planning regulations must be revised and adapted. People are more important than bats. Conservation areas should have their place, but that place should not be at the expense of uprooting our indigenous populace. Creating a massive museum and blocking small businesses from advancing and increasing employment opportunities is a misconceived policy and has about as much vision and hope as a mole in a concrete tunnel with both ends blocked. Time is running out and we need to act positively.

As for the future, politically, I can only in reality speak as a native of Gwynedd and as leader of Llais Gwynedd. I wouldn't wish to bore the reader by being repetitive, but I must again reiterate my belief that addressing the economic issue is imperative. I hope to pursue this issue through the party I represent, since the whole fabric of the rural communities is determined by this single matter.

On several occasions previously I have endeavoured to highlight the importance of bringing the various departments within the county council together to hammer out a solution, rather than each doing their own thing with their own separate agenda. Personally, I believe it's a disgrace that some of those who represent our rural communities at Assembly level have done sweet nothing to justify their existence, since they are more concerned in furthering their own political careers than helping to revive our dying communities.

There is obviously a massive vacuum in Welsh politics. The public are sick and tired of the political hide and seek games played by the four 'established' parties. It's sad that Plaid Cymru no longer leads by example, since they have slipped into the trap of emulating Labour, Lib Dems and Tories. We must be bold and set a true agenda. We must involve the public, especially young people. We must demonstrate that they count and convince them that all politicians are not self-serving crooks.

Finally, Llais Gwynedd must move forward here in Gwynedd and secure control, following the next Council elections. The party should start spreading its wings and move beyond the boundaries of Gwynedd, not only into other rural areas but also into the valleys of south-east Wales – everywhere the people have similar problems of poverty and unemployment, and exist in a climate of hopelessness and frustration. Llais Gwynedd should also contest and win its first seat in the Assembly. That seat would be the Dwyfor-Meirionnydd seat, where the party is strongest, since they already hold ten out of the twenty wards in Dwyfor.

Let's do it! Let's show that the seeds of the risen nation planted at Tryweryn fifty years ago have taken root and are growing strongly with branches in full foliage. That is my dream, not for the sake of any political party, but for my nation and its people.

Afterword and Acknowledgements

I DECIDED TO write my memories because I felt I had a story to tell, but there is rather more to it than that, since my involvement in the politics of Wales over around fifty years means I am attempting to unravel most of the complicated issues that have occurred.

Many authors and journalists have tried to probe the veneer of events that took place during this comparatively short period. While some have contributed in some ways towards understanding, and analysing the reasons for, the turmoil and dissent, I don't believe that many had the inside knowledge that would allow them to fully comprehend the psyche behind what became a mini-uprising. I write as an active member of a secret organisation, and as someone who took part in direct action against installations and equipment when it became clear that all democratic protests and opposition were being ignored.

It is important to remember that the story covers a period from the early 1960s – when there was not even talk of devolution – until the present. This period was a time of rebellion and revolution on a global scale. Wales and an active minority played a part in it. Prior to the moronic decision to seize a Welsh valley, and kick out its inhabitants, to create a massive dam to supply England with water, there had been no rallying point that could unite Wales, north and south, Welsh-speakers and much of the anglicised sector. Today it is generally acknowledged that it was a result of direct action by the few that galvanised opposition, which developed over a few years into

271

open rebellion, when various acts of sabotage were to become the norm. Almost without exception, these actions were the result of careful planning and co-ordination, organised by a secret underground movement, MAC; the movement's first act was to plant the Tryweryn dam site bomb. The repercussions of that explosion were far-reaching and profound. Not only the dam site was shaken to its foundations, but the whole nation, which had been in a deep slumber since the War of Independence of Owain Glyndŵr. Five hundred and fifty years is a long time to sleep.

One final question: why write this book in English, since I was brought up as a monoglot Welsh-speaker? I had already written a book in Welsh dealing with the flooding of Capel Celyn, *Cysgod Tryweryn* (the shadow of Tryweryn), which was made into a film, *Y Weithred* (the action) later. I had the feeling that non-Welsh-speakers within Wales, and hopefully further afield, would like to learn about the events that took place during this time. After all, many people in Wales who do not live in Welsh-speaking areas, or have no provision of Welsh-language schools, are still unaware of their own history. Unfortunately, the education system within our country decided long ago not to teach our history in our schools. I hope this book will go some way to rectifying that, and maybe it will encourage readers to seek more information about their own national identity – who they are, and where they belong.

Before I finish I wish to thank all those who have contributed in any way towards helping me put the book together. Obviously I haven't the space to name everyone, but in particularly I wish to thank all at Y Lolfa, especially Robat Gruffudd and his son Lefi, for their support and encouragement. Thanks also to Carole Byrne Jones for her tireless efforts in trying to create some order with the various chapters; also my thanks to Dr Jen Llywelyn for editing the book and suggesting changes here and there. Since the whole book was handwritten in the first place it had to be typed by Llinos Williams, who had to decipher my atrocious handwriting; also I thank her for the many photographs she took.

Obviously the names of persons still living have been replaced with aliases.

It's a very sad task for me to write about people who were very close to me, but are no longer with us. It's over four years since I started writing this book. My older brother, Morris, passed away in February 2012 – we were very close. My other surviving brother, John, passed away this summer, following a long period suffering from dementia. Many of my close friends, some mentioned in this book, have also recently died, among them Bryn Williams, who wrote the letter confirming his arrest and interrogation at the hands of the intelligence services; ironically, he died on the first day of 2015. Gordon Thatcher has been plagued by illness over the last few years and is currently in a nursing home near Caernarfon; Gordon's contribution is invaluable as it deals with a most sensitive and dramatic turn of events. One other important person in my life, not only my cousin but my best friend during my youth, Owen Penant Williams, died in Australia before I had the chance to fly out to visit him.

The years spent putting this book together have meant an extra strain on my family, in particular my wife Doran and my two youngest children, Rhys and Enlli, and not forgetting my youngest grandchild, Efa Teleri, who is now three and a half years old. Throughout this time everyone has been most tolerant, even during my long sessions spent scribbling and reminiscing. There are not enough words to thank them for their support and patience. DIOLCH!

Finally, a big thank you to Eifion Glyn for agreeing to write the introduction. Eifion is a long-standing friend and has only recently retired after producing several memorable editions of the Welsh-language current affairs programme, *Y Byd ar Bedwar*, for S4C.

"You don't know me but I know you and I have seen you in plenty of demonstrations" meddai, ni atebais ef.

"You are a sly spineless yellow bellied Welsh bastard" meddai. Aeth yn ei flaen "I don't care how many Birmingham pipe lines you blow up. I don't care how many offices you blow up in Cardiff or ANYWHERE IN Wales, but you come into the Cheshire area or anywhere near, I will crucify you . I'll nail you to the fucking wall, what are you trying to do - turn Wales into a fucking Cyprus?" meddai. Cymerodd ei wynt ato a cherdded o amgylch yr ystafell yna yn sydyn gafaelodd ynof a fy mhwshio o gwmpas yr ystafell. "You have a wife and a young baby. It could easily be arranged for them to be somewhere where a bomb goes off and see how you like it then"meddai. Ar ol rhyw awr o hyn daeth y lleill yn nol i'r ystafell a dechreuodd D. S. Booth fy holi eto. Yr un hen gwestiynnau ac ar ol rhyw awr o gwestiynnu heb seibiant na paned o de na dim dywedodd Booth "The next time you will see me it will be early one morning but don't worry we'll get you up and you will be going down for a long time, but before then we'll harrass you so much you will come running to us to tell us what we want to know". ac yna cerddodd allan o'r ystafell, daeth Gwyn Owen i fy nol a mynd a fi i'r car ac yna cychwyn am adref. Cyrraedd Llanaelhaearn am 9 y nos.

Ella y dylwn i ychwanegu fod Owain Williams wedi ei gael yn ddieuog o gyhuddiadau yn ymwneud a ffrwydron ac o fod yn rhan o'r ymgyrch fomio oedd yn cymeryd lle ers canol y chwedegau. Gan ei fod wedi treulio bron i flwyddyn o amser, un ai yn y carchar neu ar ffo oddiwrth special branch ayyb, ac yn y diwedd ei gael yn ddi euog, roedd yr heddluoedd yn ceisio rhoi yr argraff na doeddent yn ei erlid ymhellach. Am y rhesymau yma dwi'n meddwl fy mod wedi cael fy nhargedu, gan eu bod yn meddwl fod gen i wybodaeth am Now am ein bod yn ffrindiau. Drwy'r amser tra ' roeddant yn fy holi a'm bwlio gan soecial branch ac uwch swyddogion yr heddlu, roedd enw Owain Williams yn dod i fyny bob munud.

Cofiaf un enghraifft o hyn, ar ol cael fy holi am rhyw chwech neu saith awr. Dywedodd un ohonynt - Det. Chief Sup. Dixie Dean "Now, you're a smart lad Bryn, I'm sure you will listen to reason..... but him.. Williams, he won't see reason. and I'm telling you now. if he is within fifty miles of Caernarfon on the day before the investiture, he's going to have an accident....." Dychrynais a gofynais pwy oedd y 'Williams'.. "You know bloody well who I mean... your mate Owain Williams" oedd ei ateb.

Toc ar ol hynny, aethant a fi at un o'u ceir ac aethant a fi adra. Nid oedd gan fy ngwraig na neb o'r teulu syniad lle yr oeddwn, pan gyrrhaeddais adref, roedd yn nos.

Mae'r hanes uchod yn gywir, yn air am air fel y digwyddodd, ni allwn anghofio pe taswn eisiau gan i'r digwyddiad fy nychryn ac hefyd gwneud i mi sylweddoli pa mor ddifrifol oedd y llywodraeth a'r awdurdodau yn cymeryd y sefyllfa.

Bryn Williams   Llinos Merks
20 Mai 2014   20 Mai 2014

Part of a letter by Bryn Williams confirming his arrest by the intelligence services

AFTERWORD

Christmas 2015

SINCE STARTING TO write my book some four (if not five) years ago, so much has changed, not only in my own personal life, but in general. In a relatively short time, as mentioned earlier, I lost my two remaining brothers, Morris and John; my cousin, Owen Penant; and one of my closest friends, Bryn Williams from Llithfaen.There are but a few of the stalwarts left who have played important parts in my life over a long period. Sadly, I've also heard that Gordon Thatcher died recently.

On the political side, Wales has been left the poorer through the passing away of important figures who cast their giant shadows over our nation, and helped to mould and nourish the sense of nationhood and identity. In my belief, none will be missed more than Dr Meredydd Evans, who contributed so much and in such a variety of ways to the defence and nurture of our unique culture and language, in a life-span of over nine decades.

Depite my awareness of the fact that I will be castigated by certain sections of the comfortably-placed elitist Welsh-speaking middle class for daring to criticise Plaid Cymru – God forbid – I stick by what I have written earlier: that they are a party obsessed with trivialities and political correctness, and gobbled up by the British political system. How can a party that has the gall to term itself 'the party of Wales' justify taking up seats in the House of Lords? Or do they truly believe that by masquerading as 'champions' of the working class and downtrodden 'gwerin' they can pull the wool over the voters' eyes and continue to dwell in their pygmy world of cronyism?

Just because one lives and, if lucky enough, works in a predominantly Welsh-speaking area such as north-west Wales, that does not give anyone, or any party, the God-given right to assume they – and they alone – can represent and hi-jack the language or culture for their own ends.

It is my belief that there ar good and proud Welsh people in most areas of life, and even in most of the political parties. They are to be found amongst Labour, Lib Dem and even some Conservative politicians, just as there are some not-so-good individuals amongst all the parties, including Plaid Cymru. Labels can be very misleading and dangerous. No, I do not believe that every member of Llais Gwynedd is beyond reproach, or has the perfect credentials, or is the ideal patriotic Welshman or woman, but, on the other hand, we never pretended to be that either. We were formed as a party fo fill a vacuum and to challenge Plaid Cymru in Gwynedd, where it had established itself almost as a one-party mini-state. Elections were a joke: more than half their councillors 'walked' into seats unopposed; nobody stood against them. If we succeeded only in changing all that, and gave people the opportunity of choice, that in itself is a milestone.

Since I began by noting changes and losses it is only proper that I close on the same subject. It has not been the best year for Llais Gwynedd because during the second half of 2015 we lost five of our councillors. Three deserted us for Plaid Cymru – just after the general election – one of them was supposed to stand for us in the Assembly elections in 2016, but *c'est la vie*; his wasn't such a surprise departure as several of our members doubted his motives for coming over to us from Plaid in the first place.

As for the other two losses, they were sad. The untimely death of Bob Wright aboard the Pwllheli lifeboat was a tragedy of the worst kind. Our other loss was Llywarch Bowen Jones of Trefor, who had to resign because of serious health problems.

Both were loyal and faithful, hard-working councillors who served their communities with devotion. I would like to add they were also very close personal friends, and committed to the cause and efforts of Llais Gwynedd. Undoubtedly we will pick ourselves up from these setbacks and retrieve the lost ground by sticking together and working towards the future for the good of Gwynedd and of Wales. I wish to thank all the thousands of people who have supported and voted for us during the eight years of our existence.

Thank you all. Diolch yn fawr.

Also from Y Lolfa:

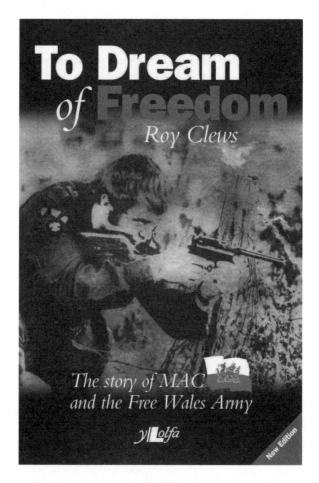

£9.95

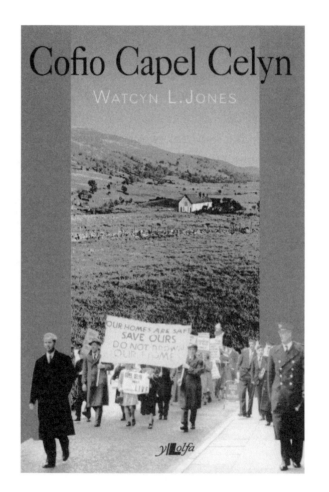

Cofio Capel Celyn

WATCYN L. JONES

y Lolfa

£5.95

Tryweryn: A Nation Awakes is just one of a
whole range of publications from Y Lolfa.
For a full list of books currently in print, send
now for your free copy of our new full-colour
catalogue. Or simply surf into our website

www.ylolfa.com

for secure on-line ordering.

TALYBONT CEREDIGION CYMRU SY24 5HE
e-mail ylolfa@ylolfa.com
website www.ylolfa.com
phone (01970) 832 304
fax 832 782